I find myself in awe of what Dr. Cherry-Paul has skillfully crafted—a true masterclass and a work of art in the field of antiracist education. This book is not just a mere publication; it symbolizes a dedicated pledge to love, intersectionality, justice, and the crucial process of repair. It goes beyond being a standard resource; rather, it stands as a testament to the transformative power of education when approached with a commitment to creating an antiracist world.

—Bettina L. Love, *New York Times* **bestselling author**
Punished for Dreaming: How School Reform Harms
Black Children and How We Heal

Rooted in the love and collective scholarship of Black women, Dr. Cherry-Paul's Six Critical Lenses are an essential (not additional) component of reading instruction in the classroom. *Antiracist Reading Revolution* meets the reader at their intersection of years of antiracist readings and equity trainings, and it extends a concrete framework for both adult and young learners to develop and apply their racial literacy and consciousness alongside one another. Beginning so beautifully with affirmation, the Antiracist Reading Framework summons every reader to continue practicing the critical and transformative conversations necessary for progress.

—Sara K. Ahmed, **educator and author**
Being the Change: Lessons and Strategies to
Teach Social Comprehension

Dr. Sonja Cherry-Paul has listened to teachers, librarians, literacy coaches, curriculum developers, teacher educators, and researchers in children's literature and antiracist teaching! *Antiracist Reading Revolution* compels all to move beyond the book lists and into liberating pedagogy—an invitation to "think deeply and possibly differently" through children's literature and, in that process, better facilitate literature and life discussions with children.

—Carla España, **assistant professor**
Bilingual Education, Puerto Rican/Latinx, and
Latin American Studies
Department of Puerto Rican and Latinx Studies
Brooklyn College, CUNY

This book is an inspiration to make a commitment. A commitment to love. A commitment to construct a classroom that is deserving of and centers BIPOC students. A commitment to push ourselves beyond representation and to use our agency to create curriculum that brings us closer to creating a more antiracist classroom. Dr. Cherry-Paul challenges us to interrogate how our identities, biases, and assumptions influence our instructional decision making. The Antiracist Reading Framework provides applicable, transferable skills that can be implemented meaningfully in the classroom. With the tools Dr. Cherry-Paul provides, *Antiracist Reading Revolution* will not only create a change in ourselves and our students in the classroom, it will help create a more antiracist world beyond.

—Angela Bae, **senior program officer**
Cotsen Foundation for the ART of TEACHING

In this creative masterpiece, Dr. Sonja Cherry-Paul centers the work of four incredible Black women scholars to create the Antiracist Reading Framework. This framework teaches educators how to select and engage youth in multicultural literature, while providing the practicality of meaningful prompts, reflection, and an actionable antiracist curriculum. *Antiracist Reading Revolution* is necessary and urgent for anyone who dreams of and seeks a better world.

—Gholdy Muhammad, **author**
Cultivating Genius **and** *Unearthing Joy*

Antiracist Reading Revolution is both a mentor and a needed companion to educators that includes an expansive foundation grounded in research, reflection, and action. Dr. Cherry-Paul's Antiracist Reading Framework provides a supportive guide that creates pathways for educators to collectively engage in necessary conversations and teach centering love and humanity within all parts of a younger reader's experience. Dr. Cherry-Paul's work will continue to thrive across time and spaces.

—Tiana Silvas, **educator**

Antiracist Reading Revolution peels back the often unquestioned layers of reading as a means for socialization and oppression. Dr. Cherry-Paul models the self-scrutiny and deliberate planning teachers must do to wield reading as an instrument for liberation. The accessible resources she provides guide teachers at any stage of their journey toward becoming antiracist educators.

—Anna Gotangco Osborn, **reading teacher**

In this powerful tool for individual and collective professional learning, Dr. Cherry-Paul demonstrates not only the self-work needed to begin—or delve deeper into—antiracist pedagogy, but also the ways to make that work actionable with students by implementing critical lenses woven together to form the Antiracist Reading Framework. Through dozens of examples applying the framework to recently published books, she provides clear pathways to teaching toward liberation.

—Keisha Smith-Carrington, **supervisor of humanities and co-author**
Read-Alouds with Heart: Literacy Lessons That Build Community, Comprehension, and Cultural Competence

Antiracist Reading Revolution is a tremendous gift for teachers everywhere and an essential addition to every literacy educator's professional library. Dr. Cherry-Paul offers a comprehensive toolkit that synthesizes decades of research in culturally responsive and liberatory instructional practices. The beauty and power of this book is the way Dr. Cherry-Paul guides teachers throughout, modeling expertly along the way what it means to be an antiracist reading teacher and teacher of young readers. The text selections, rich scholarship, and practical and engaging framework will deepen new and experienced teachers' practices. Following Dr. Cherry-Paul's lead, may we all be dandelions, planting the seeds of change that our young people deserve.

—Tricia Ebarvia, **author**
Get Free: Antibias Literacy Instruction for Stronger Readers, Writers, and Thinkers
Co-founder of the Institute for Racial Equity in Literacy, #DisruptTexts, and #31DaysIBPOC

One of our oaths as educators is to teach children how to think, not what to think. *Antiracist Reading Revolution* teaches us—teachers and librarians—how to think about the texts we lovingly place in our students' hands, heads, and hearts. More importantly, it teaches us how to center the essential work of antiracism in the classroom and in the library. This book is the educators' educator's guide, teaching readers how to use any text in ways that center activism and advocacy, love and liberation.

—Shana Frazin, **teacher librarian**
Scarsdale Middle School

It is not enough to diversify our bookshelves. How can interactions with a broader selection of voices and perspectives positively influence students' literacy development and their growth as global citizens? In this timely guide, Dr. Sonja Cherry-Paul supports and challenges teachers who are striving to dismantle historically racist pedagogies and build expansive, "identity-inspiring" learning opportunities with students. The book is rich with ancillary resources, practical strategies, and extensive ideas for teaching reading using critical, antiracist lenses.

—Donalyn Miller, **educator, reading advocate, and author**

Antiracist Reading Revolution is a powerful gift for educators and serves as a guide on how to take an antiracist teaching stance to create classrooms that center affirmation, joy, love, and liberation. This is a must-have book for all educators and schools to have in their professional library—and one I will be sharing in my work with my teachers.

—Michelle Yang-Kaczmarek, **K–8 literacy coordinator**

What does it mean to be an antiracist educator? In *Antiracist Reading Revolution*, Dr. Cherry-Paul skillfully and artfully leads educators through a framework that provides the necessary skills that work to build interpersonal relationships, establish affirmational environments, and present the important questions and language needed to teach and engage with literacy that is both loving and critical. The moves she shows teachers are not only grounded in the research but also practical and inspiring. Above all else, Dr. Cherry Paul teaches us how to bring an antiracist lens to all books that we read. This book will not only support educators in building stronger readers but it will also help us all be better humans.

—Amanda Hartman, **deputy director of**
primary literacy, advancing literacy
Teachers College, Columbia University

Antiracist Reading Revolution has the power and potential to create just that, a reading revolution. In this book, Dr. Cherry-Paul does more than make an argument for the need for books in classrooms that reflect and represent a diversity of human beings. She gives us the tools to use those books with our students in a way that will allow every single student to better enter into the world ready to view themselves and others in a positive way and to create positive change. This book is more than a road map for better reading instruction; it is a heart map for better living and better existing in the world.

—Jess Lifshitz, **fourth-grade ELA teacher**

This gift transcends the boundaries of traditional education, equipping educators with tools to foster liberation in the classroom that go beyond mere representation. It uplifts and empowers the souls of educators, igniting a powerful wave of change for a brighter and more beautiful tomorrow.

—Gary Gray, **author**
I'm From

This is such an important book for teachers! School is about education. Education is about creating critical thinkers. Critical thinkers need to have all the facts. The facts are that this is a culturally diverse world filled with people of all colors and cultures. All colors and cultures must be SEEN by children, and adults, in the classroom as fully functioning and contributing members of society. Test scores will sort themselves out just fine if Black and Brown children are SEEN in the classroom.

—Carole Lindstrom, **author of books for young people**

As an antiracist classroom elementary educator, I know the importance of my growth and having tools to improve my pedagogy. Dr. Sonja Cherry-Paul's *Antiracist Reading Revolution: A Framework for Teaching Beyond Representation Toward Liberation* demands we self-interrogate the development of our racial identity in a racialized society and reflect on how that influences our instruction. The framework's six critical lenses of Affirmation, Awareness, Authorship, Atmosphere, Activism, and Accountability require thoughtful and purposeful creation of lessons on social justice that even our youngest learners deserve to receive. The tools and guiding lessons Cherry-Paul offers have strengthened how I teach all my students to recognize the humanity of others and be agents of change in our diverse world. I am even more intentional about selecting books that provide opportunities to teach students how to be racially literate, using specific language, and increasing their awareness of recognizing, analyzing, and discussing injustice, race, and racism. I believe it is essential that our current and future generations of learners be empowered thinkers and activists, and Cherry-Paul's framework is a powerful means to get us there.

—Kyrie Gilmore, **NYC public school elementary educator**

Sonja Cherry-Paul provides a powerful antiracist reading framework that compels educators to lead with love, seek and state the truth, and teach toward liberation. Guided by six critical lenses, the reader is inspired to imagine what is possible—especially important during a time where professional autonomy is increasingly challenged. Sonja lights a path for antiracist educators and we are emboldened to act—centering humanity, justice, and hope.

—Jane Hsu, **principal**
P.S. 116 Mary Lindley Murray, NYC

I have never met an educator who does not want to make their teaching match their values. But the reality of teaching today means teachers are inundated with mandates, theories, and student needs with very little offered in terms of practical, step-by-step lessons, explanations, and resources to meet the avalanche of demands and very real concerns. *Antiracist Reading Revolution* is the book I dreamt of but never thought possible. Cherry-Paul gives us clear definitions and explanations of foundational scholarship while also holding our hand and walking us through lessons we can teach our students tomorrow, all within a framework that keeps our teaching from feeling disjointed. This is a gift of a book for educators and their students.

—M. Colleen Cruz, **educator and bestselling author**
Writers Read Better: Nonfiction

Dr. Sonja Cherry-Paul's *Antiracist Reading Revolution* is such a powerful book for all educators. Grounded in the latest culturally responsive research that centers the possibilities of Black and other children, Dr. Cherry-Paul has crafted a thorough handbook that provides educators with the *how* they are often searching to find. This robust text offers up resources and guidance for educators at all levels of their work with children; thus, with *Antiracist Reading Revolution*, there's no excuse not to do the work—immediately—that gets us closer toward truly equitable literacy practices. Dr. Cherry-Paul is leading the way. May we all follow!

—Kimberly N. Parker, **cofounder #disrupttexts cofounder and author**
Literacy Is Liberation: Working Toward Justice
Through Culturally Relevant Teaching

ANTIRACIST READING
REVOLUTION

To Zoe for the question that I hope this book answers.
And to all of the young people I've been fortunate enough to learn from.
You have always been poised and ready to lead the revolution.

SONJA CHERRY-PAUL

#1 New York Times Bestselling Author

ANTIRACIST READING
REVOLUTION

A Framework
for Teaching
Beyond
Representation
Toward Liberation

Foreword by **YOLANDA SEALEY-RUIZ**
Art by **PORSCHE JOSEPH**

GRADES K–8

CORWIN **Literacy**

FOR INFORMATION:

Corwin

A SAGE Company

2455 Teller Road

Thousand Oaks, California 91320

(800) 233-9936

www.corwin.com

SAGE Publications Ltd.

1 Oliver's Yard

55 City Road

London EC1Y 1SP

United Kingdom

SAGE Publications India Pvt. Ltd.

Unit No 323-333, Third Floor, F-Block

International Trade Tower Nehru Place

New Delhi 110 019

India

SAGE Publications Asia-Pacific Pte. Ltd.

18 Cross Street #10-10/11/12

China Square Central

Singapore 048423

Vice President and
  Editorial Director: Monica Eckman

Executive Editor: Tori Mello Bachman

Content Development Editor: Sharon Wu

Product Associate: Zachary Vann

Project Editor: Amy Schroller

Copy Editor: Gillian Dickens

Typesetter: C&M Digitals (P) Ltd.

Proofreader: Lawrence W. Baker

Indexer: Molly Hall

Cover Designer: Scott Van Atta

Marketing Manager: Margaret O'Connor

Printed in Canada

ISBN 978-1-0719-1535-6

This book is printed on acid-free paper.

24 25 26 27 28 10 9 8 7 6 5 4 3 2 1

Contents

A NOTE ON THE ARTWORK   xv

FOREWORD BY YOLANDA SEALEY-RUIZ   xix

ACKNOWLEDGMENTS   xxiii

ABOUT THE AUTHOR   xxvii

INTRODUCTION: THERE'S NO SUCH THING AS
ANTIRACIST FAIRY DUST   1

CHAPTER 1: BE A DANDELION: A METAPHOR AND
VISION FOR ANTIRACIST TEACHING   23

CHAPTER 2: CENTER BIPOC IN TEXTS   43

     Lesson: *I Am Every Good Thing,*
        by Derrick Barnes and illustrated by Gordon C. James   52

     Lesson: *Tía Fortuna's New Home,* by Ruth Behar and illustrated
        by Devon Holzwarth   56

     Lesson: *My Two Border Towns,* by David Bowles and illustrated by
        Erika Meza   60

     Lesson: *I Am Golden,* by Eva Chen and illustrated by Sophie Diao   64

     Lesson: *Wild Berries,* written and illustrated by Julie Flett   69

     Lesson: *I'm From,* by Gary R. Gray Jr. and illustrated by Oge Mora   73

     Lesson: *A Day With No Words,* by Tiffany Hammond and illustrated by
        Kate Cosgrove   77

     Lesson: *Homeland,* by Hannah Moushabeck and illustrated by Reem Madooh   81

     Lesson: *My Rainbow,* by Trinity and DeShanna Neal and illustrated
        by Art Twink   86

     Lesson: *My Papi Has a Motorcycle,* by Isabel Quintero and illustrated by
        Zeke Peña   90

     Lesson: *I Can Write the World,* by Joshunda Sanders and illustrated by
        Charly Palmer   94

CHAPTER 3: RECOGNIZE CULTURAL, COMMUNITY, AND COLLECTIVE PRACTICES   99

Lesson: *Uncle John's City Garden*, by Bernette G. Ford and illustrated by Frank Morrison   110

Lesson: *Berry Song*, written and illustrated by Michaela Goade   114

Lesson: *A Crown for Corina*, by Laekan Zea Kemp and illustrated by Elisa Chavarri   118

Lesson: *The Night Before Eid: A Muslim Family Story*, by Aya Khalil and illustrated by Rashin Kheiriyeh   123

Lesson: *My Powerful Hair*, by Carole Lindstrom and illustrated by Steph Littlebird   127

Lesson: *Dancing the Tinikling*, by Bobbie Peyton and illustrated by Diobelle Cerna   132

Lesson: *Plátanos Are Love*, by Alyssa Reynosso-Morris and illustrated by Mariyah Rahman   136

Lesson: *My Bindi*, by Gita Varadarajan and illustrated by Archana Sreenivasan   140

Lesson: *Luli and the Language of Tea*, by Andrea Wang and illustrated by Hyewon Yum   144

Lesson: *Amy Wu and the Perfect Bao*, by Kat Zhang and illustrated by Charlene Chua   148

CHAPTER 4: SHATTER SILENCES AROUND RACISM   153

Lesson: *Unspeakable: The Tulsa Race Massacre*, by Carole Boston Weatherford and illustrated by Floyd Cooper   168

Lesson: *When We Say Black Lives Matter*, written and illustrated by Maxine Beneba Clarke   172

Lesson: *The 1619: Project Born on the Water*, by Nikole Hannah-Jones and Renée Watson and illustrated by Nikkolas Smith   176

Lesson: *Build a House*, by Rhiannon Giddens and illustrated by Monica Mikai   181

Lesson: *We Are Still Here! Native American Truths Everyone Should Know*, by Traci Sorell and illustrated by Frané Lessac   185

CHAPTER 5: HELP STUDENTS ACQUIRE RACIAL LITERACY   189

Lesson: *Stamped (For Kids): Racism, Antiracism, and You*, by Sonja Cherry-Paul, Ibram X. Kendi, and Jason Reynolds, and illustrated by Rachelle Baker   200

Lesson: *Skin Again*, by bell hooks and illustrated by Chris Raschka   204

Lesson: *The Antiracist Kid: A Book About Identity, Justice, and Activism*, by Tiffany Jewell and illustrated by Nicole Miles   207

Lesson: *Our Skin: A First Conversation About Race*, by Megan Madison, Jessica Ralli, and illustrated by Isabel Roxas   211

Lesson: *Where Are You From?* by Yamile Saied Méndez and illustrated by Jaime Kim   215

CHAPTER 6: LEARN ABOUT COMMUNITY ACTIVISTS   219

Lesson: *We Have a Dream: Meet 30 Young Indigenous People and People of Color Protecting the Planet*, by Dr. Mya-Rose Craig and illustrated by Sabrena Khadija   228

Lesson: *Autumn Peltier, Water Warrior*, written by Carole Lindstrom and illustrated by Bridget George   232

Lesson: *Resistance: My Story of Activism*, by Frantzy Luzincourt   236

Lesson: *Young Water Protectors . . . A Story About Standing Rock*, by Aslan Tudor and Kelly Tudor   240

Lesson: *The Light She Feels Inside*, by Gwendolyn Wallace and illustrated by Olivia Duchess   244

Lesson: *More Than Peach: Changing the World . . . One Crayon at a Time!* by Bellen Woodard and illustrated by Fanny Liem   248

CHAPTER 7: SUSTAINING THE REVOLUTION   253

EPILOGUE: BUILDING THE MOVEMENT FOR HUMAN LIBERATION   265

APPENDICES

Appendix Contents   271

Appendix A: Antiracist Reading Framework (Chapter 1)   272

Appendix B: Recalling Reading Experiences in School (Chapter 2)   273

Appendix C: Historical and Sociocultural Understandings Chart (Chapter 3)   274

Appendix D: Every Book Is About Race! (Chapter 4)   275

Appendix E: What I Learned in K–12 Schooling (Chapter 5)   276

Appendix F: Racial Literacy Development and Reading Instruction (Chapter 5)   280

Appendix G: Considering Curriculum, Books, and Activism (Chapter 6)   281

Appendix H: Student Toolkit of Critical Lenses for Antiracist
    Reading for Older Readers (Chapter 7)   282

Appendix I: Student Toolkit of Critical Lenses for Antiracist
    Reading for Younger Readers (Chapter 7)   284

Appendix J: Educator Toolkit of Critical Lenses for Antiracist
    Reading Instruction (Chapter 7)   286

Appendix K: Middle Grade and YA Recommendations   289

AUTHOR'S NOTE   291

REFERENCES   293

INDEX   301

A Note on the Artwork

Like a dandelion seed, allow a gust of wind to carry you to fertile ground and take root, believing firmly that antiracist teaching is not about uniformity; it's about possibility.

Writing this book was an opportunity for me to communicate the beautiful complexity of the work of antiracism. I'm grateful to my friend and brilliant educator and thought-partner M. Colleen Cruz, who listened to my goals for this book. Understanding that antiracism is living, fluid work, she suggested I come up with an organic symbol that could be a metaphor for what I was trying to achieve. I thought about this for weeks, considered several options, but nothing seemed quite right.

One spring morning, I looked through my kitchen window and noticed the first dandelions of the season emerging in my backyard. I thought about the resilience of dandelions despite the efforts of many to destroy them. I visited my local library and bookstore to learn as much as I could about dandelions. I had no idea how important they are to the environment. Soil, grass, and many organisms including human beings benefit from dandelions. I learned that the word *dandelion* comes from the French phrase *dent de lion* (which translates in English as "lion's teeth") because of its teeth-like leaves. My research helped me to understand dandelions as strong, noble perennials concerned not only with their survival but also with helping other organisms around them to thrive. I knew I had found the perfect symbol to represent my ideas.

Across this book you'll see images of dandelions painted by the brilliant artist Porsche Joseph, who also designed the cover of this book. You'll learn facts about dandelions in each chapter and you'll discover why I've used them as a metaphor for antiracism. Each chapter begins with an image of a dandelion from the stages of its life lifecycle. Not only is the dandelion a metaphor for antiracism, but it is also a symbol of our growth, our progress, and our journey as antiracist educators.

▶ "Much as dandelions must resiliently shed their leaves as a part of their natural life cycle, educators must be willing to discard nonessential beliefs. This shedding process involves conscious and subconscious recognition that certain beliefs have outlived their purpose and must be buried and released to permit new growth." ~ Yolanda Sealey-Ruiz

▶ *There's no such thing as antiracist fairy dust, glittery sparkles we can blow into the air that can magically transform society. To be antiracist requires us to utilize our powers of ongoing commitment and action.*

▶ *Dandelions are the perfect metaphor for antiracist teaching. Like dandelions, the work of antiracism has been viewed negatively—as an invasive, unlikeable, useless weed. It is true that antiracism does not fit the standard; it is disruptive of it.*

▶ *Antiracist teaching, however, isn't just about the books we make available to students, but about our stance as antiracist educators.*

▶ *A commitment to antiracist teaching requires us to be brave enough to ask: What are the unwritten rules determining what and how I teach? And it requires that we are willing to interrogate what we uncover.*

▶ *Antiracist reading instruction helps readers understand that every author's identity, experiences, and perspectives are imbued with race, which informs the ways in which they write and that every reader's identity, experiences, and perspectives are imbued with race, which informs the ways in which they read.*

▶ *As educators, we can acknowledge that facilitating conversations about race and racism can be uncomfortable. But we must also recognize that collectively, we remain stuck when we lean away from the discomfort rather than confront it and work to dismantle inequity in all of its forms.*

▶ *Activists amplify the voices of those who are marginalized and work alongside them to fight for change. In order for students to develop such understandings, educators must see themselves as activists whose work is about much more than teaching students to decode words.*

▶ *Antiracist teaching fertilizes the soil where children are planted and nurtures their souls, making it possible for them to thrive within schools and beyond them.*

▶ *Solidarity means we confront, challenge, and change ourselves, even and especially when the work is hard, fully understanding that the journey to justice is not simple or linear.*

Sowing Seeds of Equity

Nurturing Antiracist Practices in Reading Instruction

"*In embracing the wisdom embedded in this book, educators themselves can transform as teachers, breaking through the confines of the classroom, shaping how students read and perceive their community, their world, and their place within both.*"

—Yolanda Sealey-Ruiz, Ph.D.

Like dandelion seeds scattered by the gentle breath of possibility, young people possess an innate capacity to travel vast distances, guided by the winds of their dreams and aspirations. Dr. Sonja Cherry-Paul, in exploring the profound transformative power of literature, invites educators to be the wind that propels these seeds of potential forward movement; a goal of this book is to build their racial literacy and equip them with a justice-centered consciousness. "Be the wind that carries them forth," she writes with poetic eloquence, a guiding principle that echoes through the pages of this groundbreaking book.

As I read Dr. Cherry-Paul's book, *Antiracist Reading Revolution: A Framework for Teaching Beyond Representation Toward Liberation*, I imagined three of my favorite thinkers and writers—James Baldwin, Toni Morrison, and Maya Angelou—sitting for tea and discussing the great offering that is this book. All of them were giants in their craft and icons in the writing of the self and the seeing of others—particularly those who are pushed to the margin. I imagined them discussing how their own lives were representational dandelions; how they did their best to both create and ride on the seeds of change to bring forth love, joy, justice, and beauty, in the midst of struggle. I imagined them talking about this book as an excellent resource to help educators do what they sought to do in their own books—to see all people as flowers in human form who deserve nurturing so that their lives may flourish. Dr. Cherry-Paul understands that it is an honor to teach children and help them mold ideas about themselves and the world. As a seasoned educator of literacy, she knows very well that reading books is a privileged pathway to help children do this.

In this beautifully articulated and transformative book, Dr. Cherry-Paul has offered a vital tool for educators to recognize, validate, and amplify the voices of students who have been marginalized by school systems and culturally irrelevant and unresponsive curricula. Drawing from her wellspring of experience as a literacy educator, she is a thoughtful guide, illuminating the way with personal anecdotes and examples. The book offers the opportunity to explore the layers that shape one's identity as a reader and, by extension, an educator. In the realm of education, where decoding and fluency are crucial, Dr. Cherry-Paul incites a paradigm shift, emphasizing the profound importance of connecting literature to students' lives, dreams, and challenges. Reading, she asserts, extends beyond the decoding of words; it is a vital terrain that shapes a child's educational journey and should offer a connection to their ancestral roots and guidance for their current experiences. She reminds us that literature must be used as a mirror reflecting the diverse tapestry of human experiences. Dr. Cherry-Paul passionately advocates for culturally relevant education, emphasizing the urgency of incorporating the life histories and current experiences of all students in the curriculum—a nonnegotiable aspect of humanizing pedagogy.

Dr. Cherry-Paul's examples are a true gift that highlight the importance for teachers to engage authentically with their students and foster a reading environment where both educators and students are visible. The book's unique approach to building a community of antiracist thinkers through the lens of literature is a powerful mechanism for honing the lenses of humanity. The blending of classic and contemporary research with personal scholarship enriches the book's narrative and generously offers multiple entry points for educators to engage the transformative work of building antiracist reading classrooms. In the spirit of scholar activism, this book is a compelling testament to the importance of creating and sustaining inclusive and empowering educational spaces.

The significance of culturally relevant education and building racial literacy emerges as guiding principles throughout the book. In a world where representation is important but liberation is paramount, the book becomes a testament to the necessity of curricula that mirror all students' life histories and unique experiences. It is not a choice but an imperative—a pedagogy that humanizes and empowers every child toward personal liberation within a collective struggle for freedom. Dr. Cherry-Paul reminds educators that this advocacy is an unyielding commitment they must uphold, and her book reinforces the transformative potential inherent in culturally relevant, antiracist teaching.

Dr. Cherry-Paul generously applies the six critical lenses of her **Antiracist Reading Framework** to an array of diverse books that offer teachers and students reflective pathways to understanding the many lessons within a text. The carefully curated books she includes serve as vehicles to navigate teachers and students along meaningful reflective pathways.

Additionally, she offers creative ideas on how to connect the book and characters to teachers' and students' lives while building their antiracist vision for reading. This book is so timely in how it empowers teachers to construct a meaningful library reflective of the current moment while also teaching the crucial skill of selecting books that resonate with students. Through Dr. Cherry-Paul's guidance, educators will not only build mirrors that reflect their students' diversity but also open windows and doors to a world of perspectives and experiences beyond their immediate surroundings. Dr. Cherry-Paul's meticulous application of the six critical lenses testifies to her commitment to reshaping the landscape of reading instruction. This book is not merely an exploration of diverse literature; it is a call to action, an encouragement for educators to connect these literary offerings to the worlds of their students and change the way reading is taught in the majority of classrooms across the nation. Her **Antiracist Reading Framework** will be a powerful tool for educators who are guided by a vision of inclusivity and justice. By applying these critical lenses, educators become equipped to hold reflective discussions in their classrooms, lead students to explore narratives, and connect stories to their own lives. Dr. Cherry-Paul's approach is a multidimensional journey that builds bridges between the literature and the readers, creating spaces for profound self-reflection and growth across grade levels and teacher experience. It is also an immensely practical book. Dr. Cherry-Paul transcends theoretical discussions, providing reflection and accountability questions that help educators cross the terrain of antiracist teaching.

In embracing the wisdom embedded in this book, educators themselves can transform as teachers, breaking through the confines of the classroom, shaping how students read and perceive their community, their world, and their place within both. Much as dandelions must resiliently shed their leaves as a part of their natural life cycle, educators must be willing to discard nonessential beliefs. This shedding process involves conscious and subconscious recognition that certain beliefs have outlived their purpose and must be buried and released to permit new growth. Dr. Cherry-Paul accompanies readers into this cycle of renewal, in which they can confront their assumptions, biases, and preconceptions and dig through deeper layers to understand their origins and implications. As individuals shed old beliefs and embrace new perspectives, they can flourish in their personal growth and help their reading students do the same. The message in *Antiracist Reading Revolution: A Framework for Teaching Beyond Representation Toward Liberation* is clear: "Be a dandelion, embrace openness, flourish in change, and bring beauty to the lives of others." This book reclaims the reading classroom as the inviting space it was meant to be, supporting and nourishing new life.

Acknowledgments

Archbishop Desmond Tutu has explained that we cannot be human on our own. We become human through relationships. This spirit of Ubuntu—I am, because you are—is a reflection of what it means to work, live, and thrive together. And it is this traditional African philosophy that I draw upon to give thanks to the many people I come from.

I am blessed to be Black and to come from Black women who raised me. Mary. Barbara. Big Ma. Ellen. So much of how I carry myself and move through the world is rooted in your love, your knowing, your prayers, your laughter, your resourceful hands.

The brilliance, strength, and leadership of Black women sustains me. Dr. Yolanda Sealey-Ruiz, my mentor, friend, sissy—I've never met anyone like you. Yolie, you are light and love personified. You are what excellence looks like from all angles. I am in constant awe of you—your scholarship and your nurturing spirit. I will forever be grateful for the two-year inquiry course at Columbia that led me to you. Thank you for not just seeing me, but for noticing me. Thank you for writing such a beautiful fore-word. Thank you to Dr. Rudine Sims Bishop, Dr. Gloria Ladson-Billings, Dr. Barbara Love, Dr. Bettina Love, and Dr. Gholdy Muhammad. Your intellect and fierce advocacy are roadmaps for liberation. The ancestors dance at the very sound of your names.

Porsche Joseph, you dreamed up a gorgeous cover! I tear up every time I look at this beautiful child. I am so thankful that your art graces this entire book. Thank you my friend, my sister.

Jason Reynolds, Dr. Ibram X. Kendi, and Lisa Yoskowitz, thank you for the invitation to adapt Stamped (For Kids). I'm honored to be part of the legacy of Stamped and I'm grateful for your continued support of me and my work.

I am fortunate to have incredible friendships that make my life beauty—FULL. Portia James, it has been three decades of friendship and love. I am so grateful for our contin-ued laughter and joy. Colleen Cruz, my brilliant friend. Thank you for being an incred-ible thought-partner. It is because of you that I came up with the dandelion as a symbol and metaphor in this book. I love that we have entire conversations in GIFs—no words needed. Elmo/Zoe flames is forever ours. Tricia Ebarvia, my sister, your brilliance and talents are abundant. I love freedom-dreaming with you. Thank you for all of the ways you challenge and stretch me. Our ice cream shop on that island will happen.

Dana Johansen, Joanne Marciano-Watson, and Tara Lencl, I am so thankful for the squad we became at Columbia University—how we supported each other and continue to do so.

Carolyn Denton, Melissa Garcia, Erica Willimas, and Michelle Yang-Kazmarek, thank you for cheering me on, for your loving patience when I haven't communicated as much as I should, for dragging me away from work and reminding me of the importance of friendship. Jackie Marcus, I would not have survived my first years as a teacher without your friendship, guidance, leadership, love, and solidarity.

Sara Ahmed, my baby bear, and Fred Joseph, my brother, thank you for the fierce ways you love and look out for me. Shana Frazin and Amanda Hartman, my friends and co-conspirators, you've had my back so many times, in so many ways. Thank you for being in community with me.

To all of my IREL family—Aeriale Johnson, Anna Osborne, Tiana Silvas, Keisha Smith-Carrington, Jessica Lifshitz, Dulce-Marie Flecha, Chris Hall, shea martin, Dr. Cody Miller, Min Pai, LaMar Timmons-Long, and Josh Thompson—you've challenged and changed me. I'm grateful for all of the ways you've helped me grow. Kim! Dr. Parker, thank you for your generous heart and warm spirit. We WILL finish our project.

Farah Khan and the House9 Family, you've made building Red Clay Educators an absolute joy. Thank you for dreaming big with me and for being such a beautiful force for good in the world. Jordyn Aponte and Clare Landrigan, thank you for your generous support of Red Clay Educators.

Angela Bae, Julie Graham, Jerry Harris, Jodi Manby, and the entire Cotsen Family, thank you for inviting me into this incredible community of educators. I enjoy every opportunity to work alongside you to create more equitable and antiracist curriculum, classrooms, and schools.

I am incredibly appreciative of the Corwin team. Tori Bachman, thank you for shepherding this writing from the beginning and for the thoughtful ways you pushed me throughout. Thank you Sharon Wu, Margaret O'Connor, Rose Storey, Zack Vann, Amy Schroller, Lisa Leudeke, and Scott Van Atta for all of the work and details you've managed along the way.

To all the reviewers and endorsers of this book, I am so grateful. Thank you for the time you've taken to read my work. Your feedback, affirmations, and critiques are deeply appreciated as the work of antiracism is a journey where none of us just simply arrive. I'm humbled to continue the ongoing, complex work of learning and unlearning and I'm honored to do so in community with you.

Mom and Dad, thank you for your enduring love and sacrifices. I'm proud to be your daughter. And thank you Eddie for being my big brother my whole life—always protecting and championing me.

Finally, to Frank and Imani. We have always known that "three is the magic number." Thank you for the ways you nourish and love me. I am always happiest when I'm with you. Everything I do is done with the intention of making you proud.

PUBLISHER'S ACKNOWLEDGMENTS

Corwin gratefully acknowledges the contributions of the following reviewers:

Melissa Black
Teacher, Whittier Elementary School (DCPS)
Washington, DC

Chris Hass
Asst. Professor, Early, Elementary, and Reading Education
James Madison University
Harrisonburg, VA

Tinisha Shaw
Educator/Equity Coordinator and Coach, Diversity Equity Inclusion Department,
Guilford County Schools
Greensboro, NC

Viviana Tamas
Literacy Coach
White Plains, NY

About the Author

Dr. Sonja Cherry-Paul is the founder of Red Clay Educators, co-director of the Institute for Racial Equity in Literacy, co-director of the Teach Black History All Year Institute, and executive producer and host of The Black Creators Series. She is an educator with more than 20 years of classroom experience who has written several books that support reading and writing instruction and has adapted the #1 *New York Times Bestseller, Stamped (For Kids)*. Sonja leads professional development for schools and organizations in equity and antiracism. She invites you to visit her online at sonjacherrypaul.com.

There's No Such Thing As Antiracist Fairy Dust

When we commit to antiracist ideas, we commit to love. This commitment moves us from the arbitrary use of this word, often limited to a feeling. Instead, we begin to perceive love as an action.

During a virtual author's visit, Jason Reynolds and I met with a group of incredible young people. The entire evening was designed as a Q&A for students to ask us questions about *Stamped: Racism, Antiracism, and You* and *Stamped (For Kids): Racism, Antiracism, and You.* The brilliance of the students radiated across our Zoom screens. The first question of the night was from a young Black girl who asked, "When can we move beyond representation to liberation?" I was not ready for this beautiful, audacious question and fumbled my way into a response that was woefully insufficient. I wish I'd said, "You are right. Representation is not liberation. This alone is *not* how we get free."

This book is in essence my response to this young person's question. It offers a vision for antiracist teaching as well as tools to move beyond representation—from simply having books by and about BIPOC in classrooms—to liberation—where students learn to radically and unabashedly love themselves and their communities, as well as learn what it means to work for the good of the collective.

There's no such thing as antiracist fairy dust, glittery sparkles we can blow into the air that can magically transform society. To be antiracist requires us to utilize our powers of ongoing commitment and action. Scholar, educator, and author Dr. Angela Davis says, "In a racist society it is not enough to be non-racist, one has to be antiracist." Davis distinguishes between rhetoric that aims to be neutral and passive and a mind-set that is intentional and active. With an intentional and active mind-set, antiracists understand that equity does not mean equality. Rather than striving for balance and sameness, there is acknowledgment of imbalance, recognition of the historical legacy of inequities and its enduring consequences, and a clear focus to redress this. This includes an understanding that pathways for repair must be intersectional; they must reject anti-Blackness, anti-immigrant, transphobia, homophobia, ableism, antisemitism, sexism, anti-Muslim hate, anti-Asian hate, xenophobia, ageism, and any discrimination and hate toward an individual or group of people. To be antiracist is to commit to a lived, liberated practice of continuous work toward the goal of equity, justice, and freedom. To be antiracist is to commit to love.

> To be antiracist is to commit to a lived, liberated practice of continuous work toward the goal of equity, justice, and freedom. To be antiracist is to commit to love.

Black students, however, have had to endure the absence of love throughout the history of schooling in the United States. In *Punished for Dreaming* (2023), Dr. Bettina Love spotlights the decades-long educational policies and practices that cause stark racial disproportionality in school suspension and dropout rates, arrest, and incarceration of Black children as well as the lifelong impact such absence of love has on Black people and

Black communities. The polarization of Black students and White students has been the sturdy foundation from which the institution of schooling has been built (Cherry-Paul, 2020). But even in the face of these data along with the ways the 2020 COVID-19 pandemic has supposedly opened our eyes wider to such polarization, inequities, and racism, there have been few efforts to confront this with antiracist solutions. Today's learning loss narrative, for example, has been repackaged and emerges "from a long history of performance-based narratives and policies in education such as the achievement gap, A Nation at Risk, 'failing schools,' No Child Left Behind, and Race to the Top" (Cherry-Paul, 2023).

So what does it mean for educators to be antiracist and to commit to love? Dr. Gholdy Muhammad (2023) explains that "we have given attention, care, and nurturing to some children and neglected others" and calls on us to water the genius of students even and especially as we urgently work to dismantle educational environments that are dry from systemic racism and oppression (p. 19). A commitment to love is a commitment to redressing injustices that impact the lives of children and their communities. It is to nurture, feed, and protect. Young people are nourished when they are supported, encouraged, and have opportunities to activate their learning in meaningful ways. This book is for educators who fortify and fuel students who enter classrooms already brilliant—brimming with ideas, dreams, and possibilities. It is a charge for educators to connect with parents and caregivers who are their children's first teachers, the first to love them and to know their hearts. And this book is also for young people, like the person I met that night during that virtual author's visit, who are poised and ready to lead the revolution for love and liberation.

One only has to look across history to see that young people have led the revolution for justice and equality. In the 1950s and 1960s, youth empowerment transformed the nation. After learning about Black leaders such as Harriet Tubman, 15-year-old Claudette Colvin refused to give up her seat on a bus in Montgomery, Alabama, months before Rosa Parks's notable arrest. Ernest Green, Elizabeth Eckford, Jefferson Thomas, Terrence Roberts, Carlotta Walls La Nier, Minnijean Brown, Gloria Ray Karlmark, Thelma Mothershed, and Melba Pattillo Beals—also known as The Little Rock Nine—desegregated their high school in Little Rock, Arkansas. At just six years old, Ruby Bridges desegregated her all-White elementary school in New Orleans, Louisiana. North Carolina A&T State University students, Ezell Blair Jr., David Richmond, Franklin McCain, and Joseph McNeil became known as the Greensboro Four who launched a movement when they sat at a "Whites only" Woolworth's lunch counter. Huey P. Newton and Bobby Seale met in college and started the Black Panther Party to challenge police brutality, confront corrupt politicians, protect Black people, and promote social change. Inspired by the Black Panther Party, 15-year-old David Sanchez launched the Young Chicanos for Community Action, which became the Brown Berets and gave way to the Chicano Movement. The work of young leaders of the past continues to inform movements today such as the Water Protectors of Standing Rock, Black Lives Matter, intersectional environmentalism, and the young people who lead within these movements. Movements where young people assert their humanity and are essentially fighting for and to be loved.

Students in classrooms right now are the young revolutionaries of today and tomorrow who deserve love and who are ready to plant the seeds of change.

The ascent to a democracy grounded in liberation begins by recognizing the brilliance, beauty, and full humanity of Black and Brown people who make up the global majority. Antiracist reading instruction brings about such recognition through purposeful, powerful acknowledgment of this. When cultivated, readers are able to resist persistent attempts to go backward or stand still in the work of equity and instead move forward in the fight for justice. Understanding the work and pitfalls that have come before is essential to informing where we are now, what antiracist teaching is, and how it can help us get where we need to go.

Disrupting a "Heroes and Holidays" Curriculum

The push for including racially and culturally diverse texts in classrooms and antiracist teaching stems from the work of many revolutionaries, including those from the multicultural education movement. In 1989, Dr. James Banks, notable scholar of this movement, theorized about the approach most frequently used to teach beyond mainstream curriculum. He called it the Contributions Approach where a White, Eurocentric curriculum and teaching focus remains intact and students learn only about the contributions made by famous Black and Brown people during specific days of the year. Ultimately, this is an additive and appendage approach that teaches students that people of color must be extraordinary to be worthy of inclusion. Students learn canned narratives that silence racism and oversimplify the realities of oppression. This stance is about perpetuating a belief in meritocracy, not antiracism. Rather than education being used as a tool for liberation, a Contributions Approach uses education as a tool to evade societal inequities and

Learn more about teaching Black history year-round.

instead socializes children into believing that if individuals just work hard, they can succeed. A further consequence of this stance is that students miss out on learning to understand the nuanced and complex lived realities of Black and Brown people and to see them in complete, dynamic ways.

This problematic teaching stance, also known as a Heroes and Holidays approach, continues today in classrooms across the United States. The most observable example of this is Black History Month, when many students learn about Dr. Martin Luther King Jr. and Rosa Parks only during the month of February through reassuring narratives that obscure the realities of racism past and present. This is not to say that Black History Month does not have value in schools and should not be acknowledged. We must also teach about the histories and accomplishments of Black people all year.

Disrupting additive approaches toward curriculum and teaching has been decades in the making by education scholars, teachers, and caregivers concerned about BIPOC students' ability to thrive in an institution that was never built with them in mind. These activists recognize that the curriculum is our most radical tool. Curriculum is not simply a mechanism to teach content. It is a tool for teaching ways of thinking about whose histories, experiences, and ways of knowing and being in the world are valid and have value. For many Black and Brown students, the curriculum has been identity-silencing—perspectives that mirror their racial and cultural identities are included in superficial ways or not at all. There are numerous obstacles in the way of disrupting the Heroes and Holidays approach, specifically in reading instruction, including resistance, discomfort, and misunderstandings.

SYSTEMIC RESISTANCE

Whenever there have been efforts to make things more just in the United States, these efforts have been embroiled in struggle. In 2020, the nation seemed to finally be willing to reckon with the realities of racism as a result of a health and racial pandemic. COVID-19 disproportionately ravaged the lives of Black and Brown people. White rage and police brutality were on display when Ahmaud Arbury was murdered by White men while jogging, and Breonna Taylor and Geroge Floyd were murdered by police officers. As a result of this reckoning, there were concerted efforts by many White Americans to buy and read all of the books that could help the country realize an antiracist future. Books that were written by and about people of color were in high demand in bookstores around the country.

But "a racist system always seeks to correct itself," educator and author Dr. Yolanda Sealey-Ruiz reminds us. History teaches us that backlash, resistance, and organized opposition designed to undermine racial-justice sentiments and policies have been a constant pattern. And by 2021, the sentiment in the country shifted from "buy all of the antiracist books" to "ban all of the antiracist books." By 2022, more than 30 states had adopted misguided "anti-CRT" policies and legislation, which police what teachers can teach, display, or discuss in classrooms (CRT Forward Tracking Project Team, 2023). The ripple effects of this have been swift. As a result of political pressures, for example, African American studies curriculum for advanced placement courses has been stripped of content in Florida, with several other states working to review the course and possibly impose similar restrictions (Pendharker, 2023). The American Library Association has tracked a record number of book bans across the United States implemented by schools and public libraries that target books about race, racism, gender, and LGBTQIA+ identities (Pendharker, 2023). These policies and practices are designed to deny truths about inequities and oppression that make White people in positions of power uncomfortable. Book bannings designed to block students from accessing books that don't fit into a White, heterosexual, cisgender roadmap are harming teachers, students, and families across the country. Activists, communities, students, educators, and authors fight against these barriers, locally and nationally, that, if left unchallenged, perpetuate the Contributions Approach that the nation had grown comfortable with—the kind of teaching that silences and erases.

The acronym CRT is sometimes used to refer to critical race theory or culturally relevant teaching or culturally responsive teaching, depending on the context of what is being written or spoken about. They are each distinct, although there are common ideas about injustice across this scholarship. I suggest researching more about these concepts from legitimate sources as you move forward in your antiracist teaching journey.

Resources

- *Dreamkeepers: Successful Teachers of African American Children,* by Gloria Ladson-Billings

- *Culturally Responsive Teaching: Theory, Research, and Practice,* by Geneva Gay

- *Culturally Sustaining Pedagogies: Teaching and Learning for Justice in a Changing World,* edited by Django Paris and H. Samy Alim

- *Critical Race Theory: The Key Writings That Formed the Movement,* edited by Kimberlé Crenshaw, Neil Gotanda, Gary Peller, and Kendall Thomas

[Reflect]

- Have there been times when there has been momentum for talking and teaching about race and racism in your school?

- Have these moments been reactive to local, national, or global events or proactive, grounded in beliefs about equity?

- In what ways are race and racism silenced in your school and curriculum?

TEACHER DISCOMFORT

In states where educators are not legally bound by oppressive policies and laws to cause teachers to turn away from an inclusive and antiracist stance in their classrooms, there can be other barriers. Such as teacher discomfort. More than 80% of educators in the nation are White (NCES, 2020), and echoed across the research is that many White teachers are uncomfortable talking and teaching about racism and other social injustices

Read more about #DisruptTexts here.

(Cherry-Paul, 2019). When teachers cling to their discomfort rather than interrogate it, teaching that silences identities and inequities is perpetuated. One way this occurs in reading instruction is an unyielding allegiance to canonical texts that erase or distort the identities and lived experiences of Black and Brown people. The #DisruptTexts movement led by four educators and women of color, Tricia Ebarvia, Lorena Germán, Dr. Kim Parker, and Julia Torres, has shifted the consciousness of many educators when it comes to the literary canon. They challenge educators to consider that "the traditional 'canon'—at all grade levels—has excluded the voices and rich literary legacies of communities of color. This exclusion hurts all students, and especially students of color" (#DisruptTexts, n.d.). In addition to noting the harm such allegiances cause, they remind us that it is not only high school texts that are part of the traditional canon. Elementary and middle school reading curriculums are also implicated.

I remember working with sixth-grade educators who were mired to the practice of teaching whole-class novels. I suggested the ways this approach could disengage readers, particularly when the texts always centered on White characters. One teacher declared, "I would rather die than give up *The Giver*!" This educator was not simply a devoted Lois Lowery fan. She had lost sight of the fact that as teachers of reading, we don't teach books; we teach children. She had not thought about the ways reading one book with the whole class over multiple weeks took time away from students being able to read more books—and that reading volume is one of the key aspects of developing reading skill and autonomy. Halting students' reading lives is not liberation. Yet this teacher was unwilling to interrogate her racial consciousness for the ways her practices were specifically hindering Black and Brown readers from feeling more connected to reading in their classroom as well as visible and validated in the world.

[Reflect]

- What books would make you think you would rather "die" than let go of them? Why?
- How can you adjust your thinking to honor the lived experiences of your students?
- What changes can you make in your reading curriculum and instruction that move you closer toward teaching for liberation?

MISUNDERSTANDINGS ABOUT THE WORK OF ANTIRACIST TEACHING

Another obstacle to being firmly rooted in antiracist teaching is misunderstandings by teachers about what this actually entails. As a classroom teacher, I felt incredibly proud about having an abundance of powerful, racially, and culturally diverse books for students to read. Books literally surrounded my classroom. They were on displays, on countertops, on magnetic shelves. They were floating off the wall on invisible shelves. They were in bookcases and in baskets. I just had to have the latest Jacqueline Woodson picture book. I rushed to bookstores to find Margarita Engle's newest gorgeous prose novel to add to the basket. The latest Kwame Alexander and Jason Reynolds books could always be found in my classroom. I was particularly proud of the books I'd curated for students to read in book clubs.

When I look back and reflect on my teaching in reading, I can see that for a time, I was simply focused on collecting books. I recognized that these authors are indeed among the greatest writers of young people's lives. I wanted my students to have access to incredible literature. And I understood the importance of readers seeing themselves reflected in the books they read, which is part of an antiracist approach shaped by the scholarship of multicultural educator and scholar Dr. Rudine Sims Bishop.

Dr. Bishop (1990) writes about the ways books can serve as mirrors, windows, and sliding-glass doors for readers. She intentionally focuses on the importance of Black and Brown children having access to books that serve as mirrors, reflecting their identities and their lives. While this metaphor has increasingly grown popular, Dr. Bishop's touchstone essay was published more than 30 years ago, which demonstrates how long it takes and how difficult it can be for scholarship that centers Black and Brown children to be applied in educational practices. Also, amid such popularity, I've noticed the way many people, specifically White educators, lead with windows. In conversations about books and teaching, I frequently hear the phrase "windows and mirrors," rather than educators leading with mirrors the way Dr. Bishop has done in her scholarship and in the title of her article. Dr. Bishop begins by theorizing about the experience of non-White readers who, she explains, when seeking access to books that reflect their lives, have "frequently found the search futile" and discusses the impact of Black and Brown children lacking mirrors. She writes,

> When children cannot find themselves reflected in the books they read, or when the images they see are distorted, negative, or laughable, they learn a powerful lesson about how they are devalued in the society of which they are a part. Our classrooms need to be places where all the children from all the cultures that make up the salad bowl of American society can find their mirrors.

And Dr. Bishop names clearly who the readers are who need windows.

> Children from dominant social groups have always found their mirrors in books, but they, too, have suffered from the lack of availability of books about others. They need the books as windows onto reality, not just on imaginary worlds. They need books that will help them understand the multicultural nature of the world they live in, and their place as a member of just one group, as well as their connections to all other humans. In this country, where racism is still one of the major unresolved social problems, books may be one of the few places where children who are socially isolated and insulated from the larger world may meet people unlike themselves. If they see only reflections of themselves, they will grow up with an exaggerated sense of their own importance and value in the world—a dangerous ethnocentrism.

The repositioning of "mirrors and windows" to "windows and mirrors" that I'm noticing in educational spaces and in publishing may not seem like such a big deal to some. But I see it as a mischaracterization of her work. This worries me because we've seen the way language and theories are so easily co-opted. And weaponized. Leading with windows seems to be an attempt to center Whiteness. To put an emphasis on the importance of White children reading about the "other." This jeopardizes our focus on Black and Brown children seeing themselves in texts and the ways this continues today. Research on children's literature reveals the longevity, persistence, and pervasiveness of this challenge. This research also demonstrates the misrepresentations, distortions, and misappropriations that too often occur in children's literature and the need to add "curtains" to Dr. Bishop's metaphor, as suggested by Dr. Debbie Reese, founder of American Indians in Children's Literatures (AICL), in order to protect cultures. Dr. Reese (2020) explains,

> One result of these long-standing misrepresentations and exploitations is this: For some time now, Native people have drawn curtains (in reality, and in the abstract) on what we do and what we share. As a scholar in children's literature, I've been adding "curtains" to Rudine Sims Bishop's metaphor of books as mirrors, windows, and sliding glass doors. There are things people do not share with outsiders. (para. 71)

Kügler, Tina (2013).

Diversity in Children's Books 2015

Percentages of books depicting characters from diverse backgrounds, based on the 2015 publishing statistics compiled by the **Cooperative Children's Book Center**, School of Education, University of Wisconsin-Madison: ccbc.education.wisc.edu/books/pcstats.asp

0.9% American Indians/ First Nations

2.4% Latinx

3.3% Asian Pacifics/ Asian Pacific Americans

7.6% African/ African Americans

12.5%* Animals, Trucks, etc.

73.3%* White

* About a quarter of the total children's books published in 2015 were picture books, and about half of those depict non-human characters, like animals & trucks.
** The remainder depict white characters.

Illustration by David Huyck, in consultation with Sarah Park Dahlen & Molly Beth Griffin. Released under a Creative Commons BY-NC-SA license: https://creativecommons.org/licenses/by-nc-sa/4.0/

Huyck, David, Sarah Park Dahlen, and Molly Beth Griffin. (2016 September 14). Diversity in Children's Books 2015 infographic. sarahpark.com blog. Retrieved from https://readingspark .wordpress.com/2016/09/14/picture-this-reflecting-diversity-in-childrens-book-publishing/. Statistics compiled by the Cooperative Children's Book Center, School of Education, University of Wisconsin-Madison: https://ccbc.education.wisc.edu/literature-resources/ccbc-diversity-statistics/books-by-about-poc-fnn/. Released for noncommercial use under a Creative Commons BY-NC-SA 4.0 license.

Consider the graphics shown on pages 10–14. A clear pattern emerges when we look across the data on diversity in children's books that shows the persistent challenge for Black and Brown children to access books that reflect them and their lives accurately and humanely. In response to this research, along with the importance of citing the scholarship of Black women accurately, I'm calling for a recentering of race in Dr. Bishop's metaphor and for intentionality around leading with mirrors. And that in this recentering, educators do more with racially and culturally diverse books and develop reading instruction that is identity-inspiring rather than identity-silencing. In identity-inspiring educational spaces, Black and Brown children can see themselves reflected in their full humanity in books and curriculum.

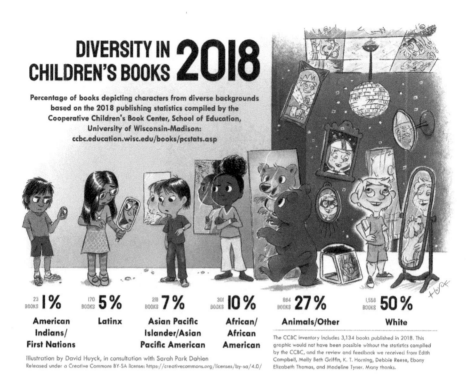

DIVERSITY IN CHILDREN'S BOOKS 2018

Percentage of books depicting characters from diverse backgrounds based on the 2018 publishing statistics compiled by the Cooperative Children's Book Center, School of Education, University of Wisconsin-Madison: ccbc.education.wisc.edu/books/pcstats.asp

23 BOOKS 1%	170 BOOKS 5%	218 BOOKS 7%	30(BOOKS 10%	884 BOOKS 27%	1,558 BOOKS 50%
American Indians/ First Nations	Latinx	Asian Pacific Islander/Asian Pacific American	African/ African American	Animals/Other	White

The CCBC inventory includes 3,134 books published in 2018. This graphic would not have been possible without the statistics compiled by the CCBC, and the review and feedback we received from Edith Campbell, Molly Beth Griffin, K. T. Horning, Debbie Reese, Ebony Elizabeth Thomas, and Madeline Tyner. Many thanks.

Illustration by David Huyck, in consultation with Sarah Park Dahlen
Released under a Creative Commons BY-SA license: https://creativecommons.org/licenses/by-sa/4.0/

Huyck, David, and Sarah Park Dahlen. (2019 June 19). Diversity in Children's Books 2018. sarahpark. com blog. Created in consultation with Edith Campbell, Molly Beth Griffin, K. T. Horning, Debbie Reese, Ebony Elizabeth Thomas, and Madeline Tyner, with statistics compiled by the Cooperative Children's Book Center, School of Education, University of Wisconsin-Madison: https://ccbc .education.wisc.edu/literature-resources/ccbc-diversity-statistics/books-byabout-poc-fnn/. Retrieved from https://readingspark.wordpress.com/2019/06/19/picture-this-diversity-in-childrens-books-2018-infographic/.

When I look back on my teaching, I can recognize that part of my intention around the *collection approach* I was taking toward books in my classroom was ensuring that the students I taught saw themselves in the books they read. Because I understood deeply that representation matters. Representation is important, and yet, it's insufficient. We must do more. What we do with the books we make central in our teaching moves us forward. Antiracist teaching is what helps us and students to do more.

2019 by the Numbers:
MAIN CHARACTERS IN U.S. CHILDREN'S LITERATURE

* statistics from the Cooperative Children's Book Center

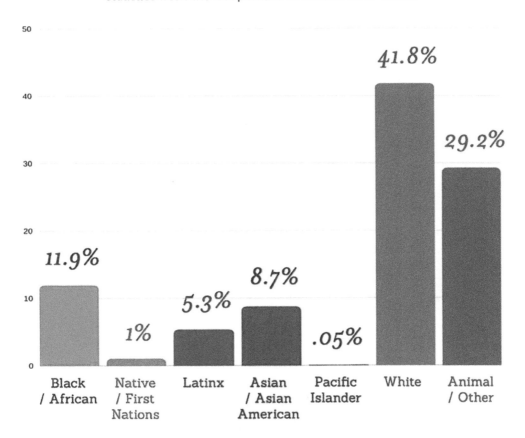

diversebooks.org

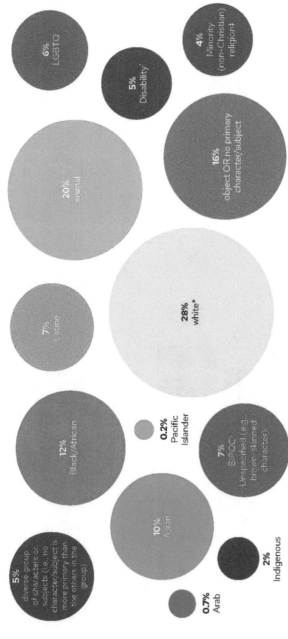

2023 CCBC Diversity Statistics: PRIMARY CHARACTER/SUBJECT
Race/Ethnicity, Disability, LGBTQ, Religion

6% LGBTQ

5% Disability†

4% Minority (non-Christian) religion‡

20% animal

16% object OR no primary character/subject

7% Latine

28% white*

12% Black/African

0.2% Pacific Islander

7% BIPOC Unspecified (e.g. brown-skinned character)

5% diverse group of characters or subjects (i.e., no character/subject is more primary than the others in the group)

10% Asian

0.7% Arab

2% Indigenous

40% of 3,491 total books received have at least one BIPOC§ primary character (fiction) or human subject (nonfiction).

Individual books with multiple primary characters/subjects or primary characters/subjects with multiracial or intersectional identities will be counted in all applicable categories. Percentages are not mutually exclusive and cannot be combined to calculate a total of the whole.

Last updated: 04/02/2024

* "White" is not counted for multiracial characters/subjects so as not to misrepresent a BIPOC§ individual as white.

†"Disability" includes physical, cognitive, neurological, and psychiatric disabilities.

‡2% Jewish, 1% Muslim, 0.3% other minority religion

§Black, Indigenous, and People of Color

©2024 Cooperative Children's Book Center
Please see our media kit to access the most recent version of this image, and for additional information about our work documenting diversity. The most recent version of this image available can be used without permission as long as it is reproduced in its entirety.

CCBC

Source: Cooperative Children's Book Center, 2024.

Reflect

- What does the word *diverse* mean to you?

- In what ways is the word *diverse* used as coded language in your school to mean "not White" when referring to students as well as books?

- How is this usage problematic? (See educator Chad Everett's post: There is no diverse book: qrs.ly/lffrdtv)

- In what ways has a focus on "collecting" racially and culturally diverse books and curating "diverse" libraries contributed to avoidances around teaching about race and racism?

- Why is it important, even in predominantly White schools, to center Black and Brown students and provide books as mirrors?

A Foundation of Love, Joy, Validation, and Healing

I believe that many teachers can locate themselves in one or more of these examples. In my work with educators across the nation, I can't help but notice the ways the latter example—misunderstandings—is where reading instruction is stuck. As a classroom teacher for 20 years, there was a time when I mistakenly believed that just having racially and culturally diverse books in my classroom would be enough. That this alone meant I was a culturally relevant and antiracist educator. That my students would read these books and this alone would help them understand what it means to be antiracist. I was operating from an *antiracist fairy dust approach,* teaching as if I could just sprinkle a bit of it on top of my reading curriculum and teaching. But as I've shared, there is no such thing as antiracist fairy dust. The kind of teaching that is truly antiracist involves actively nurturing students with unyielding love and care, which includes helping them to directly confront what works to harm them and their communities.

Antiracist teaching fosters identity-inspiring experiences where students can show up fully as themselves and recognize the full humanity of all people.

Antiracist teaching fosters identity-inspiring experiences where students can show up fully as themselves and recognize the full humanity of all people. Antiracist teaching centers and acknowledges the lived experiences of those most impacted by racism: Black and Brown people. And because antiracism is about love, love is the foundation from which all instruction emerges. Too often the work of antiracism is falsely positioned as divisive work that teaches students to hate. This is a harmful misconception by those especially who are least invested in and most resistant to addressing racism. For any curriculum or teaching to be antiracist, it must acknowledge the marginalization and oppression of Black and Brown people and other minoritized populations past and present and it must also love them.

Also and critically important, antiracist teaching must spotlight the important role of joy in the collective liberation of Black and Brown people. As the fifth pursuit in her powerful Historically Responsive Teaching Framework, Dr. Muhammad (2023) positions joy as the ultimate goal of teaching and learning. She asserts that educators must "understand how to connect beauty, aesthetics, wellness, wholeness, solutions to problems, and/or happiness to their curricular, instructional, and leadership practices" (p. 50). In doing so, we fully recognize the totality of the human experience, the brilliance, and audacious resilience of those who have been oppressed instead of positioning Black and Brown people as perpetual victims. Antiracist teaching helps teachers, students, and communities to align their words about equity and justice with their actions. Together, as we engage this work, we tap into the deepest part of our humanity. An antiracist reading revolution takes root when students are able to fellowship with each other in ways that are validating, loving, healing, and joyful.

APPLICATIONS OF THIS BOOK

It is critical to note the work before the work of antiracism. In *Get Free: Antibias Literacy Instruction for Stronger Readers, Writers, and Thinkers,* author and educator Tricia Ebarvia challenges educators to reflect prior to engaging in conversations about race and racism, writing, "If we are going to enter into conversations about race or racism, how much have we ourselves read and learned and reflected? How much have we examined our own racial identity or racialized experiences?" (Ebarvia, 2023, p. 159).

Ebarvia (2023) alerts educators of the dangers of skipping this work and details the work of creating conditions in classrooms for brave and safe discussions:

> Asking students to engage in self-reflection related to any one of their identities—particularly regarding race, gender, social class, among others—without the safety net of a supportive community can do more harm than good. For some students, it can even be traumatic. (p. 63)

Because historically it has not been commonplace to have conversations about race in K–8 schools, establishing community agreements can help nurture classroom environments where powerful and productive discussions can thrive. The place to begin is with self-reflection around your own racial and cultural identity and how this shapes your instructional practices. Dr. Erica Buchanan-Rivera (2002) says this "mirror work" for educators is essential in understanding "how we see the world through our ideologies and beliefs." Such reflection can help us recognize problematic stances that must be interrogated and disrupted. We can then prepare our classrooms to be psychologically safe spaces for talking and teaching about race and racism in ways that mitigate harm to Black and Brown students.

Resources for Teachers, Parents, and Caregivers That Support Conversations About Race and Antiracism

Online Resources

- EmbraceRace—embracerace.org

- Facing History & Ourselves: Classroom Contract Teaching Strategy—qrs.ly/jtfrdua

- Learning for Justice: Let's Talk—qrs.ly/nrfrdub

- Mindful Schools: Creating a Safe Container for Students With Community Agreements—qrs.ly/pcfrduh

(Continued)

(Continued)

- National Museum of African American History and Culture: Race and Racial Identity— qrs.ly/nvfrduu

- Raising Race Conscious Children—www.raceconscious.org

Books

- *Get Free: Antibias Literacy Instruction for Stronger Readers, Writers, and Thinkers,* by Tricia Ebarvia

- *Identity-Affirming Classrooms: Spaces That Center Humanity,* by Erica Buchanan-Rivera

- *Raising Antiracist Children: A Practical Parenting Guide,* by Britt Hawthorne with Natasha Yglesias

- *Courageous Conversations About Race: A Field Guide for Achieving Equity in Schools,* 2nd edition, by Glenn Singleton

As you engage with this book, you'll notice I use a dandelion metaphor to represent antiracist teaching and the interconnectedness of each of the chapters that are designed to support antiracist reading instruction. I provide opportunities for you to stop and reflect on teaching practices. I hope you will also use these prompts to enter into discussions with colleagues about ways this book may be affirming, challenging, and/or changing your ideas about antiracism and reading practices.

In this introduction, I've worked to provide a backdrop of where we are in this moment in education around reading instruction and curriculum that is inclusive and affirming of racially and culturally diverse students, what has brought us here, and the urgent need to move beyond where we seem to be stuck. The time is now for an antiracist reading revolution that moves our teaching beyond representation and toward liberation.

In Chapter 1, I draw upon scholarship that has consistently demonstrated the ideological, spiritual, and practical pathways to teaching with love, community, justice, and solidarity at the core to provide an **Antiracist Reading Framework** that empowers educators to engage an antiracist reading stance. Because teaching that is truly antiracist does not involve one-size-fits-all approaches, I offer characteristics of antiracist teaching as well as critical lenses that emerge from research to demonstrate the kind of teaching, discussions, reflection, and actions both educators and students might take up around books that move us beyond a representation approach to one that is liberatory.

Chapters 2 to 6 are formed around five characteristics of antiracist teaching. I locate myself in this work by sharing experiences from my personal and professional life and invite you to consider yours as well. In each of these application chapters, I put ideas into action with six critical lenses and model with several books as a way of creating opportunities for you to see how antiracist teaching opens up opportunities for transformative reading and discussions in classrooms.

I conclude this book with an offering in Chapter 7: toolkits that can support the continued work of antiracism by teachers and students in reading.

Although I more specifically outline my vision of an antiracist reading classroom in Chapter 1, we can begin with a common understanding of what is typically occurring in reading classrooms, which can help you to imagine various ways to implement the ideas in this book. In reading classrooms, there are texts centered in curriculums that are read by all students. These short stories, picture books, novels, poems, informational texts, digital texts, and images can be designated for particular units focused on helping students learn to read and write in specific genres such as personal narrative, memoir, poetry, fiction, and nonfiction. In reading classrooms, students have opportunities to read communally—in partnerships and in book clubs—as well as independently. Teachers are supporting readers in these various circumstances and configurations with mini lessons, small group instruction, and reading conferences. The popular saying "Every teacher is a teacher of reading" is used to remind educators across content areas about the importance of understanding how to teach reading in ways that support their content, such as social studies, science, math, art, music, and technology. So reading classrooms are inclusive of content areas as well.

Because I recognize educators as skilled professionals, I am confident that you will use your own knowledge of the curriculum to apply the strategies I'm offering in your work. Rather than creating fully developed lesson plans, I include prompts and pathways that can provide insight into the discussions you might facilitate and to support your teaching. I imagine using this book to understand more deeply what antiracist teaching entails in reading and the kind of teaching, learning, and community experiences that can occur across parts of the day, week, month, and year. There are several possibilities.

1. Implementing Read-Alouds

    Consider reading a book aloud to students more than once. During the first read aloud, students can enjoy the story, getting to know the characters and setting. Subsequent readings provide opportunities for scaffolding students' comprehension and for them to apply critical lenses from the **Antiracist Reading Framework** that enable them to see more in the text and in the world. During subsequent readings, you'll want to plan for places to prompt students prior to reading aloud, so they are able to listen with a specific focus in mind. Then, stop strategically to provide time for students to respond to a prompt during a brief discussion with a peer. An intentional cycle of prompts and turn and talks is a powerful way to engage the six critical lenses.

2. Developing Mini Lessons

    Across the year, you may want to spotlight one of the critical lenses of the **Antiracist Reading Framework** at a time, demonstrating how you and students might apply this lens as readers. For example, a mini lesson on ways readers' identities influence how they read may focus intentionally on *affirmation*. You might construct a mini lesson where you model thinking about your own personal and social identities, naming some of them, and then invite students to watch you as you read and think about how these identities influence your reading. And in this mini lesson, you can model thinking about the identities of the characters/people in a text in powerful, affirming ways.

Breathing New Life Into Book Clubs can support you in this work.

3. Coaching Into Reading Partnerships/Groups and Book Clubs

    As students read in community with each other, the **Antiracist Reading Framework** critical lenses can support reading and discussion. In *Breathing New Life Into Book Clubs* (2019), Dana Johansen and I write that as educators, we want to ensure that students don't become the kind of readers where texts just wash over them. Further, we recognize that students need autonomy over what and how they read. Achieving this balance can feel tricky for educators. Rather than telling students what to think or what to talk about, these lenses can inform students' thinking, foster deeper comprehension of the books they read and the world as text, and elevate their conversations. If discussions seem to fade and fizzle, students might lean into the six lenses to consider what they might add to their conversation in ways that help them to understand the work of antiracism in a text and in their lives.

4. Supporting Independent Readers

Recent discussions around independent reading have focused primarily on the science of reading, specifically the teaching of reading skills such as phonics and decoding. It has been challenging to locate and connect the critical role of culturally relevant and antiracist teaching practices in discussions about the science of reading and, further, to see antiracism as an essential skill worthy of teaching within the context of reading. In response to this absence, Dr. H. Richard Milner IV (2020) invites educators to take part in what he calls a "disruptive movement," where we address questions such as: Is there knowledge that all students should know? If so, what knowledge is that? And who determines that? How can we build knowledge in ways that disrupt and dismantle racist ideas, practices, and systems? In order for students to deepen their comprehension of and think critically about texts requires educators to ask these questions and interrogate what has been the dominant response. Milner provides a conceptual framework for the purpose of disrupting the ways Whiteness maintains hierarchies of injustice. Antiracist educators understand that all of the skills of reading need to come together to support comprehension—that comprehension is based on vocabulary and background knowledge as much as it is on phonics, decoding, and fluency. Further, educators understand the importance of seeking out books that foster a love of reading within their students. As we encourage students to explore a variety of texts and topics, we can invite students to use the critical lenses of the **Antiracist Reading Framework** to explore who builds knowledge, what counts as knowledge, and why knowledge is constructed. And challenge students to address these questions in ways that are inclusive and antiracist.

5. Creating Text Sets

The **Antiracist Reading Framework** can support educators in choosing books and creating text sets across genres and formats. These text sets can provide students with both a broader perspective and in-depth knowledge about identity and injustice. For example, to encourage students in learning more about the Civil Rights Movement, you might use the critical lenses to develop essential questions and guide your selection of picture books, interviews, images, newspaper articles, podcasts, websites, artwork, and songs that you invite students to explore.

6. Planning Curriculum and Units

You might use this book to help you plan curriculum and reimagine existing curricular units. This book can help you (re)consider the work you do around identity and ways you plan to thread that work across curriculum and the school year. You might use this book to support unit planning. For example, an environmental justice unit can be developed that begins by listening to and learning from local activists. You might use this book to develop a curriculum about musicians and artivists who use their talents to speak out about the humanity and beauty of groups of people and the injustice they face. You might use this book to help students explore the work of BIPOC scientists, mathematicians, and engineers who are typically not centered in mainstream curriculum.

7. Facilitating Whole School and Community Reads

The work of antiracism must extend beyond what children learn and do in classrooms and schools. It must branch out into their communities and into the world. One powerful way to nurture home–school connections is when reading serves as a bridge that builds a community of readers. During the year, educators might select a book that every child reads and discusses at school and also at home with parents and caregivers. Using the critical lenses of the **Antiracist Reading Framework**, educators, students, and caregivers can engage in experiences that affirm their identities and help students to become more aware of ways inequities work systemically while considering ways a community can be more committed and accountable to each other.

When we commit to antiracist ideas, we commit to love. This commitment moves us from the arbitrary use of this word, often limited to a feeling. Instead, we begin to perceive love as an action. Strengthening our understanding of love as an action, bell hooks (2001) offers, "To truly love we must learn to mix various ingredients—care, affection, recognition, respect, commitment, and trust, as well as honest and open communication" (p. 5). In an antiracist reading classroom, reading helps us to dream, experience joy, engage in collective struggle, liberate our minds, and love. Let's move forward together to realize our vision of an antiracist reading classroom rooted in love and liberation.

CHAPTER ONE

Be a Dandelion

A Metaphor and Vision for Antiracist Teaching

In a world that often fails to hold fast to a vision of teaching and learning for liberation, I urge educators to be like dandelions. Abundant. Unmovable. Resilient. Refuse to allow anyone to dismiss this work as weeds. Like a dandelion seed, allow a gust of wind to carry you to fertile ground and take root, believing firmly that antiracist teaching is not about uniformity; it's about possibility. There are seeds of hope we can plant everyday through intentional antiracist reading instruction practices.

When I was a kid, like many children, I loved picking dandelions during the fifth stage of their life, when their tiny florets turned into a mass of fluffy, cloud-like seeds. The once-single yellow flower transformed and became delicate, airy works of art. All it took was a gust of wind or a gentle puff of breath from my mouth to send transparent seeds traveling through the air. New dandelion seedlings would land in the soil, and in time, new plants would appear with the same transformative power and potential.

While my love for dandelions was a marker of my childhood, in *The Bluest Eye* by Toni Morrison (1970/1999), Pecola, the novel's protagonist, observes, "*Nobody loves the head of a dandelion. Maybe because they are so many, strong, and soon.*" Morrison uses dandelions symbolically to represent what we've been socialized into believing them to be. Imperfect. Unattractive. Useless. To some, dandelions represent weeds of resistance. I challenge you to see them instead as symbols of resilience.

While ubiquitous in the natural environment, dandelions are often overlooked and disregarded. They are commonly considered an irritant to remove from the desired homogeneity of green backyard lawns, parks, and professional landscapes. But across cultures, time, and space, dandelions have benefited many. Several ancient cultures used dandelions for food, medicinal, and spiritual purposes. Today, they continue to be used in traditional medicine by some cultures, and experts note the dietary and health benefits that result from consuming dandelions. When we shift our perspective beyond the dominant construction, it is undeniable that dandelions are significant.

Dandelions are the perfect metaphor for antiracist teaching. Like dandelions, the work of antiracism has been viewed negatively—as an invasive, unlikeable, useless, weed. It is true that antiracism does not fit the standard; it is disruptive of it. Symbolically, dandelions represent hope, power, light, optimism, and healing. For these reasons and more, I believe the dandelion is a humble and admirable symbol to use for an **Antiracist Reading Framework** that I introduce in this chapter and for all that becomes possible when we operate from an antiracist teaching stance.

As you read this book, you'll see key characteristics of antiracist teaching highlighted throughout. While there may be a specific focus on one or more in a section, page, or chapter, know that a characteristic is never actually alone. Like a dandelion, one part cannot survive without the other. We cannot ever truly talk about any one of these characteristics separated from the whole. While I work to spotlight their distinctions and the books and teaching that can support cultivation of each, it is critical to always keep in mind the interconnectedness of these characteristics. Therefore, you will see the **Antiracist Reading Framework** in each of the following chapters with each antiracist teaching characteristic named even as one or more is being highlighted. This serves as a reminder of how all of the characteristics work together to create liberatory outcomes for young people. As I provide an **Antiracist Reading Framework** to ground our understandings in this chapter, in chapters to come, I also demonstrate antiracist teaching practices with books that open up worlds of possibilities for young people. (See Figure 1.1.)

FIGURE 1.1   Antiracist Reading Framework

A Vision of Antiracist Teaching in Reading

During a read-aloud of *My Papi Has a Motorcycle* by Isabel Quintero, I observed a group of fifth graders dig into the kind of *Mind Work* they do whenever they read fiction. They discussed the characters of the text and named traits that described them. They wondered where the story was taking place as they took in the setting. I interrupted them briefly. "In addition to this *Mind Work*, there's *Heart Work* we always do as readers. But we're not always thinking about this." Several students looked at me quizzically. "Part of this Heart Work is thinking about our identities as we read. Parts of my identity are that I am Black. I am a Black woman. I am a Black woman and a teacher. I am a Black woman who is a teacher and a mother. I bring each of these identities to every text I read. As you read, try remaining alert to this *Heart Work*. Pay attention to how your identities influence your understanding of this text. *How do they help you to perceive more in a text, about characters and issues they face? And also, how might your identities limit your understanding? Notice parts of the text that make you think, might I be missing something?*"

Reflect

- How often do you reflect on your identities and share this reflection with students?

- How do you demonstrate ways your identities influence how you read and understand a text?

- How do you help young readers discover how their identities inform their interpretation of a text and to understand this as a powerful reading strategy?

I listened in carefully while students tried this work. They applied the scholarship of Dr. Rudine Sims Bishop (1990), discussing parts of the text that were mirrors for them (refer to the introduction for more on Dr. Bishop's crucial work). Like speaking Spanish and English like the characters or, more broadly, having the ability to speak more than one language. Like enjoying spending time with their fathers, just like the main character, Daisy, does. Like being an immigrant like the character Papi or being part of a family of immigrants. Affirmations about identity were abundant. Students also shared parts of the text that were windows for them. Like not really realizing and recognizing the hard work of immigrants and the challenge of living in a country that isn't always appreciative of the work and sacrifices immigrants make. Like not understanding the importance and joy of multilingualism.

We read a bit more before I paused again. "I'd like to discuss a word that may be unfamiliar to you. That word is *gentrification*. Gentrification is the process of making a neighborhood more appealing to people moving in who have more money than those who were already living there. As a result, rent prices increase and people from the community who can't afford to live there anymore are pushed out. This mostly affects Black and Brown people in neighborhoods who are pushed out when White people with more resources move in. Talk with your partner about how the word *gentrification* helps you to understand this part of the story. And also, tell your partner if you've seen any signs of *gentrification* in your neighborhood or in neighborhoods you are familiar with." I listened intently while students continued to apply Dr. Bishop's metaphor:

> *Well this is a mirror for me because I have seen signs of this in my neighborhood. There used to be a bodega. We all went there. And now there's Starbucks. That bodega is gone now.*

> *Whenever a Whole Foods shows up it seems like the whole community changes.*

> *They're building luxury apartment buildings in my neighborhood. Already several of my friends have moved away.*

> *I never knew about gentrification at all.*

This experience with fifth-grade students illustrates my vision of the role and work of educators in moving beyond teaching approaches that are just about representation to teaching approaches that are about liberation. The classroom becomes fertile ground for students to more closely examine their identities and the world around them. Truth-seeking and truth-telling become students' common, collective practice of community, solidarity, love, justice, and freedom. This work requires educators to do more with racially and culturally diverse books beyond simply collecting them.

FIVE CHARACTERISTICS OF ANTIRACIST TEACHING

While there is no one way to define antiracist curriculum or instruction, several characteristics emerge from the existing and growing body of scholarship on antiracism. I have identified five that can inform instruction and shape the educational experiences of students. Each of these characteristics works together as a whole to construct a vision of an antiracist reading classroom—the work of teachers and the work of students—that leads to liberation.

FIVE CHARACTERISTICS OF ANTIRACIST TEACHING

- **Center BIPOC in texts.** Antiracist educators select texts by and about BIPOC that reflect the fullness of their lives without exclusively locating their histories, experiences, and backgrounds in oppression.

- **Recognize cultural, community, and collective practices.** Antiracist educators highlight powerful ways of knowing and being in the world that are rooted in the knowledge of racially, culturally, and linguistically diverse groups of people.

- **Shatter silences around racism.** Antiracist educators name racism, Whiteness, and White supremacy and help students recognize oppressive ideologies and how they function.

- **Teach racial literacy.** Antiracist educators provide opportunities for students to have critical and constructive conversations about race and racism where they develop their ability to apply language to examine racial and cultural identities; question ideas, assumptions, and the status quo; and work to resist racist ideas, practices, and policies.

- **Learn about community activists.** Antiracist educators provide opportunities for students to learn about, explore, and reference voices of color in their communities and activists in the world who are advancing the work of racial justice.

Although I discuss each of the characteristics individually and one at a time, it is important to note that they are not linear, but circuitous and interconnected. Looking at them individually can, I hope, provide a greater understanding of antiracist teaching as lived, liberatory practice.

CENTER BIPOC IN TEXTS

Antiracist educators work to affirm racially and culturally diverse people and communities lovingly and joyfully. One way to achieve this is through transparent, intentional text selection, understanding that otherwise, books and texts are powerful ways young people can be socialized into racist and inequitable ideas. In *Stamped (For Kids): Racism, Antiracism, and You* (Cherry-Paul et al., 2021), I ask young readers to look out for mainstream representations that too often provide limited, deficit, harmful perspectives of Black and Brown people. **Therefore, antiracist teaching seeks to powerfully reflect those who have been minoritized and marginalized in depth rather than in superficial breadth that can proliferate stereotypes.** Books and texts written by BIPOC creators who share the same racial and cultural identity as the people and characters they are writing about are more likely to present important, nuanced perspectives.

In response to noticings around identity and authorship, Corinne Duyvis started a grassroots effort using the social media hashtag #ownvoices to seek out texts where the author's identities and lived experiences are reflected in the characters, settings, and themes of a story. In 2015, Duyvis tweeted the following in Figure 1.2.

FIGURE 1.2 Corinne Duyvis Tweet

On 6 September 2015, I made a suggestion on Twitter:

Corinne Duyvis ✅ @corinneduyvis · Sep 6, 2015
Glad important discussions are being had. Would love to be able to walk away with book recommendations. How about a hashtag?

Corinne Duyvis ✅
@corinneduyvis

#ownvoices, to recommend kidlit about diverse characters written by authors from that same diverse group.

♡ 57   1:55 PM · Sep 6, 2015   ⓘ

💬 91 people are talking about this   ❯

Recently, there has been tension around the term *ownvoices*—which has blossomed beyond a hashtag into a movement. Because of the ways words and terms in the work of equity and antiracism are co-opted, misused, diluted, and commercialized, it is important to remain vigilant. It's important to recognize how words that are about tweaking systems are more susceptible to being misconstrued and co-opted versus words that are about disrupting systems. Intentionality in their usage is critical when it comes to words and terms such as *ownvoices, diverse, BIPOC, POC,* and others. It is also crucial to call out those who misuse and capitalize on them.

As a Black educator whose parents were born in Georgia, whose father, aunts, and uncles grew up there and navigated segregation from childhood until young adulthood, I use the terms *BIPOC* and *ownvoices* in this book intentionally and with care. I recognize that tension around their usage is really about colonialism, imperialism, and centuries of White supremacy that have and continue to work to

(Continued)

(Continued)

erase, silence, invalidate, and marginalize identities. With this profound understanding, I use *ownvoices* to call attention to the collective struggle among groups of people and communities who've been marginalized while also working to spotlight their distinct, rich identities. I use *ownvoices* to call attention to structural and systemic racism while working to avoid minimizing the lived experiences of individuals and group identities. I use *ownvoices* to call attention to the ways we must continue to work together to collectively get free.

RECOGNIZE CULTURAL, COMMUNITY, AND COLLECTIVE PRACTICES

Antiracist educators recognize the importance of truly knowing their students—their personal identities, such as favorite TV shows, movies, sports, and music, and also their social identities, which include their racial, cultural, and linguistic identities as well as knowing the communities in which they live. Antiracist educators see this work of knowing as continuous, and it helps them to develop instruction and curriculum that are closer fits between students' home and school cultures. Dr. Kimberly Parker (2022) asserts, "We see the world through our own racialized, gendered, complicated lenses" and the importance of educators reframing our thinking. To accomplish this, she recommends we lean into the scholarship around "funds of knowledge" to develop multidimensional understandings of the children in teachers' care (pp. 53–54). **Therefore, antiracist teaching is grounded in historical and contemporary experiences and issues of people and community.** Rather than revering individualism and competition, books and texts that are centered in curriculum support collectivism and communal practices and are those that value multiple ways of knowing across cultures.

SHATTER SILENCES AROUND RACISM

Educators name racism proactively and explicitly and help students develop a working definition of racism. This definition deepens across space, time, and context, making it possible for students to recognize social, economic, and political factors that create environmental conditions that oppress BIPOC and communities. Each summer, Tricia Ebarvia and I co-facilitate the Institute for Racial Equity in Literacy (IREL), a unique professional development experience that supports educators in the work of antiracism and equity in their classrooms, schools, and communities. This work demands critical reflection and action. We challenge educators to identify the ways in which racism has been embedded throughout history and in every societal institution, including schools.

And we ask educators to reflect on questions such as these: *How can we ensure that our educational practices are not just inclusive but equitable? How can we use our power and position as educators to transform systems, whether those systems be our individual classrooms, districts, or greater communities? How can we help students read, write, and speak up for justice?* **Therefore, antiracist teaching helps students recognize ways racism is entrenched in institutions and systems such as education, housing, health care, media, government, law enforcement, and more and ways we can work to dismantle oppressive systems.**

Learn more about the IREL here.

TEACH RACIAL LITERACY

Antiracist educators acquire racial literacy themselves and help their students become racially literate. This involves teaching that invites students to recognize race as a social construct, acknowledge racism as a contemporary problem and not just a past condition, and interrogate the ways Whiteness drives the values, structures, and systems in the United States and beyond. Dr. Detra Price-Dennis and Dr. Yolanda Sealey-Ruiz (2021) convey the urgency for educators to not just talk about race and racism "but to learn how to examine carefully how race is lived in our society" (p. 21). When educators acquire this skill, they are able to support the racial literacy development of their students so they are able to navigate and interrupt racist structures, systems, policies, and practices. Dr. Yolanda Sealey-Ruiz (2021) explains that "a desired outcome of racial literacy in an outwardly racist society like America is for members of the dominant racial category to adopt an antiracist stance and for persons of color to resist a victim stance." **Therefore, antiracist teaching supports authentic, critical, and constructive conversations as students apply racial literacy skills to read and discuss texts and develop tools to disrupt racism in their lives.**

LEARN ABOUT COMMUNITY ACTIVISTS

Antiracist educators learn about folx locally as well as globally who are working to dismantle racism. They recognize that those who make this their life's work aren't always heralded in books for students to access. Also crucially important is the recognition of ways activists work in community with others. Dr. Parker (2022) defines community as "a group of people who come together around shared purposes" that includes "members' needs for connection, interdependence, and the belief that a community—and the work required to create and maintain it—are necessary and possible" (p. 50). The work of antiracist educators cannot flourish without cultivating community in our classrooms. Community, Dr. Parker asserts, "must be intentional if we want it to be liberatory" (p. 51). The nurturing of our classroom communities must also include connecting students to the people and organizations in the wider school community who work to make life more equitable in their neighborhoods and in the world. Such connection is one way students maintain hope for a more just world—a hope that is underpinned by intention, commitment, and action. **Therefore, antiracist teaching creates community and connects young people to activists that empower them to consider how they locate themselves in the longevity of work for liberation and ways they will cultivate new ideas that become seeds of change.**

Six Critical Lenses to Support Antiracist Reading Instruction

To help implement these antiracist teaching characteristics in reading, I provide six critical lenses that support the instructional approaches of educators and the insights of students as they read and discuss books. These lenses are demonstrated throughout the remaining chapters in this book, which will guide you through texts and practices that provide a foundation for an antiracist reading revolution in your classroom. While they do not have to be implemented in any particular order, there is one exception. I urge you to always begin this work with affirmation, that you begin in ways that lets students know they are loved. This is essential for the emotional and spiritual well-being of Black and Brown students who have often received messages in education that are the antithesis of this. Use each, any, and all of the critical lenses as you develop your antiracist teaching practice. The six critical lenses I offer extend from the research of Black women scholars who shape my knowledge and practice of antiracist teaching (Table 1.1).

To nurture an antiracist reading revolution, we can apply two overarching lenses from the scholarship of culturally relevant and critical pedagogies to inform the ways we teach reading: affirmation and awareness.

Antiracist educators work intentionally to affirm the racial and cultural identities of students. This work is not left for chance or for students to solely experience from reading a particular text. Instead, antiracist educators help students understand the ways characters and people are fully recognized and validated in a text and the importance of recognizing

TABLE 1.1 Scholarship of Black Women Who Shape Antiracist Teaching

SCHOLAR	SCHOLARSHIP	FRAMEWORK
Dr. Rudine Sims Bishop *Mirrors, Windows, and Sliding Glass Doors* (1990)	"When there are enough books available that can act as both mirrors and windows for all our children, they will see that we can celebrate both our differences and similarities, because together they are what makes us all human."	Mirrors · Books can be . . . · Windows · Sliding Glass Doors
Dr. Gloria Ladson-Billings "Toward a Theory of Culturally Relevant Pedagogy" (1995)	"Culturally Relevant Pedagogy is a theoretical model that not only addresses student achievement but also helps students to accept and affirm their cultural identity while developing critical perspectives that challenge inequities that schools (and other institutions) perpetuate."	Critical Consciousness · Culturally Relevant Pedagogy · Cultural Competence · High Expectations

(Continued)

SCHOLAR	SCHOLARSHIP	FRAMEWORK
Dr. Barbara Love *Developing a Liberatory Consciousness* (2010)	"With a liberatory consciousness, every person gets the chance to theorize about issues of equity and social justice, to analyze events related to equity and social justice, and to act in responsible ways to transform society."	Awareness Analysis Action Accountable Ally-ship
Dr. Yolanda Sealey-Ruiz *Racial Literacy: A Policy Research Brief*, produced by the James R. Squire Office of the National Council of Teachers of English (2021)	"Research has revealed that conversations about race, when done effectively, provide education professionals with the confidence they need to alter their pedagogy in more culturally responsive and culturally sustaining ways. They become skillful at engaging their students in essential conversations that relate to their learning and social development."	**RACIAL LITERACY DEVELOPMENT** INTERRUPTION — Interrupting racism & inequality at personal and systemic levels THE ARCHOLOGY OF SELF — Deep excavation & exploration of beliefs, biases, and ideas that shape how we engage in the work HISTORICAL LITERACY — Develop a rich & contextual awareness of the historical forces that shape the communities in which we live and work, as well as the society in which we live CRITICAL REFLECTION — Think through the various layers of our identities and how our privileged and marginalized statuses affect the work CRITICAL HUMILITY — Remain open to understanding the limits of our own worldviews and ideologies CRITICAL LOVE — A profound ethical commitment to caring for the communities in which we work

people in these ways in their lives. One aspect of culturally relevant pedagogy as theorized by Dr. Gloria Ladson-Billings is educators working to affirm students' cultural identities. Dr. Ladson-Billings (2009) explains that for Black students in particular, affirmation has not been easy to access in schools:

> The typical experience in the schools is a denigration of African and African American culture. Indeed, there is a denial of its very existence. The language that students bring with them is seen to be deficient—a corruption of English. The familial organizations are considered pathological. And the historical, cultural, and scientific contributions of African Americans are ignored or rendered trivial. (p. 151)

There should be no surprise, then, when Black students do not trust schools and find them to be "spirit-murdering" (Love, 2019) spaces rather than humanizing, liberatory spaces. For educators who wonder about the importance of culturally relevant and sustaining teaching in predominantly White contexts, Drs. Django Paris and H. Samy Alim (2017) address the inclination of White teachers to avoid this work with White students.

Whenever working to make structures, systems, and institutions more racially just, it is those who have experienced the most racial injustice that must be centered.

They convey that "developing a multicultural, multilingual perspective or competence means that all students (including white, middle-class students) broaden their cultural repertoires so that they can operate more easily in a world that is globally interconnected" (p. 145). Further, whenever working to make structures, systems, and institutions more racially just, it is those who have experienced the most racial injustice that must be centered.

The work of affirmation in reading instruction provides opportunities for BIPOC students to appreciate their own culture and "make connections between their community, national, and global identities" (Ladson-Billings, 2009, p. 38). Such teaching demands that educators have an in-depth knowledge of their students—their racial and cultural identities, the values instilled in them by their families and communities, their joys, hopes, and dreams. Dr. Yolanda Sealey-Ruiz (2021) names this kind of commitment Critical Love, "a profound commitment to the communities we work in."

Antiracist educators also work to help students develop an awareness of racism and an understanding of how racism functions systemically. As a result, students are better able to make antiracist decisions in their own lives that are a disruption of the status quo, and they can determine how they want to move through the world in ways that promote equity and justice. Educators tend to shy away from this work because of their own discomfort confronting issues of inequities. And they tend to avoid instruction about race and racism, believing that children are too young or too tender for such conversations. However, research disrupts the myth that children are too young to discuss issues related to race and the importance of educators developing the skills needed to facilitate these discussions (Sullivan et al., 2020).

The work of awareness in reading instruction involves raising students' sociopolitical consciousness. Students acquire language and tools to discuss and disrupt injustice (Ladson-Billings, 1995; Sealey-Ruiz, 2021). Such teaching makes it possible for students to live their lives from what Dr. Barbara Love (2010) calls "a waking position" in an oppressive society with "awareness and intentionality, rather than on the basis of the socialization to which they have been subjected" (pp. 599, 600).

Antiracist educators work alongside students to develop a "liberatory consciousness" and racial literacy. Love (2010) says, "A liberatory consciousness enables humans to maintain awareness of the dynamics of oppression characterizing society *without giving in to despair and hopelessness about that condition*, to maintain awareness of the role played by each individual in the maintenance of that system *without blaming them for the roles they play*, and at the same time practice intentionality about changing the systems of oppression" (p. 599). Racial literacy development, Sealey-Ruiz (2021) shares, is critical for educators, particularly those teaching in racially diverse contexts. Critical Love, she theorizes, is the foundation of racial literacy development and involves educators working to recognize and reckon with their own biases and racist assumptions, in order to fully and authentically love Black and Brown children as they are.

With Affirmation and Awareness as cornerstone concepts, the six critical lenses I provide build upon this scholarship to support antiracist teaching and learning in reading. Educators can use these lenses to examine curriculum and plan instruction that centers BIPOC students—their lives, their experiences, their communities—and strives toward liberation. I cannot emphasize enough the importance of always beginning with affirmation. When Black and Brown students can only see themselves reflected in the curriculum through the lens of oppression, this is not humanizing. This is not liberation. So it is critical that the work of affirmation is where your work starts in order for BIPOC students to see the fullness of who they are. The remaining lenses do not have to be implemented in any particular order, though I urge you to use each, any, and all of the critical lenses as you develop your antiracist teaching practice.

FIGURE 1.3   Six Critical Lenses

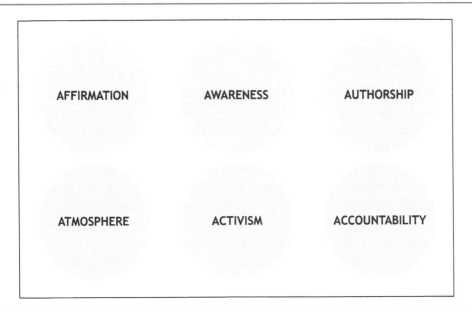

AFFIRMATION

Always begin with affirmation. Simply put, affirmation makes readers feel that they matter, not only in classrooms, but in the world. Identity-inspiring texts make it possible for readers to see themselves reflected in powerful ways. Educators can foster affirmation in students' reading lives by considering: Do the books in their classrooms make children feel seen, valued, cherished, loved, and that they matter? And in what ways do the books accomplish this? It's important to know and understand this, so we can teach into this. Educators can facilitate in ways that help students to recognize this in the books they read and discuss with peers.

AWARENESS

We're living in a time where truth is weaponized. And the truth is not a weapon. The truth is love. The truth is liberation. Educators can help raise students' awareness by considering: In what ways are the books in their classrooms truth-tellers about racism? About White supremacy? About what it means to engage in collective struggle? To labor for freedom together? About what it means to be antiracist? Educators can coach in ways that help students to understand the meaning of solidarity and what it means to work as a collective in the greatest sense.

AUTHORSHIP

Who writes the story matters. The research around children's publishing led by educators and scholars such as Dr. Sarah Park Dahlen, Edith Campbell, Dr. Ebony Elizabeth Thomas, and Dr. Debbie Reese demonstrates the misrepresentations and distortions that are prevalent in books written by White authors who do not know the Black and Brown people and communities they are writing about. At best, many books can demonstrate a lack of nuance and care. These data reveal the ways Black and Brown people are systematically erased from their own narratives. It's critical that students learn to question when identities do not mirror the characters or people being written about, what work has been done to do so with accuracy and care? Antiracist educators recognize deeply that who authors a text (fiction and nonfiction) significantly matters and utilize reading instruction as opportunities for students to understand this as well.

ATMOSPHERE

Atmosphere relates to the setting and context of the books educators share with students. As a result of doing an audit of my classroom library, I realized that the overwhelming majority of books on my shelves that were about BIPOC characters were historical fiction. This is not to say that historical fiction isn't valuable. It absolutely is! However, if Black and Brown children could only ever see themselves in the past, how could they imagine their place in the world right now or in the future? When thinking about atmosphere, educators consider questions such as: How are Black and Brown people positioned in the books students have access to? What is the context? Are the circumstances around the issue of oppression? Students need access to all kinds of books including contemporary books that speak to their lives right now.

ACTIVISM

A commitment to antiracism is a commitment to action. For some students, their understanding of activism is about the big, bold actions they see from individuals and groups that may be well known through the media. Antiracist educators can help students understand that the actions students take in their daily lives may seem small, but are mighty. Actions such as building relationships with peers from various racial and cultural identities, taking an inclusive approach in their reading lives, and learning about issues that impact the lives of those who have been marginalized help to expand students' perspectives. Educators invite students to consider what they are learning about people and society in the texts they read. What are they being invited to challenge and change? And how might they do this within and beyond the four walls of the classroom and school?

ACCOUNTABILITY

The work of antiracism relies on evaluating how our words align with our actions. Educators and students consider the implications of what they've learned through reading and work to apply these learnings in ways that benefit the collective. Together, they consider how they will hold themselves accountable for sustaining their new understanding about justice to care for each other and their communities.

ANTIRACIST READING FRAMEWORK

Together, the characteristics and critical lenses work as an **Antiracist Reading Framework** that cultivates and sustains reading instruction and reading practices of students. This framework provides the structure for the following chapters that are organized around each of the five characteristics of antiracist teaching. I model ways to apply the **Antiracist Reading Framework** to a carefully curated collection of mostly picture books about racially and culturally diverse characters and people from various backgrounds. (Because I model with mostly picture books, I have included in the Appendix a list of middle-grade and young adult (YA) books that are examples of wonderful longer fiction and nonfiction books to include in classroom libraries and to center in curriculum and instruction.)

You may be wondering why picture books? First, picture books are for all ages. I repeat: Picture books are for readers of all ages. What I have observed and continue to notice is this—the higher the grade, the fewer (if any) picture books students seem to have access to. Picture books are enjoyable to read; they are exceptional models of craft, structure, and art; and they help readers develop empathy. Further, picture books are excellent to teach with because they can be read in one sitting. Of course, volume and stamina matter in order for students to blossom as strong readers. This involves them reading longer texts. I hope that modeling with picture books can provide insights for applying the **Antiracist Reading Framework** when teaching with novels and longer nonfiction and informational books that students may be reading independently, in book clubs, or as part of a whole class shared reading experience.

In my work with thousands of educators and caregivers, I am often asked if I can provide a book list—the titles and authors of texts I recommend for the kind of vision I discuss and teach about. Earlier in my career, I obliged. In thinking more about this, I've come to recognize that providing these lists can be problematic. First, lists may give the impression that only the titles on it are *the* books to teach with and include in libraries. There are wonderful new books that are released each year that deserve to be read, loved, and made accessible to children. Second, providing a list can be dangerous. They can reinforce the *collection approach* I discussed in the introduction when these titles are purchased and educators assume that simply having them in the classroom is enough. So it is my goal that the **Antiracist Reading Framework** supports the application of antiracist teaching and also serves as a guide for book selection by educators, caregivers, and students.

You may have the urge to purchase the books referenced for your classroom or to ask a school leader to do so. Lean into that temptation! Even though this book selection is not intended to serve as a finite list, the authors and illustrators highlighted deserve your patronage. These books deserve to be centered in curriculum, read, discussed, and loved by children. However, I discourage the belief that antiracist teaching isn't possible without the specific books featured. Remember, antiracist teaching is not a checklist, and these are not the only books to teach with and make available to students. Book lists can lead to fixed collections instead of living libraries that have the potential to fortify students in myriad ways. With the **Antiracist Reading Framework,** I aim to provide you with a set of transferable skills that make it possible for you to do this work with various books—the ones featured across these pages and beyond.

The pages that follow are not curriculum or lesson plans, although ideas may be developed into this. What follows is insight that I hope helps to sharpen our lenses when selecting, reading, and teaching with books; guidance that supports seeing and doing more with books; and tools that activate our minds and galvanize us to actions that move us closer to an antiracist future. If you are planning to use any of the books I model with, please read them first, prior to using them in instruction. This creates an opportunity for you to both bring your insights and perspectives as well as interrogate the ways you may be responding to a text with biases and assumptions that can cause harm.

The prompts I provide as students read and discuss books are not the *only* prompts that can be used. Consider your learners and the fullness of who they are and what they bring to your classroom as you consider what might spark rich, vibrant conversations. Every text is informed by our own identities, backgrounds, and experiences.

The pathways included are based on discussions I've had with children and their responses that can help you to imagine the possibilities that can occur in your classroom, and they are insights into ways you might further support thinking and discussions. Many of the books I model with could be placed in more than one chapter, as they address more than one characteristic of antiracist teaching. Antiracist teaching is not a binary; it is layered, interconnected, and iterative. The presence of the **Antiracist Reading Framework** serves as a reminder of this. The purpose of the organization of this book is to deepen your understanding about antiracist teaching. I hope you'll consider the implications and applications of this work as you develop an antiracist reading stance.

In a world that often fails to hold fast to a vision of teaching and learning for liberation, I urge educators to be like dandelions. Abundant. Unmovable. Resilient. Refuse to allow anyone to dismiss this work as weeds. Like a dandelion seed, allow a gust of wind to carry you to fertile ground and take root, believing firmly that antiracist teaching is not about uniformity; it's about possibility. There are seeds of hope we can plant everyday through intentional antiracist reading instruction practices.

CHAPTER TWO

Center BIPOC in Texts

Seeds, also called parachutes, are located at the center of a dandelion. If you look closely, you'll notice that each seed has an umbrella-like structure that helps to keep it upright and ready to soar far and wide on a gust of wind.

Think back to when you were a young person in elementary or middle school. What are some of the titles of books that were seen and celebrated in your classrooms? Which books were centered in the curriculum? Now jot down some of your identities that were particularly important to you as a young person. As you do this work, include not only personal identities, such as favorite sports, but also your social identities that informed and influenced your lived experiences, such as race, ethnicity, language, gender, dis/ability, family, sexuality, and so on. Jot your notes in the grid that follows.

RECALLING READING EXPERIENCES IN SCHOOL	
BOOK TITLES	IDENTITIES
Which books do you remember reading when you were in elementary or middle school?	What were some of your personal and social identities that felt important to you when you were a kid?
Which books were used in instruction?	Personal identities (talents, skills, abilities, hobbies, interests)

RECALLING READING EXPERIENCES IN SCHOOL	
BOOK TITLES	**IDENTITIES**
Which books were seen and celebrated in classrooms and libraries?	Social identities (race, ethnicity, gender, religion, language, economic status, family, dis/ability, sexuality, etc.)

Here's a collage of some of the book titles that were at the center of reading curriculums and in my school library when I was in elementary school.

FIGURE 2.1   School Book Collage

Sonja's Elementary School Book Collage

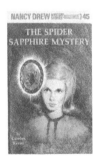    

  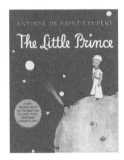  

Some of the personal and social identities that were important to me during this time were that I loved to jump rope, especially Double Dutch. I played the piano and loved to read. As a Black girl born in the Northeast with southern roots, I traveled between New York and Georgia to maintain a connection to the birthplace of my parents and family. For the first 10 years of my life, I lived in public housing (aka "the projects") in Brooklyn, New York. My grandparents, who had migrated north before I was born, lived across the street from me, and I saw them almost daily. When they moved to the borough of Queens, so did my parents. As well as my uncles, aunts, and their families. The proximity to family during my elementary years—grandparents, cousins, aunts, uncles—is one of the most defining aspects of my childhood.

When I think about these identities and look across my book collage, there is a tension. With the exception of one, I cannot really locate myself in the books that were a part of my formative years, a time when the construction of self is critical in a young person's development. *Roll of Thunder, Hear My Cry* by Mildred D. Taylor was the first book I'd ever read with characters who looked like me. And not only did they look like me, the setting is the U.S. South. It meant EVERYTHING to me to hold that book in my hands. I stumbled across it myself in my school library in fourth grade. I read it. And then again in fifth grade. And sixth grade. Never could I have imagined then that one day, I'd have the honor of writing a teacher's guide for this beloved book and author.

Roll of Thunder, Hear My Cry teacher's guide.

The experiences I've described as a young reader occurred decades ago. It would be easy to dismiss them, arguing that today there are more books featuring racially and culturally diverse characters. There are. And yet, too often, many Black and Brown students are having the same experience I had as a young person. Books are chosen by educators that render students invisible or provide limited, harmful depictions of Black and Brown people, particularly when they are not written by BIPOC authors who are able to write with greater specificity, nuance, and care. Books in classrooms around the country are not always reflective of "the salad bowl of American society" Dr. Bishop (1990) calls for where BIPOC students "can find their mirrors." This national moment of book banning and soft censorship contributes to this issue. Students today continue to experience significant challenges accessing books and curriculum in schools that center their lived experiences in full, dynamic ways.

When you look at your own book collage and consider the identities you've jotted, are you able to see yourself in your reading in powerful ways? What patterns can you notice as you recall your reading experiences in school? How might this be similar or different for students today, particularly those who are members of BIPOC, multilingual, LGBTQ+, dis/ability communities, and those who hold multiple intersecting identities that are marginalized within a White-dominant, heteronormative, Christian hegemonic society? Write your notes in the grid that follows.

RECALLING READING EXPERIENCES IN SCHOOL		
BOOK TITLES	**IDENTITIES**	**PATTERNS**
Which books do you remember reading when you were in elementary or middle school?	What were some of your personal and social identities that felt important to you when you were a kid?	How many ways can you locate yourself on your book collage?
Which books were used in instruction?	Personal identities (talents, skills, abilities, hobbies, interests)	What patterns and truths are revealed as you look back at the books you read?

(Continued)

(Continued)

RECALLING READING EXPERIENCES IN SCHOOL		
BOOK TITLES	IDENTITIES	PATTERNS
Which books were seen and celebrated in classrooms and libraries?	Social identities (race, ethnicity, gender, religion, language, economic status, dis/ability, sexuality)	How might this be similar/ different for students who are members of BIPOC/ multilingual/LGBTQ+/ dis/ability communities?

Cultural competence, as theorized by Dr. Ladson-Billings (2009), means students are firmly grounded in their own culture as well as fluent in at least one other culture. This tenet is dropped in education when a White, Eurocentric approach to curriculum is what's centered. When this occurs, BIPOC students learn that their culture, their histories, are irrelevant. The essence of who they are is extinguished by books, curriculum, and teaching that do not reflect or affirm them. To center BIPOC students, those who are most marginalized in education, involves doing just that—putting them at the core of curriculum and teaching. It requires a willingness to recognize how students of color have historically experienced and continue to experience schooling. It requires a willingness to recognize the impact and perpetuation of Whiteness in education. And it requires a willingness to know and implement the scholarship of Black and Brown people in curriculum and teaching.

As you select texts that center BIPOC and reflect the fullness of their lives without exclusively locating their histories, experiences, and backgrounds in oppression, it is critical to avoid superficial breadth. This looks like using a single text as a stand-in to represent an entire group that has been marginalized. Instead, the goal is depth. Begin by questioning: "Why THIS book?"

Reflect

In what ways do the books centered in curriculum and my teaching:

- Affirm and celebrate racially and culturally diverse people and communities?

- Portray racially and culturally diverse people and their lived experiences beyond mainstream representations?

- Focus on joy, love, and the full humanity of Black and Brown people?

Antiracist teaching, however, isn't just about the books we make available to students but also about our stance as antiracist educators. Take note of the instructional strategies demonstrated that cultivate and sustain antiracist reading classrooms. The six critical lenses help us to center BIPOC using texts by and about BIPOC that reflect their lives fully and humanely.

Like dandelion seeds, young people have the ability to go the distance. When readers see themselves and others in powerful ways, they move through the world upright, conscientious, and justice-centered. Be the wind that carries them forth.

Center BIPOC in Texts: Prompts and Pathways

Facilitating conversations about race and racism requires that you plan to mitigate harm to those in your care who are most impacted by racism—BIPOC students. Ongoing reflection on your own racial identity and racial socialization along with interrogating biases is necessary, critical work. To avoid doing this often results in causing more harm to Black and Brown students. Please refer to resources shared in Chapter 1 that can support you in this work.

There is a tendency for teachers and students to say that oppression, specifically racism, happened or happens because of the racial identity of the individual or group being oppressed (e.g., "This happened because they're Black."). This leads students, especially BIPOC students, to believe that there's something wrong with being Black, Latinx, Asian American, Indigenous, and so on. It is important to shift such language so that students understand that racial oppression occurs because of racist ideas—that Black and Brown skin is not the problem, White supremacy is.

BOOKS FEATURED IN THIS CHAPTER

I Am Every Good Thing, by Derrick Barnes and illustrated by Gordon C. James	Page 52
Tía Fortuna's New Home, by Ruth Behar and illustrated by Devon Holzwarth	Page 56
My Two Border Towns, by David Bowles and illustrated by Erika Meza	Page 60
I Am Golden, by Eva Chen and illustrated by Sophie Diao	Page 64
Wild Berries, written and illustrated by Julie Flett	Page 69
I'm From, by Gary R. Gray Jr. and illustrated by Oge Mora	Page 73
A Day With No Words, by Tiffany Hammond and illustrated by Kate Cosgrove	Page 77
Homeland, by Hannah Moushabeck and illustrated by Reem Madooh	Page 81
My Rainbow, by Trinity and DeShanna Neal and illustrated by Art Twink	Page 86
My Papi Has a Motorcycle, by Isabel Quintero and illustrated by Zeke Peña	Page 90
I Can Write the World, by Joshunda Sanders and illustrated by Charly Palmer	Page 94

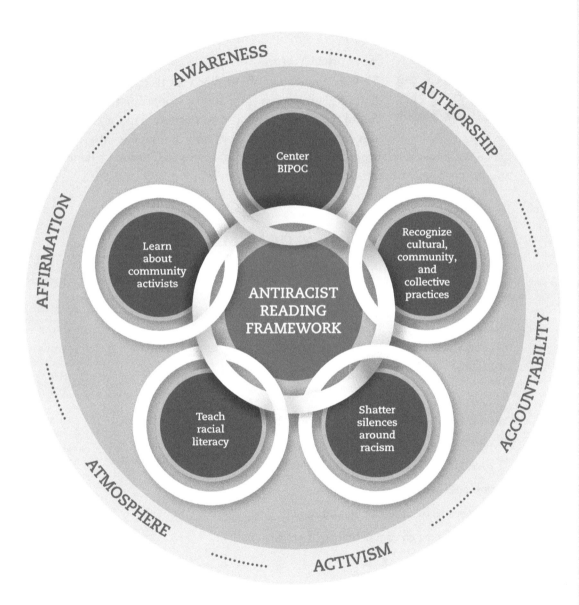

I Am Every Good Thing, written by Derrick Barnes and illustrated by Gordon C. James, is about a boy and all of the powerful ways he sees himself as a person and in the world.

About the Creators

To learn more about the author, visit Derrick Barnes's website, derrickdbarnes.com. The author's note for the book can be found there, and it is not to be missed. (Tip for educators and caregivers: Print the author's note and tape it into the back of the book for easy reference.) Learn more about the illustrator Gordon C. James on his website, gordon-james-pkrs.squarespace.com.

SIX CRITICAL LENSES

Prompts are provided to nurture students' thinking as they read in partnerships, groups, or independently.

Pathways capture the details and ideas that students may notice and think about as they read and respond to the text, and they can be used as guidance for educators to teach into.

AFFIRMATION

PROMPTS

- What are you learning about the main character?
- How does he feel about himself?
- What seems to make him feel this way?
- What are some character traits to describe him?

PATHWAYS

- The main character is confident, energetic, and fun.
- He likes to skateboard, he likes science, and he likes learning new things.
- He sees himself as a leader—someone who can make a difference in the world.

- He's curious and wants to explore the world around him.

- He's kind and polite, funny, and cool.

- His family and friends are important to him and that contributes to how he sees himself.

AWARENESS

PROMPTS

Racism is the harmful idea that a person's race, cultural background, or skin color is better than another's, resulting in individual and systemic mistreatment.

- Perhaps some of you have heard about or seen racism. Maybe you've experienced this. It's important for all of us to know about this.

- Let's think about this character's identity as we read this part: *"Although I am something like a superhero, every now and then, I am afraid. I am not what they might call me, and I will not answer to any name that is not my own. I am what I say I am."* What might make him afraid? Why might he be called a name that isn't his own?

- What shapes a person's identity?

- What messages are learned about racial identity in society?

- How can people resist harmful messages about race?

PATHWAYS

- Our family and the ways we see ourselves and the way the world sees us shape our identity.

- A person's identity is shaped by everything that makes them who they are—funny, kind, the things they like to do such as their favorite sports or music, their skin color, race, ethnicity, culture, and more.

- The main character may have been teased or bullied.

- Racism is a specific kind of bullying that involves people having false and unfair ideas about others based on skin color.

- Racist ideas about skin color affect Black and Brown people like this character.

- The main character resists harmful messages about race by refusing to allow anyone to change how he feels about himself and refusing to accept harmful ways others might see him. He practices resistance by saying, "I am what I say I am."

AUTHORSHIP

PROMPTS

- Who are the creators of this text?

- How do their identities influence this work?

- What is their motivation for creating this text?

PATHWAYS

- Derrick Barnes is the author of this text.

- In his author's note, Derrick Barnes states that he is the father of four strong, beautiful, brilliant Black boys.

- Derrick Barnes's identity as a Black father of Black boys influences this book by showing Black boys as they truly are and not in the inhumane ways society often makes them out to be.

- Derrick Barnes and Gordon C. James have also created the picture book *Ode to the Fresh Cut.*

ATMOSPHERE

PROMPTS

- How does this text reflect the identities and lived experiences of the characters/people?

- How does it reflect your identities and lived experiences?

- In what ways does this book convey and bring you joy?

PATHWAYS

- Setting: The book shows the main character in his neighborhood, at school, at church, at home, in his community—a full representation of his life.

- Perspective: Readers get to learn about all of the ways this character sees himself, his identity, and how he feels about himself and his life; his confidence, strength, creativity, brilliance, bravery, beauty, and his love.

- Figurative Language/Imagery:

  - Discuss the recurring line—"I am . . ." and how it serves as a mantra of self-confidence for this young boy.

  - Notice the many similes and metaphors throughout the book—"I am good to the core, like the center of a cinnamon roll." "I am a roaring flame of creativity."

- Mood/Tone: The feeling of joy, power, and triumph radiates across the book. The mood changes when the character reflects on times he feels afraid. Racism causes fear, uncertainty, and doubt.

- Theme: Black joy, self-love, self-confidence

ACTIVISM

PROMPTS

- In what ways does this book call attention to injustice?

- In what ways does this book affirm that Black lives matter?

- On the dedication page, Derrick Barnes lists the names of seven Black boys he dedicates this book to, boys who were victims of police shootings; then Gordon C. James provides an illustration of their likeness at the end of the book.

- This book affirms that Black lives matter by showing that Black children, specifically Black boys, matter—they are "worthy of success, of respect, of safety, of kindness, of happiness" and they deserve to be loved.

ACCOUNTABILITY

PROMPTS

- How can this book influence your thinking and actions now and in the future?

- How will you remain alert for the ways your particular identities help you to understand a text and the world?

PATHWAYS

- Reflect on ways this text makes a difference to your heart and in your life. Consider commitments you'll make to care for people and communities.

- This text is an invitation for me to think deeply and possibly differently about

  _____ and to apply this in my life (when/how)

  _____.

Reflection and Accountability for Antiracist Educators:

This text is an invitation for me to think deeply and possibly differently as a reader

_____ and challenges me to make radical changes in my personal and

 (in what ways?)

professional life _____.

 (in what ways?)

Tía Fortuna's New Home

Tía Fortuna's New Home, written by Ruth Behar and illustrated by Devon Holzwarth, is a heartwarming, intergenerational, multicultural story that explores Sephardic Jewish and Cuban heritage along with the true meaning of family and home.

About the Creators

To learn more about the author, visit her website, www.ruthbehar.com, which includes her biography and interviews.

Read this interview to learn more about the illustrator, Devon Holzwarth.

SIX CRITICAL LENSES

Prompts are provided to nurture students' thinking as they read in partnerships, groups, or independently.

Pathways capture the details and ideas that students may notice and think about as they read and respond to the text, and they can be used as guidance for educators to teach into.

AFFIRMATION

PROMPTS

- What are we learning about Estrella and Tía Fortuna?

- What brings them joy?

- What are we learning about their identities and how they see the world?

PATHWAYS

- Estrella loves spending time with her Tía Fortuna in the pink casita.

- Being near the ocean brings joy to Estrella and Tía Fortuna.

- The characters speak multiple languages—English, Spanish, Hebrew, Turkish, Arabic.

- Tía Fortuna shares her gratitude for the environment, for spending time with family, for friendships.

- Tía Fortuna believes in hope.

AWARENESS

PROMPTS

Antisemitism is prejudice and hatred toward Jewish people that has led to violence in the past and presently.

- What does this book help you to understand about the power of intersecting identities such as race, ethnicity, language, and cultural and religious beliefs?

- What does this book help you to understand about the ways people with intersecting identities can experience oppression?

PATHWAYS

- There are beautiful, powerful, cultural traditions that are observed and honored by people with intersecting identities such as the Jewish Cuban characters in this story.

- Antisemitic and racist ideas cause people with intersecting identities to experience hate and oppression in various ways. In the author's note, Ruth Behar explains, "The Sephardim descend from Jews who once lived in Spain and were forced to leave in 1492 because of their religious beliefs."

AUTHORSHIP

PROMPTS

- Who are the creators of this text?

- How do their identities influence this work?

- What is their motivation for creating this text?

PATHWAYS

- In the author's note, Ruth Behar explains her personal connection to this story. She writes, "I am a child of two Jewish civilizations—Ashkenazi on my mother's side, inheriting powerful Yiddish traditions, and Sephardic on my father's side."

- Behar's identities informed her writing of this story. This book is a way to ensure that her Sephardic heritage and traditions are preserved.

- The book jacket shares that Devon Holzwarth was "born in Washington, D.C., grew up in Panama," and now lives in Germany. Her background helps her to bring a multicultural lens to her art.

ATMOSPHERE

PROMPTS

- How does this text reflect the identities and lived experiences of the characters/people?

- How does it reflect your identities and lived experiences?

- In what ways does this book convey and bring you joy?

PATHWAYS

- Setting: From her home by the sea to the La Casa de los Viejitos where she moves to, the natural environment is important to Tía Fortuna—the ocean, the banyan trees.

- Perspective: Tía Fortuna makes the transition from one place to the next by reminding herself of what's most important—her cultural identity, the love of her family, her memories, and the opportunity to make new friends.

- Figurative Language/Imagery: Explore the power and purpose of symbolism in this text: the key, the mezuzah, the lucky-eye bracelets, the names Estrella and Fortuna, and so on.

- Mood/Tone: This book celebrates Jewish and Cuban culture.

- Theme: culture, home, tradition, family, love

ACTIVISM

PROMPTS

- What does this book help you to understand about the multiculturalism of Jewish people?

- How does this story help you to recognize the importance of learning about the stories and experiences of those who have been marginalized?

- How does this story help you to recognize the importance of writing our own stories and experiences?

PATHWAYS

- There is racial, ethnic, cultural, and linguistic diversity of Jewish people around the world.

- Writing our own stories and experiences is one way to work against the erasure of people who have been marginalized past and present.

- Writing our stories, especially if we have been marginalized, is a way to resist erasure.

ACCOUNTABILITY

PROMPTS

- How can this book influence your thinking and actions now and in the future?

- How will you remain alert for the ways your particular identities help you to understand a text and the world?

- Reflect on ways this text makes a difference to your heart and in your life. Consider commitments you'll make to care for people and communities.

- This text is an invitation for me to think deeply and possibly differently about

  _____ and to apply this in my life (when/how)

  _____.

Reflection and Accountability for Antiracist Educators:

This text is an invitation for me to think deeply and possibly differently as a reader

_____ and challenges me to make radical changes in my personal and
(in what ways?)

professional life _____.
                       (in what ways?)

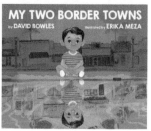

My Two Border Towns, by David Bowles and Erika Meza, is the story of a father and son, their weekend ritual driving across the U.S.–Mexico border, and ways they care for their community. This book is available in English and in Spanish.

About the Creators

Visit the author's and illustrator's website www.david bowles.us and www.erikameza.com and listen to the creators discuss their process of creating this story.

SIX CRITICAL LENSES

Prompts are provided to nurture students' thinking as they read in partnerships, groups, or independently.

Pathways capture the details and ideas that students may notice and think about as they read and respond to the text, and they can be used as guidance for educators to teach into.

Watch as David Bowles and Erika Meza, author and illustrator of *My Two Border Towns,* answer students.

Download a free educator's guide here.

AFFIRMATION

PROMPTS

- What are you learning about the ways these characters spend time together?

- What are you learning about the ways these characters interact with their communities?

PATHWAYS

- The characters have a father and son ritual that is important to them.

- They speak Spanish and English.

- Both characters think about others. The boy has gifts for friends in his special bag.

- The boy loves his community; there are favorite places he loves.

- They live in a Spanish-speaking community.

- Dad teaches his son important history during trips—"Coahuiltecans once lived here, before all this was Mexico—both riverbanks."

- They eat breakfast at their favorite *restorán* and the boy plays soccer with his cousins.

- The characters have family in both towns.

- They purchase Mexican items and foods to bring back home, and they purchase items and medicine to give to refugees from the Caribbean and Central America: "We have a duty to care for our gente."

AWARENESS

PROMPTS

Amnesty International (**Refugees, Asylum Seekers, and Migrants—Amnesty International**), a global organization working to protect human rights, provides the following definitions:

Refugee—"A person who has fled their own country because they are at risk of serious human rights violations and persecution there. The risks to their safety and life were so great that they felt they had no choice but to leave and seek safety outside their country because their own government cannot or will not protect them from those dangers. Refugees have a right to international protection."

Asylum seeker—"A person who has left their country and is seeking protection from persecution and serious human rights violations in another country, but who hasn't yet been legally recognized as a refugee and is waiting to receive a decision on their asylum claim. Seeking asylum is a human right. This means everyone should be allowed to enter another country to seek asylum."

- What do these definitions help you to understand or wonder about the story?

- What is the purpose and function of a border?

- What can be noticed about how refugees and asylum seekers from the Caribbean and Central America are treated?

PATHWAYS

- What happens when people are stuck between two countries?

- Dad says, "It's unfair to make him wait, since our country has room for his family right now."

- If the United States has room, why doesn't the country invite refugees and asylum seekers in?

- Dad reminds his son, "Coahuiltecans once lived here, before all this was Mexico—both riverbanks. Now we're two countries."

- Borders are a way to separate land and people.

AUTHORSHIP

PROMPTS

- Who are the creators of this text?

- How do their identities influence this work?

- What is their motivation for creating this text?

PATHWAYS

- The bio in the book shares that David Bowles grew up in the Rio Grande Valley of South Texas, the same setting as the book. Like the characters, he regularly crossed the border with his father.

- The illustrator, Erika Meza, was born in Mexico.

- In a discussion about the book, both creators share that both of their families "come from the border," and David Bowles says he wanted to write a book that shows the experiences of those who live on the border and what people are really like.

ATMOSPHERE

PROMPTS

- How does this text reflect the identities and lived experiences of the characters/people?

- How does it reflect your identities and lived experiences?

- In what ways does this book convey and bring you joy?

PATHWAYS

- Setting: Consider the similarities and differences between the two towns (boy describes the town in Mexico as a twin of the one where he lives, "with Spanish spoken everywhere just the same but English mostly missing till it pops up like grains of sugar on a chili pepper."). In both towns Spanish is important to the identities of the characters.

- Perspective: This story offers the perspectives of people who live and work to help asylum seekers and refugees.

- Figurative Language/Imagery: Take note of the author's use of symbolism across the story (e.g., eagle, river, passport, the boy's bag, etc.), metaphors (e.g., "Before I know it, we reach the broad river, a watery serpent that glints with the dawn"), and vibrant illustrations throughout.

- Mood/Tone: The complexities and joys of life are shown.

- Theme: community care, displacement

PROMPTS

- What does it mean to be part of a transnational community?
- What are you learning from this book about the meaning of community care?

PATHWAYS

- Many people maintain connections to loved ones, communities, and issues across national borders. These connections can lead to an exchange of ideas and cultures that increases diversity in many ways (food, the arts, politics, education, etc.).
- The characters in this story feel it is their duty to connect with their communities, as well as support and care for each other's well-being.

ACCOUNTABILITY

PROMPTS

- How can this book influence your thinking and actions now and in the future?
- How will you remain alert for the ways your particular identities help you to understand a text and the world?

PATHWAYS

- Reflect on ways this text makes a difference to your heart and in your life. Consider commitments you'll make to care for people and communities.
- This text is an invitation for me to think deeply and possibly differently about

  _____ and to apply this in my life (when/how)

  _____.

Reflection and Accountability for Antiracist Educators:

This text is an invitation for me to think deeply and possibly differently as a reader

_____ and challenges me to make radical changes in my personal and
(in what ways?)

professional life _____.
(in what ways?)

I Am Golden

In *I Am Golden,* written by Eva Chen and illustrated by Sophie Diao, Mei's parents provide foundational lessons about her Chinese identity, emphasizing the richness and beauty of her culture, particularly in a world where anti-Asian hate threatens to harm her physical and psychological safety.

About the Creators
Visit Sophie Diao's website to learn more about her art: www.sophiediao.com.

Watch this YouTube interview to learn more about the author and her motivation for writing *I Am Golden,* which she calls "a manifesto for Asian joy."

Six Critical Lenses

Prompts are provided to nurture students' thinking as they read in partnerships, groups, or independently.

Pathways capture the details and ideas that students may notice and think about as they read and respond to the text, and they can be used as guidance for educators to teach into.

AFFIRMATION

PROMPTS

- What are you learning about the characters?
    - Mei?
    - Mei's parents?
- What are you learning about Mei's identity?

PATHWAYS

- Mei's name means *beautiful.*
- There are Chinese words (e.g., Mei Guó—May Gwah) in the story.
- Mei's parents love their daughter and they tell Mei she's beautiful.
- Mei's parents are immigrants and they are raising their daughter in America, a country that isn't always an easy place to live in.
- Mei listens to her parents and sees herself the way they see her.

- Mei is smart.

- Mei helps her parents navigate living in the United States by translating between English and Chinese.

- Mei teaches her parents about the United States.

AWARENESS

PROMPTS

Microaggressions are discriminatory statements and actions that are intentionally or unintentionally directed toward individuals or groups of people who are marginalized. There are a few major types of racial microaggressions. The use of a racial slur or symbol like offensive racial name-calling, swastikas, or the Confederate flag is called a *microassault*; *microinsults* are subtle verbal and nonverbal communications that come from racist stereotypes, like saying to someone who is Black and tall, "You must play basketball"; and exclusionary comments like saying to someone who isn't white, "No, where are you really from?" are *microinvalidations*.

- What can get in the way of Mei's positive sense of self?

- What might prevent Mei from seeing herself the way her parents do?

- What are you learning about racial microaggressions and how they impact people's lives?

- How do Mei's parents help her understand their racial and cultural identity in order to cultivate self-love and to help her resist harmful microaggressions?

PATHWAYS

- Mei is targeted by peers who express racist ideas toward her.

- People who call Mei "different" and treat her differently threaten Mei's positive sense of self.

- Racial microaggressions are an affront to a person's identity and damage their self-esteem.

- Mei's parents provide a counternarrative that functions as a shield to protect Mei.

- Our family and the ways we see ourselves and the way the world sees us shape our identity.

AUTHORSHIP

PROMPTS

- Who are the creators of this text?

- How do their identities influence this work?

- What is their motivation for creating this text?

PATHWAYS

- The identities of the author and illustrator shape this story.

- Eva Chen authored this book. The endnote shares that Eva Chen is a first-generation Chinese American.

- In the author's note, Eva Chen describes being bullied by her classmates and the racial microaggressions they targeted her with.

- One personal motivation for creating this text is that the author is a mother. She writes, "I hope that they will never experience that sting of otherness, the swirl of confusion, of questioning whether they belong."

- Another motivation for writing this book is in response to the rise in anti-Asian hate during the COVID-19 pandemic.

- Eva Chen wrote this book as "a love letter" to Chinese Americans and in celebration of Chinese American joy.

- Sophia Diao is the illustrator of this book. In the illustrator's note, she shares that her parents immigrated from China to Germany and then to the United States, where she was born.

- The illustrator was also targeted in school by peers and teachers, and as a result, she shares, "It wasn't until I got much older that I learned to cherish my Chinese heritage."

- The illustrator hopes this book helps children learn to "embrace all the things that make them unique and brilliant."

ATMOSPHERE

PROMPTS

- How does this text reflect the identities and lived experiences of the characters/people?

- How does it reflect your identities and lived experiences?

- In what ways does this book convey and bring you joy?

PATHWAYS

- Setting: Whether at home or at school, Mei listens to and carries within her the history, knowledge, and messages of strength and beauty of her identity provided by her parents.

- Perspective: Mei's parents share stories and affirmations of love that strengthen Mei's sense of self.

- Figurative Language/Imagery: Discuss the meaning and significance of the author's use of gold/golden across the book.

  ○ "We see skin brushed with gold"

  ○ "You carry a golden flame inside you, and it's always with you"

  ○ "But they don't know that each of our golden flames flickers distinctly"

  ○ "You are power. You, Mei, are golden."

  ○ "I am golden."

- Mood/Tone: This book provides a counternarrative that serves as "a manifesto of self-love for Chinese American children."
- Themes: self-love, identity, resistance

ACTIVISM

PROMPTS

Anti-Asian hate has increased during the COVID-19 pandemic due to the misattribution of the coronavirus to the Asian American community. But anti-Asian hate did not begin in 2020; it has existed since the time Asians first immigrated to the United States. Asian Americans experience racism in a variety of forms such as verbal and physical abuse, harassment, and anti-Asian laws and policies.

- What does this book help you to understand about the difference between bullying and racism?
- How does this story help you to recognize the ways racism occurs at school between peers?
- What can you do to interrupt racism and anti-Asian hate when you see it in action at school and in your daily life?

PATHWAYS

- All bullying is harmful, but race-based harassment increases harm—emotionally, mentally, and physically.
- Kids who target their peers based on aspects of their identity—this is racism in action.
- If racism at school is witnessed, focus on the person being harmed and the impact of this. Don't laugh as if this is just a joke. Ask how I can support them. Include them in your friend group. Speak to a trusted adult. Get help.
- Commit to being antiracist by learning language (e.g., microaggressions, anti-Asian hate) to speak out against racism; broaden your circle of friends to be inclusive of a wider group of people; learn about the values, cultures, and identities of people beyond your own by reading books and engaging media by and about BIPOC.

ACCOUNTABILITY

PROMPTS

- How can this book influence your thinking and actions now and in the future?
- How will you remain alert for the ways your particular identities help you to understand a text and the world?

PATHWAYS

- Reflect on ways this text makes a difference to your heart and in your life. Consider commitments you'll make to care for people and communities.

- This text is an invitation for me to think deeply and possibly differently about

  _____ and to apply this in my life (when/how)

  _____.

Reflection and Accountability for Antiracist Educators:

This text is an invitation for me to think deeply and possibly differently as a reader

_____ and challenges me to make radical changes in my personal and
(in what ways?)

professional life _____.
(in what ways?)

Wild Berries, written and illustrated by Julie Flett, is the story of Clarence, who spends the day with ōkoma, his grandmother, picking wild blueberries and interacting with nature and wildlife in their beautiful woodland. Cree language is centered reflecting the cultural identities of the characters. There are two versions of this book. One version is written in Cree language. Another version is in English with Cree syllabary and in a Cree dialect.

About the Creator

Visit the author's website, www.julie flett.com.

Read this online interview to learn more about the author/illustrator.

There are important distinctions and nuances around the words *Indigenous, Native American, American Indian, tribe,* and *nation.* In my discussion of texts, I use the language and terminology the author uses. It's important to listen for who people tell us who they are and to teach children to listen as well and to respect what they are learning. Learn more here about the impact of words and using accurate terms: qrs.ly/cufrdvt.

Six Critical Lenses

Prompts are provided to nurture students' thinking as they read in partnerships, groups, or independently.

Pathways capture the details and ideas that students may notice and think about as they read and respond to the text, and they can be used as guidance for educators to teach into.

AFFIRMATION

PROMPTS

- What are you learning about the characters?
- How do they enjoy spending time together?
- What are you noticing about the use of language in this book?

PATHWAYS

- Clarence spends lots of time with ōkoma, grandma.
- Ōkoma knows how to pick blueberries in the forest and teaches Clarence.
- Clarence enjoys this time and enjoys nature.
- Clarence respects the insects and animals in the woods.
- Ōkoma and Clarence are grateful for nature and the forest.

AWARENESS

PROMPTS

- Why might the author have written a version of this book in English with Cree language?
- How is language a key part of identity?

PATHWAYS

- Cree language is alive in parts of the United States and Canada.
- Language matters! Language is a key part of cultural identity and in protecting cultural knowledge.
- It is important that Indigenous languages such as Cree are promoted, protected, taught, and preserved.
- Language is preserved when it is spoken and used in books, in the media, and in schools.
- Colonization and White supremacist policies have threatened Indigenous and Native languages.
- Indigenous and Native children were forced to attend boarding/residential schools in the United States and Canada for the purpose of erasing their cultural identities, including languages, and replacing this with White, mainstream culture.

AUTHORSHIP

PROMPTS

- Who are the creators of this text?
- How do their identities influence this work?
- What is their motivation for creating this text?

PATHWAYS

- Julie Flett is the author and illustrator.
- The About Julie Flett section shares that Julie Flett is Cree-Métis and lives in Vancouver, British Columbia, which is in Canada.
- Julie Flett's Cree-Métis identity has likely shaped her writing of this text, including Cree language, that is used in the story.

- The book blurb shares that the setting of this book is Julie Flett's ancestral home.
- Julie Flett may have wanted to share the beauty of her home, language, and Indigenous knowledge and traditions with readers.

ATMOSPHERE

PROMPTS

- How does this text reflect the identities and lived experiences of the characters/people?
- How does it reflect your identities and lived experiences?
- In what ways does this book convey and bring you joy?

PATHWAYS

- Setting: Ōkoma and Clarence enjoy time together in the beautiful woods they love, which is connected to their identity, culture, and traditions.
- Perspective: Knowledge of, respect, and honoring nature are part of the characters' identity.
  - "They say thank you nanākomowak."
- Figurative Language/Imagery: The art follows a specific color scheme that brings the forest to life. Some words are pulled out from the text and are bolded or italicized in black or red to spotlight Cree language, a particular object, wildlife, or action.
- Mood/Tone: There is a powerful sense of peace, connection, and joy between the characters, their tradition, and the natural environment.
  - "Grandma likes sweet blueberries *ininimina*, soft blueberries, juicy blueberries. Clarence likes big blueberries, sour blueberries, blueberries that go POP in his mouth."
- Theme—It's not just relationships with people that are important but also people's relationships with the natural environment.

ACTIVISM

PROMPTS

- What does this book help you to consider about relationships with family? With the natural environment?
- How does this book help you to consider the power and purpose of language?

PATHWAYS

- Intergenerational relationships are powerful.
- Family, elders, and youth influence how we see the world.
- Language helps us do more than communicate; it preserves our identity, cultural values, and sense of belonging.

PROMPTS

- How can this book influence your thinking and actions now and in the future?
- How will you remain alert for the ways your particular identities help you to understand a text and the world?

PATHWAYS

- Reflect on ways this text makes a difference to your heart and in your life. Consider commitments you'll make to care for people and communities.
- This text is an invitation for me to think deeply and possibly differently about

  _____ and to apply this in my life (when/how)

  _____.

Reflection and Accountability for Antiracist Educators:

This text is an invitation for me to think deeply and possibly differently as a reader

_____ and challenges me to make radical changes in my personal and
     (in what ways?)

professional life _____.
          (in what ways?)

I'm From, written by Gary R. Gray Jr. and illustrated by Oge Mora, is the story of the everyday small yet mighty moments of a young boy's life that define where he's from and shapes how he sees himself in the world.

About the Creators

Visit the author's and illustrator's websites, to learn more about these creators:

- www.garyrgrayjr.com

- www.ogemora.com

SIX CRITICAL LENSES

Prompts are provided to nurture students' thinking as they read in partnerships, groups, or independently.

Pathways capture the details and ideas that students may notice and think about as they read and respond to the text, and they can be used as guidance for educators to teach into.

Read this interview, "In Conversation: Gary Gray Jr. and Joanna Ho," to learn more about the author and illustrator.

Watch Oge Mora discuss the power and freedom of representation in her art in this online conversation.

AFFIRMATION

PROMPTS

Identity is all of the parts of us that make us who we are—funny, kind, the things we like to do such as our favorite sports or music, our skin color, race, ethnicity, and culture—these are all important parts of our identity.

- What are you learning about the main character?

- Which identities seem particularly important to him?

- What are the various ways he shares where he's from?

- The main character enjoys his family and friends.

- Parts of his identity that are important to him include his family, friends, his hair, music, drawing, writing stories, and his community.

- He comes from places, people, sayings, food, and love.

AWARENESS

PROMPTS

Stereotypes are unfair and often untrue beliefs about people who share a particular characteristic such as racial identity and expectations that people will look and behave in certain ways.

Let's think about the main character's identity as we read this part: *"And the other kids . . . can I touch your HAIR? / you don't sound BLACK! . . . do you play BASKETBALL?"*

- What are you learning about the ways parts of his identity are challenged?

- What are you learning about assumptions made about his identity?

- Why is this harmful to his self-esteem?

PATHWAYS

- Some of his peers have limited ideas about what it means to be Black that are based on stereotypes.

- His peers have made decisions about his identity without really knowing who he is.

- Asking to touch his hair is a way of making him feel different, when really everyone is different and unique.

- Asking if he plays basketball is a stereotype—a judgment about him simply because he is Black and the belief that if you are Black and a boy that you like to play basketball.

- These questions are harmful and hurtful. They make him feel like he's an outsider and like there's something possibly very different and wrong about him.

AUTHORSHIP

PROMPTS

- Who are the creators of this text?

- How do their identities influence this work?

- What is their motivation for creating this text?

- In an interview (**In Conversation: Gary Gray Jr. and Joanna Ho**), Gary R. Gray identifies as Black Canadian.

- On his website, Gray explains that he didn't consider himself much of a reader when he was a young person. In *I'm From,* he writes that he's from "Books that don't click with me: one or two that do."

- On his website, Gray shares that sometimes it takes more work to develop a reading identity and encourages readers not to give up.

- In a discussion with children's book illustrators, Oge Mora discusses the pressure she's felt to fit into expectations of what it means to be Black and Nigerian. She shares how freeing it is to let go of these expectations and be herself and how this shows up in her art.

ATMOSPHERE

PROMPTS

- How does this text reflect the identities and lived experiences of the characters/people?

- How does it reflect your identities and lived experiences?

- In what ways does this book convey and bring you joy?

PATHWAYS

- Setting: The book shares the places, people, and experiences that are important to the character.

- Perspective: Readers learn about the main character's identity and all of the things that shape who he is and how he feels about this.

- Figurative Language/Imagery: The book *I'm From* is the author's poem, and it is an invitation for readers to think about where they're from and to write their own poem and stories.

- Mood/Tone: This text centers the everyday joys that warm the heart of this main character as well as experiences that frustrate him.

- Theme: identity, joy, love, validation, community, difference

ACTIVISM

PROMPTS

- How does this book help you consider ways to avoid stereotyping?

- How does this book help you consider what to do if you commit, experience, or witness stereotyping?

- Stereotyping can be avoided by getting to know a person for who they are.

- If a person expresses a stereotype, they can apologize immediately and acknowledge the harm it caused.

- People can think about where such harmful ideas come from and commit to acting differently.

- If a person witnesses stereotyping, they can offer support to the person who was harmed and let the person who committed stereotyping know why their words/actions are harmful.

- If a person experiences stereotyping, they can speak to people they feel close to—their closest friends, families, and teachers. And they can practice resistance by refusing to believe harmful ideas about themself.

ACCOUNTABILITY

PROMPTS

- How can this book influence your thinking and actions now and in the future?

- How will you remain alert for the ways your particular identities help you to understand a text and the world?

PATHWAYS

- Reflect on ways this text makes a difference to your heart and in your life. Consider commitments you'll make to care for people and communities.

- This text is an invitation for me to think deeply and possibly differently about

  _____ and to apply this in my life (when/how)

  _____.

Reflection and Accountability for Antiracist Educators:

This text is an invitation for me to think deeply and possibly differently as a reader

_____ and challenges me to make radical changes in my personal and
  (in what ways?)

professional life _____.
                    (in what ways?)

A Day With No Words, written by Tiffany Hammond and illustrated by Kate Cosgrove, invites readers into the daily joys and challenges of a young, Black, autistic boy and his mother. Aidan is nonverbal and uses a tablet to communicate with his mom, who advocates for his full acceptance, respect, and humanity.

About the Creators

Learn more about Tiffany Hammond and her work at her website, www.fidgetsand fries.co, and to learn more about Kate Cosworth, visit her website, www.katecosgrove .com.

SIX CRITICAL LENSES

Prompts are provided to nurture students' thinking as they read in partnerships, groups, or independently.

Pathways capture the details and ideas that students may notice and think about as they read and respond to the text, and they can be used as guidance for educators to teach into.

AFFIRMATION

PROMPTS

- What are you learning about the boy and his mother?
- What brings the boy comfort and joy?

PATHWAYS

- The boy and his mother communicate using a tablet.
- The boy loves the sound of his mother's voice; it comforts him.
- His father's voice makes him feel safe.
- His mother always knows how her son feels.
- The boy knows what brings him joy, like hugging trees and spinning barefoot on the grass.

AWARENESS

PROMPTS

The American Psychiatric Association describes **autism**, or **autism spectrum disorder (ASD)**, as a broad range of conditions that can include challenges with social skills, repetitive behaviors, speech, and nonverbal communication. **Neurodiversity** is a way of explaining the range of differences in ways people's brains work.

- How does this book shed light on the various ways people's brains work?

- How does this book help you to recognize ways people can respond to differences in ways that are hurtful and harmful?

- How does this book help you to think about ways people can respond to differences in ways that are loving and kind?

PATHWAYS

- There is more than one way for our brains to work. And there's more than one way to communicate.

- Sometimes people's voices feel too loud to the main character, "like storms."

- The boy experiences less stress when there isn't a crowd of people.

- People can respond to differences through actions and words that are hurtful (e.g., staring; handicapped).

- The boy has a unique way of being, and he is judged by people who think there's only one right way to be in the world.

- People can respond to differences through actions and words that are warm (e.g., offering welcoming smiles, finding common ways to communicate).

AUTHORSHIP

PROMPTS

- Who are the creators of this text?

- How do their identities influence this work?

- What is their motivation for creating this text?

PATHWAYS

- In the author's note, Tiffany Hammond shares that she is an autistic mother, advocate, storyteller, and parent of two Autistic boys. Her personal experiences with Autism informed the writing of this story.

- Aidan is Tiffany Hammond's older son, and this book is based on him.

- The author explains that "A Day With No is a call to action. We all have a role in helping foster understanding, acceptance, love, and accommodations for those like Aidan."

ATMOSPHERE

PROMPTS

- How does this text reflect the identities and lived experiences of the characters/people?

- How does it reflect your identities and lived experiences?

- In what ways does this book convey and bring you joy?

PATHWAYS

- Setting: The story provides a window into how Aidan experiences a typical day in his life.

- Perspective: Readers understand the world through Aidan's daily experiences and broadens understandings about communication.

- Figurative Language/Imagery: Discuss why the author has titled this book *A Day With No Words* when the boy and his mother actually use many words. Discuss how people associate words with vocalized speech. Discuss the part of the story where the boy's mother says, "My son does not speak, but his ears work just fine. The words that you say go straight to his mind."

- Mood/Tone: This story calls on readers to open their hearts and imagine a world where everyone is accepted just as they are.

- Theme: acceptance, love, connection, communication

ACTIVISM

PROMPTS

- What connections are you able to make between racism and ableism?

- What does this story help you to understand about being an upstander versus a bystander?

- What can you do to be an upstander?

PATHWAYS

- People have intersecting identities such as race and dis/ability.

- Learn about the ways race and dis/ability can magnify how people experience discrimination.

- Being an upstander means accepting and appreciating people as they are and recognizing the full humanity of every person. Upstanders interrupt discrimination. Bystanders allow discrimination to continue.

- Seek out books and media that center the experiences of people with dis/abilities.

- Notice the way the world around me (my school, playgrounds, stores, transportation methods, etc.) are inclusive—making it possible or impossible for people with dis/abilities to utilize. Ask store owners, principals, and local leaders to make my environment more inclusive.

- Support the rights of all people from all backgrounds to freely express themselves.

ACCOUNTABILITY

PROMPTS

- How can this book influence your thinking and actions now and in the future?

- How will you remain alert for the ways your particular identities help you to understand a text and the world?

PATHWAYS

- Reflect on ways this text makes a difference to your heart and in your life. Consider commitments you'll make to care for people and communities.

- This text is an invitation for me to think deeply and possibly differently about

_____ and to apply this in my life (when/how)

_____ .

Reflection and Accountability for Antiracist Educators:

This text is an invitation for me to think deeply and possibly differently as a reader

_____ and challenges me to make radical changes in my personal and

(in what ways?)

professional life _____ .

(in what ways?)

Homeland, written by Hannah Moushabeck and illustrated by Reem Madooh, is a multigenerational story of Palestinian culture. A father keeps the history, cultural identity, and significance of place alive by sharing his memories of Palestine with his daughters and deepening their understanding of the meaning of home.

About the Creators

To learn more about the author, visit Moushabeck's website, www.hannahmoushabeck.com, and visit www.reemadooh.com to learn more about the illustrator.

Read this interview to learn more about the book and the author's motivations for writing this book.

Six Critical Lenses

Prompts are provided to nurture students' thinking as they read in partnerships, groups, or independently.

Pathways capture the details and ideas that students may notice and think about as they read and respond to the text, and they can be used as guidance for educators to teach into.

AFFIRMATION

PROMPTS

- What are you learning about the characters?
- What are you learning about their cultural identity?
- How can stories help us learn about our history?

PATHWAYS

- The daughters love the special time they have with their father and the stories he tells them of home.
- The father is funny and loving.

- The stories are connected to their Palestinian identity, their father's homeland, which the girls see as their home too.

- The father's stories help his daughters to know their homeland even though they have not physically been there.

- Palestine is important to the daughters because their father's memories keep their heritage, cultural traditions and foods, and relatives alive in their hearts and minds.

AWARENESS

Nakba is an Arab word for catastrophe. Al-Nakba, "the catastrophe," refers to the Israeli occupation of Palestine and dislocation of Palestinians in 1948, which created a refugee crisis that is still unresolved. *The Israeli-Palestinian conflict in 2023 has created a humanitarian issue resulting in significant loss of life, as well as a scarcity of food and medical supplies, and it has caused more than a million Palestinians in Gaza to flee their homes and seek refuge.

PROMPTS

- What information do we need to know to understand this conflict?

- How does this book help you to understand the importance of imagining and working toward a world without conflict?

PATHWAYS

- Where in the world is Palestine?

- Where in the world is Israel?

- What and where is Jerusalem?

- What and where is Gaza?

- What is Hamas?

- When and how did Israel become a country?

- Are other countries involved in the conflict?

- How is the United States involved in the conflict?

- This book helps us to learn about life in Palestine, the people, their culture, and their lives. The more we learn about people and their lives, the more we care about them, which can help us find ways to live in peace.

NOTE: Depending on students' ages, the questions they ask will vary. Because there is an abundance of misinformation readily available, anticipate that students have been exposed to this. To mitigate harm to students in your classroom, you might ask students to address these prompts in writing that you collect and then reframe questions in ways that can support safe and productive discussions. Further, it's important to distinguish between Hamas and Palestinians when discussing this conflict to avoid furthering Islamophobia and anti-Muslim hate.

AUTHORSHIP

PROMPTS

- Who are the creators of this text?

- How do their identities influence this work?

- What is their motivation for creating this text?

PATHWAYS

- In the author's note, Hannah Moushabeck shares that she and her siblings grew up hearing stories about Palestine, their homeland, from their parents and other family members. These experiences and her identities influence the writing of this autobiographical book.

- In an interview, Moushabeck provides insight around why writing this book is so important. She shares, "One of the tragedies of displaced families is that so much of what makes up your culture and identity is lost through distance, time, and assimilation. This book unlocks truths about my culture that took me many years to discover. It took years of pestering my family members for stories, recipes, and photos. I am still unlocking new wonderful parts of my culture—even now as an adult."

ATMOSPHERE

PROMPTS

- How does this text reflect the identities and lived experiences of the characters/people?

- How does it reflect your identities and lived experiences?

- In what ways does this book convey and bring you joy?

PATHWAYS

- Setting: Palestine comes to life through the characters and the memories of their homeland.

- Perspective: Readers learn the significance and definition of home through the characters' deep connection to their cultural identity.

- Figurative Language/Imagery: Admire the ways the author and illustrator help readers to visualize the sights, sounds, and vibrancy of life in Palestine. Discuss the symbolism of the key. In an interview, the author shares, "The key as a symbol is deeply important to Palestinians. Palestinians living in exile have used the key as a symbol for the 'right to return,' which is a movement that would allow indigenous Palestinians the freedom to return to their homeland. Many Palestinians still have the keys to their houses, like my family. Keys also represent an opening or unlocking, which feels particularly relevant to my story. As a second-generation Palestinian, I find myself constantly seeking out and learning more and more about my culture and ancestry" (Brechner, 2023).

- Mood/Tone: This book is a love letter to Palestine and an ode to the importance and meaning of home.
- Theme: identity, family, intergenerational relationships, significance of place and home

ACTIVISM

PROMPTS

- How is this book an invitation to learn more about Palestine, Palestinians, and Palestinian Americans?
- How does this book help you to understand the importance of stories as a way of learning about your history, culture, and identity?
- How does this book invite you to learn more about your identity and homeland?

PATHWAYS

- Learning more about Palestine and Palestinians can provide counternarratives to misrepresentations in the movies, books, and other media.
- Storytelling is an important way to make sure people, their histories, and cultures are not erased.
- Our stories are a way to keep our memories active and alive, which can fill us with pride and joy about who we are.
- Like Hannah Moushabeck has done, we can speak with our elders to learn about our backgrounds, look at photographs, and ask questions about where we're from and our connections to places.

ACCOUNTABILITY

PROMPTS

- How can this book influence your thinking and actions now and in the future?
- How will you remain alert for the ways your particular identities help you to understand a text and the world?

PATHWAYS

- Reflect on ways this text makes a difference to your heart and in your life. Consider commitments you'll make to care for people and communities.
- This text is an invitation for me to think deeply and possibly differently about

_____ and to apply this in my life (when/how)

_____.

Reflection and Accountability for Antiracist Educators:

This text is an invitation for me to think deeply and possibly differently as a reader

_____ and challenges me to make radical changes in my personal and
  (in what ways?)

professional life _____.
                      (in what ways?)

In *My Rainbow,* written by Trinity and DeShanna Neal and illustrated by Art Twink, Trinity, a Black, autistic, transgender girl, realizes she needs long hair to fully express who she is. With the love and support of her family who affirms all parts of her identity, Trinity finally gets the long hair she desires.

SIX CRITICAL LENSES

Prompts are provided to nurture students' thinking as they read in partnerships, groups, or independently.

Pathways capture the details and ideas that students may notice and think about as they read and respond to the text, and they can be used as guidance for educators to teach into.

Learn more about the authors by reading this interview.

AFFIRMATION

PROMPTS

- What are you learning about Trinity and what brings her joy?

- What are we learning about Trinity's identity and what's important to her?

- What are you learning about Trinity's family?

PATHWAYS

- Trinity loves her family. She enjoys playing with her sister and her doll.

- Trinity is autistic and loves soft things.

- Trinity is a transgender girl and wants long hair in order to fully express herself.

- Trinity's family knows what she likes—her favorite colors, textures, and so on.

- Trinity's mom and brother really listen to understand how Trinity feels.

AWARENESS

PROMPTS

In a Guide to Gender Identity Terms, developed by NPR with help from multiple organizations that focus on LGBTQ advocacy, *cisgender* and *transgender* are defined as follows:

"**Cisgender**, or simply cis, is an adjective that describes a person whose gender identity aligns with the sex they were assigned at birth."

"**Transgender**, or simply **trans**, is an adjective used to describe someone whose gender identity differs from the sex assigned at birth. A transgender man, for example, is someone who was listed as female at birth but whose gender identity is male."

This is a good resource to learn more about gender identity terms and expression: qrs.ly/dtfrdvv.

- What can be understood by really listening to Trinity?
- What does Trinity express about her experience as a transgender girl?

PATHWAYS

- Trinity communicates who she is—a transgender girl.
- She shares with her mom that "people don't care if cisgender girls like you have short hair. But it's different for transgender girls. I *need* long hair!"
- Trinity is observing how people are treated in society and specifically how challenging it is for transgender girls to experience respect and acceptance.

AUTHORSHIP

PROMPTS

- Who are the creators of this text?
- How do their identities influence this work?
- What is their motivation for creating this text?

PATHWAYS

- Trinity and her mother, DeShanna Neal, are "advocates for Black and transgender rights and awareness."
- Art Twink identifies as an "artivist" who has worked on "prison abolition, transgender liberation, and mental health issues."
- In an interview, DeShanna Neal shares that *My Rainbow* is the true story of her daughter Trinity and how she got her rainbow hair. DeShanna Neal also shares about the importance of listening to children. "Don't just listen with your ears; listen with your heart. Children have pure but really big feelings and it's our jobs as the grownups to hear them out. Validating those feelings are also very important and honestly, sometimes it's the kids who teach us a thing or two" (Pride and Less Prejudice, 2023).

ATMOSPHERE

PROMPTS

- How does this text reflect the identities and lived experiences of the characters?

- How does it reflect your identities and lived experiences?

- In what ways does this book convey and bring you joy?

PATHWAYS

- Setting: Trinity embraces her various identities and is affirmed by her loving family.

- Perspective: As a transgender girl, Trinity feels long hair will help her to fully express herself.

- Figurative Language/Imagery: Invite students to discuss the significance of this part of the story: "Trinity's gender was part of what made her a masterpiece, just like her autism and her Black skin." Invite students to discuss the symbolism of Trinity's rainbow wig.

- Mood/Tone: The complexities and intersections of identity are communicated and affirmed.

- Theme: identity, validation, inclusion, acceptance

ACTIVISM

PROMPTS

Scholar Kimberlé Crenshaw (1989) explains that **"intersectionality** is a metaphor for understanding the ways that multiple forms of inequality or disadvantage sometimes compound themselves and create obstacles that often are not understood among conventional ways of thinking."

Educator and author Britt Hawthorne distinguishes between three levels of accountability in the work of equity and justice: qrs.ly/wifrdw2.

Active Ally—"This might be changing your profile picture to say, 'I am an ally,' or writing your pronouns in your bio. While these actions support the cause visually, the solutions are stuck in the interpersonal quadrant. The actions do little to change the institutional and systemic injustices, allowing the status quo to thrive."

Accomplice—"An accomplice understands an oppressed individual cannot easily cast away the weight of their oppression on a whim. They must carry that weight every single day. You move from ally to accomplice when you understand that this is a weight you must be willing to carry and never put down."

Co-conspirator—"Being a co-conspirator means you are willing to disrupt, build, and, when necessary, dismantle for the future you want to see."

- In what ways does an understanding of the term *intersectionality* provide understandings about Trinity and her experiences?

- What can be learned about activism in this story, particularly from Trinity's mom and brother?

- As a Black, transgender girl who is autistic, Trinity has multiple identities that are each on their own marginalized in society. Trinity can experience inequities in ways that are multiplied and nuanced.

- Activism is about more than just supporting people and causes in ways that are visible (signs, protests) and expressing care about social justice issues without taking any action to create change.

- From Trinity's mother and brother, readers learn that being an ally isn't enough. They act as co-conspirators who believe Trinity when she tells them who she is and what she needs. They listen to her and work alongside Trinity to help her fully express herself.

ACCOUNTABILITY

PROMPTS

- How can this book influence your thinking and actions now and in the future?

- How will you remain alert for the ways your particular identities help you to understand a text and the world?

PATHWAYS

- Reflect on ways this text makes a difference to your heart and in your life. Consider commitments you'll make to care for people and communities.

- This text is an invitation for me to think deeply and possibly differently about

  _____ and to apply this in my life (when/how)

  _____.

Reflection and Accountability for Antiracist Educators:

This text is an invitation for me to think deeply and possibly differently as a reader

_____ and challenges me to make radical changes in my personal and
    (in what ways?)

professional life _____.
        (in what ways?)

My Papi Has a Motorcycle, written by Isabel Quintero and illustrated by Zeke Peña, is set in Corona, California, and tells the story of Daisy and all of the ways she enjoys spending time with her Papi in their loving and joyful community.

About the Creators

Visit the author's and illustrator's websites to learn more about them and their work:

- www.isabelinpieces.com

- www.zpvisual.com

For additional information about this story, access this NPR interview.

SIX CRITICAL LENSES

Prompts are provided to nurture students' thinking as they read in partnerships, groups, or independently.

Pathways capture the details and ideas that students may notice and think about as they read and respond to the text, and they can be used as guidance for educators to teach into.

AFFIRMATION

PROMPTS

- What are you learning about Daisy and Papi?

- What are you learning about the community?

PATHWAYS

- Daisy is smart; she is eager and excited to learn.

- Daisy likes to tinker around with tools; she does not embody a stereotypical girl character.

- Daisy loves spending time with her Papi.

- Papi is strong and hardworking.

- Papi works hard and still makes time for Daisy.

- Papi is an immigrant.

- Papi is a caring and loving father who shows this with his actions.

- Daisy and Papi speak Spanish and English.

- In this community, everyone seems to know and respect each other.

- The beautiful mural reminds the community of their history, which includes the hard work of immigrants, and this makes them feel proud.

- The neighborhood seems to be changing (e.g., Rudy's Raspados went out of business; new homes replacing the citrus groves).

AWARENESS

PROMPTS

Gentrification is the process of change that occurs in a neighborhood to make it more appealing to people who have more money than those who already live there. As a result, rent prices increase and people from the community have to move out. This mostly impacts people of color in neighborhoods who are pushed out when White people move in.

- How does this support your understanding of the story?

- What signs of gentrification have you noticed in your neighborhood or other neighborhoods?

PATHWAYS

- Rudy's Raspados has closed, but Don Rudy has found a way to continue selling shaved ice in the community.

- Don Rudy and the community are resilient; they support each other.

- The mural captures the history of the community and the immigrants who worked in the citrus groves, but the city is changing with new homes replacing the last of the citrus groves.

- Signs of gentrification include chain restaurants and businesses replacing smaller stores and bodegas and luxury buildings and large homes with high rent/mortgage prices.

AUTHORSHIP

PROMPTS

- Who are the creators of this text?

- How do their identities influence this work?

- What is their motivation for creating this text?

PATHWAYS

- The creators of the text are Isabel Quintero and Zeke Peña.

- Isabel Quintero writes in the author's notes that she grew up in the city depicted in this text.

- Zeke Peña says in an interview: "But I think that with Isabel and I, it's nice because a lot of our backgrounds as people who identify as Latinx or Chicanx or Chicanos, there's this really narrow definition of what that is. But the nice thing with my collaboration with Isabel is that we span like a spectrum of that, right? And it doesn't necessarily look just one way. I hope that the youth reading our book walk away with a validation of their own story, and where their own family comes from and their heritage. And their right to it, their right to express that as they wish" (Fadel & Balaban, 2019).

- The author and illustrator challenge readers to think about the perception of Latinx people, including immigrants and Latinx communities.

ATMOSPHERE

PROMPTS

- How does this text reflect the identities and lived experiences of the characters/people?

- How does it reflect your identities and lived experiences?

- In what ways does this book convey and bring you joy?

PATHWAYS

- Setting: Readers learn in the author's note that this story is based on the city of Corona in California. This story captures the community presently—the languages they speak, their interconnectedness, their values—and reflects on its history.

- Perspective: Readers learn about the city through Daisy's eyes and heart. Readers gain entry into her feelings about her community—pride, connection, joy.

- Figurative Language/Imagery: The author captures the sights, smells, and feelings of Daisy and her community:

  - "The shiny blue metal of the motorcycle glows in the sun. The sun, the sun, the bright orange sun is on its way down, turning our sky blue and purple and gold. We become a spectacular celestial thing soaring on asphalt. A comet. The sawdust falling from Papi's hair and clothes becomes a tail following us."

  - "As we ride on, I feel and hear everyone and everything we pass by. Each sound landing in my ears rebuilds whole neighborhoods inside me. No matter how far I go from this place, or how much it changes, this city will always be with me."

- Mood/Tone: Note the close-knit community, pride of people, and history create the feeling of love and joy.

- Themes: family, community, endurance, resilience

ACTIVISM

PROMPTS

- In addition to gentrification, what societal issues does this text raise?

PATHWAYS

In the author's note, Isabel Quintero writes, "History and change are always on my mind," and she asks some important questions for readers to consider: "*Who are the people who build our cities and form our communities? Who are the people who lay the asphalt? Who are the people who get streets named after them?*"

- These questions challenge readers to notice who is valued in society and who is not.
- This story disrupts harmful societal messages (the media and from others) about immigrants from Spanish-speaking countries.

ACCOUNTABILITY

PROMPTS

- How can this book influence your thinking and actions now and in the future?
- How will you remain alert for the ways your particular identities help you to understand a text and the world?

PATHWAYS

- Reflect on ways this text makes a difference to your heart and in your life. Consider commitments you'll make to care for people and communities.
- This text is an invitation for me to think deeply and possibly differently about

  _____ and to apply this in my life (when/how)

  _____ .

Reflection and Accountability for Antiracist Educators:

This text is an invitation for me to think deeply and possibly differently as a reader

_____ and challenges me to make radical changes in my personal and
(in what ways?)

professional life _____ .
(in what ways?)

I Can Write The World, written by Joshunda Sanders and illustrated by Charly Palmer, is set in the Bronx, New York, and tells the story of Ava Murray, who loves her neighborhood but has noticed that the way she sees her community isn't always what is reflected back from others. So Ava learns about the collective actions and contributions of her community and decides to take action to preserve the history, vibrancy, and culture of the Bronx.

To see the artist demonstrate his artistic process, watch Charly Palmer on YouTube.

About the Creators

To learn more about the author of this book, visit her website: joshundasanders.com. To learn more about the illustrator, visit his website www.charlypalmer.com.

SIX CRITICAL LENSES

Prompts are provided to nurture students' thinking as they read in partnerships, groups, or independently.

Pathways capture the details and ideas that students may notice and think about as they read and respond to the text, and they can be used as guidance for educators to teach into.

AFFIRMATION

PROMPTS

- What are you learning about Ava and how she feels about her community?

- What new insights are you gaining about this community?

PATHWAYS

- Ava loves the colors, sounds, and the whole vibe of the Bronx.

- Ava feels proud about her neighborhood; she wants to learn more and to protect it.

- The Bronx is a place that is rich with creativity and history.

AWARENESS

PROMPTS

- Listen for what Ava notices about how others feel about her community.
- How is power used and by whom?
- How is resistance demonstrated? How do people push against forces that create inequities?

PATHWAYS

- Ava notices that others from outside of the community don't seem to feel the way she does.
- Ava notices the news doesn't reflect what she sees and how she feels.
- The police have power that is not always used in ways that help communities.
- A pattern of injustice can be noticed in recent news coverages about police shootings that have taken the lives of Black men in particular.
- Schools have power. If art, dance, and music classes aren't offered, kids don't have access to certain types of knowledge or ways to express themselves creatively.
- People respond to injustice by taking actions such as teaching themselves, creating art, music, and dance moves, and sharing this outside of school.
- Graffiti and Hip Hop culture are examples of creativity and resistance.
- People from this community have to work hard to resist negative narratives about who they are and where they live.

AUTHORSHIP

PROMPTS

- Who are the creators of this text?
- How do their identities influence this work?
- What is their motivation for creating this text?

PATHWAYS

- The author's and illustrator's identities influence this story in several ways:
  - In the about the author section in the book, readers learn that Joshunda Sanders has been a journalist, she teaches writing, and she lives in the Bronx. In an interview she says: "I love writing about my hometown because it's a place of great beauty and potential and culture," Joshunda says on her website. "So much is alive and thriving here, and not just in the parts that people write about. But also I think writers really love writing about where they're from because they know it best. I am a Bronx expert because I know this place best, and that makes it easy" (Lyons, 2020).

- On his website, Charly Palmer's work is described in this way: "In every painting, he bears witness of African ancestry and contemporary experiences—rhythmic, visual stories that shift what each viewer believes to see—should one dare to look deeply" (Palmer, 2023).

- The author and illustrator are both Black, and they have a profound love and appreciation of Black people; they care deeply about how Black people are portrayed in the world.

ATMOSPHERE

PROMPTS

- How does this text reflect the identities and lived experiences of the characters/people?

- How does it reflect your identities and lived experiences?

- In what ways does this book convey and bring you joy?

PATHWAYS

- Setting: The Bronx, New York, is where Hip Hop was created. Hip Hop is not just music—it's a culture that includes art, fashion, and music.

- Perspective: Having an insider perspective about a community and the experiences of people who live there matters. Having an outsider perspective about a community that is not your own and the experiences of people who live there is limiting.

- Figurative Language/Imagery: Notice the language used in this text. It has a rhythm to it and some of the words rhyme. This fits in with the setting of this story. Hip Hop and rap music were created in the Bronx, and in this genre, rhyme is often used.

  - "Everything we make is connected to the past, Mom says. It's how you make the art you love last."
  - "What matters most is that we know we are connected to people who have always made the most of the world they were given making visible the beauty that otherwise might be hidden."

- Mood/Tone: The colors used in the book; the description of the sounds and block parties creates a vibrant, joyful image of the Bronx.

- Theme: pride, community, culture, resistance, resilience

ACTIVISM

PROMPTS

- Why does it matter who gets to tell the story of our lives and our communities?

- What can you learn from Ava about taking action against injustice?

PATHWAYS

- There are joys and challenges in every community.

- Insiders can shed light on the specific experiences of living in a community.

- Insiders are able to accurately and humanely name how they see themselves and their communities.

- Outsiders may only focus on the challenges within a community.

- Taking action against injustice involves becoming knowledgeable about a topic or issue:

  - Ava interviews her mother to learn more about the community, its strengths and accomplishments, and her experiences.

- Taking action against injustice involves educating others:

  - Ava shares what she's learned about the Bronx with her teacher and peers.

- Taking action against injustice involves making changes to problematic systems and structures:

  - Ava decides she will be a journalist who writes the world more completely and humanely than what she's noticed by journalists on the news.

ACCOUNTABILITY

PROMPTS

- How can this book influence your thinking and actions now and in the future?

- How will you remain alert for the ways your particular identities help you to understand a text and the world?

PATHWAYS

- Reflect on ways this text makes a difference to your heart and in your life. Consider commitments you'll make to care for people and communities.

- This text is an invitation for me to think deeply and possibly differently about

_____ and to apply this in my life (when/how)

_____ .

Reflection and Accountability for Antiracist Educators:

This text is an invitation for me to think deeply and possibly differently as a reader

_____ and challenges me to make radical changes in my personal and
    (in what ways?)

professional life _____ .
         (in what ways?)

CHAPTER THREE

Recognize **Cultural, Community,** and **Collective Practices**

Try pulling a dandelion out of the ground and you'll discover it's not so easy. That's because of its thick taproot that can penetrate hard soil a foot or more below the surface. Having done the difficult work of breaking through dry, compact earth, the taproot and its offshoot roots transport water from the surface to other plants and insects beneath the ground. They become lifelines that help other organisms survive.

There is probably no clearer representation or symbol from my childhood than a set of jump ropes. The image of Double Dutch jumping reminds me that Black girl magic can turn an ordinary object such as rope, cable chords, or telephone wire into art. Into a movement.

It was me, Samantha, Valerie, Christina, Arlene, and more girls from my neighborhood whose names I both knew and didn't know. We jumped Double Dutch in the summer heat from morning until the street lights came up to remind us when to go home. In my community, jumping rope was never a solo activity. It was us, together. The tick-tack-tick-tack sound of the rope against the concrete. The front-back and forth rocking to the rhythm of the rope, sensing just the right time to brave our way in. Braids, beads, and barrettes clicking. The synchronous energy of our footwork. The world around us faded except for our collective voices chanting in unison to keep turning the rope and jumping on time and to call out what tricks the jumper should do.

- *Let's get the rhythm of the head, ding-dong.*

- *Let's get the rhythm of the head, ding-dong.*

- *Let's get the rhythm of the head, ding-dong.*

- *Let's get the rhythm of the hands (clap clap).*

- *Let's get the rhythm of the hands (clap clap).*

- *Let's get the rhythm of the feet (stomp stomp).*

- *Let's get the rhythm of the feet (stomp stomp).*

- *Let's get the rhythm of the hot dog.*

- *Let's get the rhythm of the hot dog.*

Double Dutch was popularized in northeastern cities like my Brooklyn neighborhood in New York by Black girls and women. This practice, this way of being in community with one another, is imbued with cultural significance. In African countries and cultures, music and dance were, and continue to be, ways to cultivate reciprocal relationships between people in the community. Nsibidi signs, indigenous to the Ejagham peoples of southeastern Nigeria and southwestern Cameroon, reveal the purpose and joys of music: repetition, call and response, and correspondence (1983). Rhythmic techniques are used to tell each other's stories, to uplift the community, and to support each other in developing one's own unique gifts and talents. These values were nurtured in my community of Double Dutch jumpers, along with opportunities for self-expression and a binding commitment to one another. This shared connection is passed from Black people in African countries to Black people in the United States, across generations, by Black mothers to Black daughters. And it's what allows Double Dutch jumpers to flourish today. An aphorism that researchers believe is African in origin, as it embodies the spirit of many African cultures, is "If you want to go fast, go alone. If you want to go far, go together." The ingenuity, creativity, and collective practice of Black girls and women has turned Double Dutch jumping into much more than a game or sport that has influenced the lives of Black people in neighborhoods and communities around the world. You simply can't jump Double Dutch alone.

During my childhood, what my friends and I knew was this. Although resources were scarce, being in community was our source of strength. Double Dutch was not a summer pastime; it was a commitment rooted in cultural, collective, and community understandings. To turn, chant, jump, and fly was our collaborative practice of freedom and joy.

Considering my identity, background, and cultural connection to Double Dutch, it's not a coincidence that decades later, I would use rope as a metaphor in *Stamped (For Kids): Racism, Antiracism, and You* (2021). As an ordinary, familiar thing that holds many possibilities, I invite young readers to consider how rope can anchor and join things and how it can be used as a weapon. I ask them as readers to notice how people become tied to racist ideas and how people become bound to antiracist ones. My intention is to help young readers not only to recognize racist and antiracist ideas but to also think about how they'd like to position themselves in the world and the difference this makes to the collective.

When you look back on your childhood, the people and activities that were a significant part of your world, what historical, sociocultural commitments were you rooted in? In what ways are you shaped by cultural understandings, experiences, and expressions? What symbols, structures, and patterns emerge as you reflect? Which ideas were cornerstones of your PreK–12 grade educational experiences and beyond?

HISTORICAL AND SOCIOCULTURAL UNDERSTANDINGS		
FIVE Cs	What does this word mean to you?	What role has it played in your childhood?
Culture		
Collective		
Collaboration		
Community		
Curriculum		

As teachers of reading, we know there are common literary archetypes, familiar characters, situations, and symbols that recur in stories. We teach students to notice patterns and structures used to construct, for example, character archetypes like the hero, old wise one, villain, sidekick, and others. Such recognition leads to rich analysis of a text as well as comparison and critique of ourselves and the world.

Archetypes do not only exist in literature; they show up in our teaching. Think about the ways historical and sociocultural understandings drive teaching practices. Take a moment to consider the systems and structures of your teaching of reading. What are the dominant archetypes operating within them? How are they shaped by your beliefs about the Five Cs: culture, concern for the collective, collaborative approaches, what it means to be in community with others, and curriculum? Create a chart like the one in Table 3.1, filling in your own reflections on the concepts and questions. (Find a blank version of this chart in the Appendix.)

A commitment to antiracist teaching requires us to be brave enough to ask, *What are the unwritten rules determining what and how I teach?* And it requires that we are willing to interrogate what we uncover.

Dominant ideologies and Eurocentrism are deeply enmeshed in curriculum and teaching in the United States and are often unquestioned and uninterrogated. In *Linguistic Justice: Black Language, Literacy, Identity and Pedagogy,* Dr. April Baker-Bell (2020) intentionally links racial classifications to language to shed light on the way "linguistic hierarchies and racial hierarchies are interconnected" (p. 2).

TABLE 3.1 Sonja's Completed Chart

HISTORICAL AND SOCIOCULTURAL UNDERSTANDINGS—IMPLICATIONS AND APPLICATIONS			
THE FIVE Cs	What does this word mean to you?	What role has it played in your childhood?	What are the dominant archetypes in your reading instruction? How are they shaped by your understanding of and experiences with the Five Cs?
Culture	Knowledge, achievements, language, values, and traditions that uniquely define me and inform my identity as a Black woman	"Black is beautiful!" Cornrows with beads "Lift Every Voice and Sing"—Black National Anthem Mahalia Jackson, Stevie Wonder Kwanzaa Hip Hop culture—expression, ingenuity, creativity, power, pride *Strengthened my emotional and psychological well-being*	Individualism or collectivism? Product or process? Allegiance to canonical texts or commitment to student choice? Identity-silencing or identity-inspiring? "Culturally destructive," "culturally insufficient," or culturally relevant and sustaining? (Culturally Responsive Curriculum Scorecard Toolkit, 2023)
Collective	Moving in sync and working on behalf of the common good of the group	Volunteering for change—youth programming, political campaigns, neighborhood improvement *Helped me to understand the importance of thinking beyond myself*	
Collaboration	Partnerships/ groups working together toward a common goal	Black and Brown political alliances—local politicians, Jesse Jackson, David Dinkins, food drives/ pantries, organized sports leagues *Taught me that together we are strong and can achieve more*	

(Continued)

(Continued)

HISTORICAL AND SOCIOCULTURAL UNDERSTANDINGS—IMPLICATIONS AND APPLICATIONS			
THE FIVE Cs	What does this word mean to you?	What role has it played in your childhood?	What are the dominant archetypes in your reading instruction? How are they shaped by your understanding of and experiences with the Five Cs?
Community	A group of people tied to one another by common cultural, social, historical ties and perspectives in a particular place	Block parties Community center PTA Neighborhood watch *Provided affirmation of my identity, love, and protection*	
Curriculum	Our most radical tool!	Skill and drill Memorization of facts Teacher as "knower," student as "learner" Eurocentrism *Learned content and ideas that marginalized me and my experiences*	

Anti-Black linguistic racism impacts Black speakers and writers in classrooms around the country where White mainstream English is the expectation. Drs. Carla Espana and Luz Yadira Herrera (2020) challenge educators to learn about bilingual Latinx students' language practices. *En Comunidad: Lessons for Centering the Voices and Experiences of Bilingual Latinx Students* conveys the various ways educators can nurture rather than suppress the linguistic resources students bring into classrooms each day. Gatekeeping practices fortify educational expectations, creating the norms of curriculum and teaching. An allegiance to centering canonized books in reading instruction, for example, reinforces these norms and what readers come to believe about "good" writing, shaping their ideas about people and the world. "Craft is not innocent or neutral," Matthew Salesses (2021) asserts. In *Craft in the Real World: Rethinking Fiction Writing and Workshopping,* Salesses explains that "the way we tell stories has real consequences on the way we interpret meaning in our everyday lives"

(p. 14). Further, "Craft is the history of which kind of stories have typically held power—and for whom—so it also is the history of which stories have typically been omitted" (p. 19). Our willingness to see and interrogate one-right-way approaches in speaking, writing, reading, mathematics, the scientific method, history, classroom design, and hierarchical constructions of teacher/student roles makes possible the work of dismantling these imposed limitations.

In the 1990s, Toni Morrison spoke out about dominant perspectives toward literature. In an interview with journalist and talk show host Charlie Rose, Morrison addressed reviews of her work where critics accused her of not writing about White people. Bewildered by such thinking, she responds, "As though our lives have no meaning and no depth without the White gaze. And I have spent my entire writing life trying to make sure that the White gaze was not the dominant one in any of my books" (Rose, 1998). The work of pushing against the White gaze is just as urgent 30 years later in books, curriculum, and teaching practices.

Watch the full Toni Morrison interview.

What if we shift our lens as educators to a Black gaze? What comes into focus? Who and what is centered and for what purpose? Tina M. Campt (2021), Black feminist theorist of visual and cultural and contemporary art, explains that a Black gaze shifts dominant practices of positioning Blackness as the "elsewhere (or nowhere) of whiteness" (p. 7) to "radical forms of witnessing that rejects traditional ways of seeing blackness—ways that historically depict blackness only in subordinate relation to whiteness" (p. 17). Howell, Norris, and Williams (2019) define Black Gaze Theory as "an analytical tool that focuses on Black strength and problematizes structures that promote dominant ideologies" where Black student behaviors are seen as cultural assets and their sociopolitical consciousness is fostered by curriculum and teaching (p. 27). At the Institute for Racial Equity in Literacy (IREL), Cherry-Paul and Ebarvia (2023) build on scholarship that embraces a Black gaze stance in curriculum and teaching and convey that a Black gaze:

- humanizes Black experiences;

- creates an affirming space for Black students and students of color (Bishop, 1990);

- intentionally includes and assumes a racially diverse audience;

- validates multiple ways of knowing;

- challenges dominant, White narratives (Love, 2010);

- promotes criticality (Muhammad, 2020);

- is rooted in culturally relevant, responsive, sustaining pedagogy (Gay, 2000; Ladson-Billings, 1995; Paris & Alim, 2017); and

- centers and protects BIPOC students: "look with, through, and long side" (Campt, Howell, Norris, & Williams, 2019).

A Black gaze as stance by teachers of reading disrupts dominant ideologies and opens up antiracist possibilities.

When you make texts available that help students to recognize powerful ways of knowing and being in the world that are rooted in cultural, community, and collective practices, it's critical to consider not only the *what* (the books) but also the *how* (the teaching). What is communicated and emphasized as you teach reading? Individualism or collectivism? Process or product? Adherence to the canon or choice?

Reflect

In what ways do the books centered in curriculum and my teaching:

- Spotlight the importance of collectivism?

- Celebrate and create communal experiences?

- Connect to students' home and school cultures?

- Recognize and value various ways of knowing and being in the world?

As we dismantle and then build new reading practices and select texts, antiracist teaching calls upon us to take a collectivist approach where students are encouraged to read and discuss together. There is an emphasis on nurturing reading communities where students are strengthened, challenged, and changed by each other's ideas.

Instructional strategies are rooted in the belief that education, as scholar and author bell hooks (1994) asserts, is the practice of freedom. Pay attention to the antiracist ideas, approaches, and methods rooted in the six critical lenses that can help us realize reading as a practice of freedom.

> *A dandelion's taproot seeks not only to sustain itself; it creates an extensive root system that nurtures the community around it. When readers are taught in ways that recognize the wisdom, ingenuity, and ethos of care that exists within their communities, they bloom. They have the knowledge and capability to sustain each other and thrive.*

Recognize Cultural, Community, and Collective Practices: Prompts and Pathways

Facilitating conversations about race and racism requires that you plan to mitigate harm to those in your care who are most impacted by racism—BIPOC students. Ongoing reflection on your own racial identity and racial socialization along with interrogating biases is necessary, critical work. To avoid doing this often results in causing more harm to Black and Brown students. Please refer to resources shared in Chapter 1 that can support you in this work.

There is a tendency for teachers and students to say that oppression, specifically racism, happened or happens because of the racial identity of the individual or group being oppressed (e.g., "This happened because they're Black."). This leads students, especially BIPOC students, to believe that there's something wrong with being Black, Latinx, Asian American, Indigenous, and so on. It is important to shift such language so that students understand that racial oppression occurs because of racist ideas—that Black and Brown skin is not the problem, White supremacy is.

BOOKS FEATURED IN THIS CHAPTER

Uncle John's City Garden, by Bernette G. Ford and illustrated by Frank Morrison	Page 110
Berry Song, by Michaela Goade	Page 114
A Crown for Corina, by Laekan Zea Kemp and illustrated by Elisa Chavarri	Page 118
The Night Before Eid: A Muslim Family Story, by Aya Khalil and illustrated by Rashin Kheiriyeh	Page 123
My Powerful Hair, by Carole Lindstrom and illustrated by Steph Littlebird	Page 127
Dancing the Tinikling, by Bobbie Peyton and illustrated by Diobelle Cerna	Page 132
Plátanos Are Love, by Alyssa Reynosso-Morris and illustrated by Mariyah Rahman	Page 136
My Bindi, by Gita Varadarajan and illustrated by Archana Sreenivasan	Page 140
Luli and the Language of Tea, by Andrea Wang and illustrated by Hyewon Yum	Page 144
Amy Wu and the Perfect Bao, by Kat Zhang and illustrated by Charlene Chua	Page 148

AWARENESS

AUTHORSHIP

AFFIRMATION

Center BIPOC

Learn about community activists

Recognize cultural, community, and collective practices

ANTIRACIST READING FRAMEWORK

Teach racial literacy

Shatter silences around racism

ACCOUNTABILITY

ATMOSPHERE

ACTIVISM

Uncle John's City Garden, written by Bernette G. Ford and illustrated by Frank Morrison, tells the story of three siblings who spend the summer in the city with their uncle. From their uncle, they learn not only how to grow vegetables in the middle of tall buildings that surround the landscape but also what it means to take part in the community practice of sharing food and caring for the collective.

*Read more about
Ms. Ford here.*

About the Creators

To learn more about the author, Bernette G. Ford, be sure to read the author's note at the end of this book. Sadly, Ms. Ford passed away before this book was published. Several major news outlets, including *Publisher's Weekly*, have written to honor her life and work.

Visit Frank Morrison's website to learn about and admire his artwork: morrisongraphics.com.

SIX CRITICAL LENSES

Prompts are provided to nurture students' thinking as they read in partnerships, groups, or independently.

Pathways capture the details and ideas that students may notice and think about as they read and respond to the text, and they can be used as guidance for educators to teach into.

AFFIRMATION

PROMPTS

- What are you learning about the characters—Li'l Sissy, Brother, Sister, and Uncle John?
- How does Uncle John demonstrate and share his knowledge?
- How does Uncle John show his care and love for his community?

PATHWAYS

- Li'l Sissy and her siblings look up to Uncle John—literally and metaphorically.
- Uncle John is big and strong and uses his physical strength to grow a garden.

- Uncle John is smart and creative. He knows how to grow plants in the city surrounded by buildings.
- Uncle John is generous. He shares his knowledge of gardening with his nieces and nephew. And he shares the vegetables from his garden with his family and neighbors.
- Uncle John chooses to take care of those in the community by creating a beautiful garden and sharing the vegetables with others.

AWARENESS

PROMPTS

"Right in the middle of the projects was 'the garden.' That's what everyone called it."

The projects is a term used to describe the apartment buildings in parts of a city that provide public housing for low-income residents. The majority of residents are Black and Brown. For many residents, access to fresh fruits and vegetables can be limited in their neighborhoods.

Systemic racism describes the ways White supremacy works in institutions and structures (e.g., education, the food industry, health care). Discrimination and failure to provide equal access to services and opportunities to Black and Brown people causes them to experience fewer career opportunities, lower pay, and health issues, and negatively impacts their lives in many ways.

- How is community access to fresh fruits and vegetables an example of systemic racism?
- How does this book demonstrate ways people respond to lack of resources and injustice?

PATHWAYS

- If there aren't any or enough local supermarkets, access to fresh fruits and vegetables is challenging. If there is a pattern of this happening in mostly Black and Brown communities, this is an example of racism functioning systemically. Without enough fresh fruits and vegetables, people's health can be harmed.
- Like the character Uncle John, people take action against injustice by using their knowledge to improve conditions in their communities (e.g., Uncle John's Garden).

AUTHORSHIP

PROMPTS

- Who are the creators of this text?
- How do their identities influence this work?
- What is their motivation for creating this text?

PATHWAYS

- In the author's note, Bernette G. Ford explains that this story is partly based on her life. Her identity shapes this story. Her lived experience of having family members who were Black laborers who worked on a plantation in Louisiana informs her writing of this story.
- Frank Morrison's identity and lived experiences shape this story. On his website, he shares his intentions as an artist, which can help us understand his focus as an illustrator of this story: "My work dignifies the evolution of everyday, underrepresented

people and places within the urban landscape. I seek to both highlight and preserve the soul of the city through the lens of hip-hop culture and urban iconography. I want people to experience the visual rhythms that choreograph life for the average, everyday person."

ATMOSPHERE

PROMPTS

- How does this text reflect the identities and lived experiences of the characters?

- How does it reflect your identities and lived experiences?

- In what ways does this book convey and bring you joy?

PATHWAYS

- Setting: This story takes place in a city neighborhood.
  - "The first summer we worked in Uncle John's Garden, we thought it was the biggest garden in the city. When we looked up and up and up, all around us were tall, tall buildings—all brick, all the same. Right in the middle of the projects was 'the garden.' That's what everyone called it."

- Perspective: The author demonstrates that just because the garden is located in a city where there are tall buildings, lots of people, cars, and loud noises, a garden can thrive when the community shares their knowledge, talents, time, and hard work.

- Figurative Language/Imagery: Invite readers to notice juxtaposition, the intentional math references throughout this text, as well as symbolism.
  - Discuss juxtaposition as a literary and artistic technique in this text (e.g., Uncle John is "a great big man" who works with tiny seeds).
  - *What does the author want readers to consider about the role of math in gardening?* Point to things like height of people; length of shovel handles; number of rows in the garden; size of seeds, seedlings, and plants; and length of BBQ tables.
  - References to okra recur in this story as well as images of okra growing in the garden. *What does okra symbolize for Black people?*
    - "Brother chose corn and lima beans. Sister chose tomatoes and onions. I chose okra. When we told Mother, she laughed. She said we were growing succotash. I was glad. I love succotash!"
  - Invite students to research and learn about okra's African roots and its journey to the United States by enslaved Black people who brought okra seeds with them to carry a piece of home. Okra has a strong and symbolic place in Black American culinary history.
  - *What is the significance of succotash?* Invite students to research and learn the Indigenous roots of this dish and the historical and cultural connection to gardening—cultivating and eating plants and vegetables that are native to a place. Try out the recipe included in the back of the book!

- Mood/Tone: This book highlights the importance of intergenerational relationships and pays tribute to city gardens, Black agency, and ingenuity. It also celebrates hard work and community.

- Themes: family, nature, cultivation, ingenuity, community

ACTIVISM

PROMPTS

- How does Uncle John show care for his family and community and take action to keep the community strong?
- What communities are you a part of?
- How do you choose to take care of those communities?
- How do you show that you love those communities *and* work to keep them strong?

PATHWAYS

- Uncle John shares his knowledge and wisdom of cultivating a garden with his young nieces and nephew so this knowledge can continue across generations.
- Uncle John brings his family and the community together for a BBQ. Sharing food together is one way to demonstrate care.
- Uncle John gives some of the vegetables from the garden to family and community. Sharing vegetables with others demonstrates care and a commitment to keeping the community healthy and strong.

ACCOUNTABILITY

PROMPTS

- How can this book influence your thinking and actions now and in the future?
- How will you remain alert for the ways your particular identities help you to understand a text and the world?

PATHWAYS

- Reflect on ways this text makes a difference to your heart and in your life. Consider commitments you'll make to care for people and communities.
- This text is an invitation for me to think deeply and possibly differently about

_____ and to apply this in my life (when/how)

_____ .

Reflection and Accountability for Antiracist Educators:

This text is an invitation for me to think deeply and possibly differently as a reader

_____ and challenges me to make radical changes in my personal and
(in what ways?)

professional life _____ .
(in what ways?)

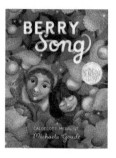

Berry Song, written and illustrated by Michaela Goade, shares the special bond between a young girl and her grandmother and the ways they honor their cultural identities, their Tlingit ancestors, and the environment.

About the Creator

Learn more about Michaela Goade on her website: www .michaelagoade.com.

Read and watch this interview with Michaela Goade.

There are important distinctions and nuances around the words *Indigenous, Native American, American Indian, tribe,* and *nation.* In my discussion of texts, I use the language and terminology the author uses. It's important to listen for who people tell us who they are and to teach children to listen as well and to respect what they are learning. Learn more here about the impact of words and using accurate terms: qrs.ly/cufrdvt.

SIX CRITICAL LENSES

Prompts are provided to nurture students' thinking as they read in partnerships, groups, or independently.

Pathways capture the details and ideas that students may notice and think about as they read and respond to the text, and they can be used as guidance for educators to teach into.

AFFIRMATION

PROMPTS

- What are you learning about the young girl and her grandmother?

- What are you learning about the various ways they spend time together and interact with their environment?

PATHWAYS

- The girl enjoys spending time with her grandmother, who teaches her about the land and their environment.
- They fish, pick berries, sing in gratitude of the land, and listen to the ocean, the forest, and their ancestors.

AWARENESS

PROMPTS

Indigenization is the process of sharing Indigenous knowledge, ways of being, and actions to educate and engage all members of a community with the purpose of respecting the land, raising awareness of Indigenous perspectives, and gaining a more in-depth, accurate, and nuanced understanding of the world.

- What can be learned from this story about Tlingit people and caring for the earth?
- What would it take to implement these lessons and to Indigenize all aspects of society?

PATHWAYS

- This story provides a vision for living in ways that respect and honor the land.
- To Indigenize our society, communities, businesses, and institutions would need to listen to and follow the leadership of Indigenous Peoples. This involves applying Indigenous knowledge to how we live, learn, and interact with the environment. It means caring about the earth, the environment, and nature more than products and making money.

AUTHORSHIP

PROMPTS

- Who are the creators of this text?
- How do their identities influence this work?
- What is their motivation for creating this text?

PATHWAYS

- Michaela Goade is the author and illustrator of this book.
- She is a member of the Tlingit Nation and lives in Alaska.
- Her identities deeply inform this text. In the author's note, Goade shares that like the character in this story, she lives in a similar setting where her grandparents lived and picked berries as a child.
- Goade captures her lived experiences in this book and provides readers with a glimpse into Indigenous knowledge, traditions, and identities. In the author's note, Goade writes, "Indigenous history and rights, land sovereignty, and environmental justice are closely intertwined, and I encourage you to listen to and lift Indigenous voices."

ATMOSPHERE

PROMPTS

- How does this text reflect the identities and lived experiences of the characters?
- How does it reflect your identities and lived experiences?
- In what ways does this book convey and bring you joy?

PATHWAYS

- Setting: Readers can appreciate the beauty of the island and environment Goade describes and illustrates.
- Perspective: Readers learn about the love and knowledge shared within intergenerational relationships.
- Figurative Language/Imagery: Throughout the story, Goade writes, "Grandma tells me. . . ."
  - Discuss what Grandma teaches and the ways her granddaughter responds.
  - Discuss the ways Goade demonstrates the reciprocal relationship between people and the land and between family members across generations.
- Mood/Tone: The story demonstrates the characters' and the author's reverence for the land, ancestors, and family.
- Themes: gratitude, family, Indigenous traditions, respect for the environment

ACTIVISM

PROMPTS

Consider these two parts of Michaela Goade's author's note:

"Protesting, contacting legislators, voting, volunteering with local environmental groups, thinking about where you spend your money, and sharing what you learn are just a few ways to get involved. Together we can unite in defense of Mother Earth, becoming caretakers and ensuring a future for all."

"In many places around the world, Indigenous peoples are leading the way in protecting our planet. I encourage you to find out whose traditional territory you call home, learn about their history and the issues they are facing today, and seek ways to engage."

- Who are some of the Indigenous activists you can learn more about?
- How might you learn about and acknowledge whose traditional territory you inhabit?
- What actions can be taken to care for the land?
- What commitments will you make to Indigenize and be caretakers of the earth?

PATHWAYS

- Learn about Indigenous activists such as Xiuhtezcatl Martinez, Autumn Peltier, Erisvan Bone, Caitlyn Baikie, Jasilyn Charger, and others.

- Learn about land acknowledgments and ways to support Indigenous communities. The guide found here is a great start: qrs.ly/59fre0f.

- Consider ways you can increase your knowledge about Indigenous Peoples as well as Indigenizing in your daily life. Some ways to do this include learning about the Indigenous roots of games and sports such as lacrosse, learning about the destruction and genocide of Native and Indigenous Peoples due to White supremacy and colonization, interacting with the environment, and working intentionally, respectfully, and with care to build relationships with the land.

ACCOUNTABILITY

PROMPTS

- How can this book influence your thinking and actions now and in the future?

- How will you remain alert for the ways your particular identities help you to understand a text and the world?

PATHWAYS

- Reflect on ways this text makes a difference to your heart and in your life. Consider commitments you'll make to care for people and communities.

- This text is an invitation for me to think deeply and possibly differently about

_____ and to apply this in my life (when/how)

_____.

Reflection and Accountability for Antiracist Educators:

This text is an invitation for me to think deeply and possibly differently as a reader

_____ and challenges me to make radical changes in my personal and
      (in what ways?)

professional life _____.
                      (in what ways?)

A Crown for Corina, written by Laekan Zea Kemp and illustrated by Elisa Chavarri, is the story of Corina, who is excited to wear a crown of flowers from her Abuela's garden for her birthday. As she delights in learning about the symbolism and traditions of the cultural practice of the Mexican flower crown, Corina discovers each flower has a special significance and represents someone she loves.

Watch this video of the illustrator teaching viewers how to draw the character, Corina, and her crown of flowers.

About the Creators

To learn more about the author, Leakan Zea Kemp, visit her website, www.laekanzeakemp.com, and read her bio and FAQ located on the About page.

Six Critical Lenses

Prompts are provided to nurture students' thinking as they read in partnerships, groups, or independently.

Pathways capture the details and ideas that students may notice and think about as they read and respond to the text, and they can be used as guidance for educators to teach into.

AFFIRMATION

PROMPTS

- What are you learning about Corina?

- What are you learning about Abuela?

- How does Corina's identity shape how she celebrates her birthday and who she is as a person?

- Which parts of Corina's identity seem to make her feel powerful? Which parts of your identity make you feel powerful?

PATHWAYS

- Corina is excited for her birthday party and to pick flowers from her Abuela's garden for her crown.

- Abuela teaches Corina about the flowers and the purpose of the birthday crown.

- Corina learns about her identity and chooses flowers that represent her family and those she loves, who she is, and who she wants to be.
- Parts of Corina's identity include her family, that she speaks English and Spanish, and the traditions that are important to her and her family.

AWARENESS

PROMPTS

Parts of a person's identity include things such as their favorite color, music, book, and sport and things they love to do. A person's identity also includes their race, culture, ethnicity, gender, age, family, language, religion, and more.

- How do people's identities shape their life experiences?
- In what ways do people hold onto their history and their stories?
- In what ways are there attempts to silence and/or erase some people's history and stories?

PATHWAYS

- Identity includes not only the way we see ourselves but also the ways others may perceive us. When people have harmful perceptions and opinions of others' identities, they might treat them in unjust ways.
- One way to hold onto the histories and stories of a people is through oral storytelling. History can be passed down this way across generations. Another way is to write down our stories, histories, and experiences. And we can intentionally seek out the stories and histories of people who we aren't taught about in order to learn about their lived experiences.
- People's histories, stories, and lived experiences are silenced and erased when they aren't taught in schools and when there aren't many books published about groups of people we don't know a lot about. Book banning is another way to attempt to erase people's histories and experiences.

AUTHORSHIP

PROMPTS

- Who are the creators of this text?
- How do their identities influence this work?
- What is their motivation for creating this text?

PATHWAYS

- The author of this text identifies as Chicana and the illustrator identifies as Peruvian. www.elisachavarri.com
- Share and discuss Laekan Zea Kemp's response in an interview with *We Need Diverse Books*, where she was asked about her identity as well as that of the characters in her novels interview here: qrs.ly/65frdwd. She was asked what the word *Chicanx* meant to her:

"To me, being Chicana means being in between. It means being several generations removed from my family's immigration history while also being close enough to my ancestral home to remain grounded in some of those traditions. It means feeling victimized by and lost in colonization while simultaneously feeling found and rescued through connection with other Chicanes. It means engaging in a life-long reclamation process while also compassionately coming to terms with all I'll never be able to get back.

"There's so much beauty and heartache and grief and resilience that exists within my identity. So much tension. And it's something that is impossible to navigate alone, which is why books featuring Chicane characters are so essential. They've been essential to my own growth and healing and all I can hope for is that my books offer Chicane readers the same as well."

- Perhaps the creators' motivation for creating this text is to make Latin cultural identities and traditions visible and to preserve the history, stories, and experiences of Latin cultures.

ATMOSPHERE

PROMPTS

- How does this text reflect the identities and lived experiences of the characters? How does it reflect your identities and lived experiences?

- In what ways does this book convey and bring you joy?

PATHWAYS

- Setting: This story takes place at Abuela's garden and home. Readers discover how family and tradition shapes one's identity. Readers discover the significance of intergenerational relationships.

- Perspective: Readers learn the tradition of selecting flowers for las coronas directly from Corina's eyes, heart, and experience.

- Figurative Language/Imagery: Invite readers to explore the symbolism of the Mexican flower crown (las coronas).

  - "When we place la corona on our head, we become its roots, reaching back through time to hold on to the things that matter. Our family. Our history."

- Mood/Tone: The author and illustrator use powerful language and bright, vivid colors to capture the excitement of Corina's birthday celebration and to show the importance of the tradition of wearing las coronas.

  - "As guests arrive for my party, I tell them the story of my crown, of all the ways that I am rooted in the people I love."

- Themes: self-discovery, family, tradition, identity

ACTIVISM

PROMPTS

- How do Corina and Abuela show how they care for their family and community and take action to keep it strong?

- What communities are you a part of?

- How do you choose to take care of those communities?

- How do you show that you love those communities *and* work to keep them strong?

PATHWAYS

- Abuela and Corina's deep connection to the natural environment and family is a way to keep their history alive.

- Abuela and Corina care for their family and community by maintaining cultural traditions that are important.

- When Corina tells everyone at her party about the story of her crown, she keeps the tradition of las coronas alive.

- When Corina vows to remember time spent with Abuela and "learning to speak the language of the flowers," she is committing to keep her family and community strong.

- By naming herself as a wishmaker and that she has time for her dreams to bloom, Corina recognizes who she is and her potential.

ACCOUNTABILITY

PROMPTS

- How can this book influence your thinking and actions now and in the future?

- How will you remain alert for the ways your particular identities help you to understand a text and the world?

PATHWAYS

- Reflect on ways this text makes a difference to your heart and in your life. Consider commitments you'll make to care for people and communities.

- This text is an invitation for me to think deeply and possibly differently about

  _____ and to apply this in my life (when/how)

  _____.

Reflection and Accountability for Antiracist Educators:

This text is an invitation for me to think deeply and possibly differently as a reader

_____ and challenges me to make radical changes in my personal and
(in what ways?)

professional life _____.
(in what ways?)

The Night Before Eid: A Muslim Family Story, written by Aya Khalil and illustrated by Rashin Kheiriyeh, is about a family's cultural practices, including a recipe and the special treat they make in honor of Eid and their Egyptian heritage.

About the Creators

Learn more about Aya Khalil and Rashin Kheiriyeh on their websites:

- www.ayakhalil.com

- www.rashinart.com

Read an interview with artist and illustrator Rashin Kheiriyeh.

SIX CRITICAL LENSES

Prompts are provided to nurture students' thinking as they read in partnerships, groups, or independently.

Pathways capture the details and ideas that students may notice and think about as they read and respond to the text, and they can be used as guidance for educators to teach into.

AFFIRMATION

PROMPTS

- What are you learning about Zain and his family?
- In what ways does this story provide a glimpse into the beauty of Muslim and Egyptian identities?

PATHWAYS

- Zain is excited to spend time with Teita and to learn a family recipe to make ka'ak.
- Zain wants to share his family's special recipe for ka'ak with his classmates at school.
- The recipe for ka'ak takes time and requires cooperation, so it's a way for the family to spend time together.
- Henna and eidiya are part of the celebration of Eid.
- Baking ka'ak is tradition and has occurred across generations. Zain's mother grew up baking ka'ak with her mom, Teita, cousins, and aunts.

- Zain learns that ka'ak is an ancient dish tracing back to pharaohs and pyramids of Egypt.
- Teita's mortar and pestle is also passed down from generations.
- Zain learns about Egyptian history, culture, and his ancestors as he bakes with Teita.

AWARENESS

PROMPTS

More than two billion people in the world identify as Muslim. Islam is the second largest religion after Christianity. Considering this:

- Which holidays are acknowledged and recognized in your school and community?
- What have you learned about Muslim identities?
- What patterns can you notice about the silencing of Muslim identities?

Anti-Muslim hate and Islamophobia is prejudice toward, as well as discrimination and fear of, Muslims that is motivated by religious, political, and institutional hostility; harassment; and abuse toward Muslims and non-Muslims. Considering this:

- What have you noticed about stereotypes in news, movies, television shows, books, and so on that target the symbols and markers of being Muslim?
- How do these stereotypes prevent us from developing a cultural literacy about Islamic beliefs and traditions and Muslim identities?

PATHWAYS

- It wasn't until 2016 that New York City public schools, the largest in the nation, officially recognized Eid al-Adha and Eid al-Fitr as holidays on the school calendar. Some schools around the country do not recognize these holidays at all.
- In many schools, curriculum and books silence Muslim identities.
- Positive representations of Muslims are limited.
- Discrimination against Muslims existed prior to the terrorist acts of 9/11 and escalated after by those who attribute collective responsibility to all Muslims based on the actions of a select few.
- Portrayals of Muslims in the media shape the public's perception of Muslims as violent.
- Negative portrayals of Muslims contribute to lack of knowledge about Islam and prevent development of cultural literacy about Muslim identities that are accurate, nuanced, and respectful.

AUTHORSHIP

PROMPTS

- Who are the creators of this text?
- How do their identities influence this work?
- What is their motivation for creating this text?

PATHWAYS

- Aya Khalil shares in the author's note that she was the only Muslim in her grade when she was growing up until her family moved to a larger city. She includes photographs of her family celebrating Eid.

- In an interview, Rashin Kheiriyeh talks about growing up in Iran before moving to the United States and says, "I think it's important that we learn to hear and understand other people's stories. That's the way to have a healthy diverse community. Authors and illustrators who are cultural insiders bring fresh air to English or American literature. The unique perspectives we bring to the work allow readers to travel, metaphorically, to different parts of the world and discover so many things that help them to become open-minded, antiracist, and just."

- Read the interview here: qrs.ly/8rfrdwr.

- The identities of the creators influence this work. They are each able to bring their lived experiences and perspectives to the story.

- In addition to being a beautiful story, this book contributes to helping young people learn more about Eid and Muslim cultures and traditions.

ATMOSPHERE

PROMPTS

- How does this text reflect the identities and lived experiences of the characters?

- How does it reflect your identities and lived experiences?

- In what ways does this book convey and bring you joy?

PATHWAYS

- Setting: Readers learn about the past and present ways a family and their ancestors celebrate Eid.

- Perspective: Readers learn about the traditions, history, practices, and significance of Eid.

- Figurative Language/Imagery: Discuss the author's use and meaning of figurative language:

  - "El sabr gameel. Patience is beautiful."

  - "But these are more valuable. They're loaded with tradition."

- Mood/Tone: Discuss the ways the words and images of the story provide a window into the beauty of Eid and Muslim culture (e.g., recipes, histories, colors, language).

- Themes: tradition, celebration, heritage, family, pride

ACTIVISM

PROMPTS

- How will you plan to access and learn more information to develop your cultural literacy about Islamic beliefs and traditions and Muslim identities?

- Why is it important to do so?

- Seek out and read more stories to learn about Eid and Muslims.
- Consider how television shows, series, and movies portray Muslims and choose to watch shows that portray Muslims in positive ways, such as *Ms. Marvel*.

ACCOUNTABILITY

PROMPTS

- How can this book influence your thinking and actions now and in the future?
- How will you remain alert for the ways your particular identities help you to understand a text and the world?

PATHWAYS

Reflect on ways this text makes a difference to your heart and in your life. Consider commitments you'll make to care for people and communities.

- This text is an invitation for me to think deeply and possibly differently about

  _____ and to apply this in my life (when/how)

  _____.

Reflection and Accountability for Antiracist Educators:

This text is an invitation for me to think deeply and possibly differently as a reader

_____ and challenges me to make radical changes in my personal and
(in what ways?)

professional life _____.
(in what ways?)

My Powerful Hair, written by Carole Lindstrom and illustrated by Steph Littlebird, tells the story of a young girl who is excited to grow her hair long, fully embracing her Indigenous ancestral and cultural practices and understanding the spiritual connection and power hair beholds.

To learn more about Carole Lindstrom, read or listen to this interview that provides more insight into Native history and culture.

About the Creators

Visit Carole Lindstrom's website to learn more about her work: www.carolelindstrom.com.

There are important distinctions and nuances around the words *Indigenous, Native American, American Indian, tribe,* and *nation.* In my discussion of texts, I use the language and terminology the author uses. It's important to listen for who people tell us they are and to teach children to listen as well and to respect what they are learning. Learn more here about the impact of words and using accurate terms: qrs.ly/cufrdvt.

SIX CRITICAL LENSES

Prompts are provided to nurture students' thinking as they read in partnerships, groups, or independently.

Pathways capture the details and ideas that students may notice and think about as they read and respond to the text, and they can be used as guidance for educators to teach into.

AFFIRMATION

PROMPTS

- What are you learning about the young girl in this text?
- What are you learning about Indigenous Peoples and the significance of hair?

- The young girl is excited to grow her hair long.

- She is centered in who she is and her Native identity.

- She feels deeply connected to her family and the environment.

- She believes all of the important moments and experiences in her life are woven into her hair.

- Hair is deeply meaningful to Native/Indigenous Peoples: "Our ancestors say our hair is our memories, our source of strength and power, a celebration of our lives."

AWARENESS

PROMPTS

Cultural genocide and forced assimilation can be described as the destruction of a culture's identity—language, customs, traditions, physical traits, names, ways of workship, values, practices, and ways of being—by a dominant group that enforces its language, educational practices, literature, religion, and values using tactics such as government-sanctioned physical and psychological violence, policies, and laws.

- How does this concept support your understanding of the story?

- Consider what you've learned about Native/Indigenous Peoples in U.S. public education. What can be noticed about the erasure of Native/Indigenous Peoples in the past as well as the present?

- How does this story help you to recognize the persistent efforts and effects of erasure of Native/Indigenous Peoples and their histories and cultures as well as their resistance and resilience?

- In what ways are Native/Indigenous People's histories and cultures cherished and maintained?

- Why is it important to learn about the nation's legacy of racism and White supremacy and confront the consequences of this today?

PATHWAYS

- Mom being told her hair was "too wild" and Nokomis not being allowed to have long hair are examples of forced assimilation—being forced to give up their practices and beliefs.

- Often Native/Indigenous Peoples and their histories, cultures, and lives today are not included in curriculum. Textbooks can present false narratives about Native/Indigenous Peoples.

- Despite the destruction and continuous efforts to exclude and erase them, Native/Indigenous Peoples still practice and preserve their customs, traditions, languages, and beliefs.

- Wearing long hair is one way Native/Indigenous culture is maintained.

- Native/Indigenous Peoples are not a monolith. Not everyone who identifies as Native/Indigenous chooses to wear their hair long.

- Without acknowledgment of wrongdoing and actions to repair and prevent further damage, reconciliation and healing isn't possible.

- White supremacy isn't just about isolated, hateful events; it's about beliefs that become embedded in practices, policies, and laws if left unchallenged.

AUTHORSHIP

PROMPTS

- Who are the creators of this text?

- How do their identities influence this work?

- What is their motivation for creating this text?

PATHWAYS

- The creators of this text are Carole Lindstrom and Steph Littlebird. Carole Lindstrom is an enrolled citizen of the Turtle Mountain Band of Ojibwe and Steph Littlebird is a member of Oregon's Confederated Tribes of Grand Ronde.

- The identities of the creators deeply influence this text. In the author's note, Carole Lindstrom shares that her grandmother and great-aunts were forced into an Indian boarding school and the ways this affected her family, including her mother, and herself, and their perceptions around hair. She writes, "Now was my chance to reclaim my identity and return the power of my ancestors to my family by growing my power."

- Steph Littlebird's website includes the following description about her work as an illustrator and as a writer: "Her works frequently engage issues related to present-day Indigenous identities, marginalized histories, and responsible land stewardship."

- Through the creation of this text, Lindstrom and Littlebird challenge readers to learn about Native/Indigenous Peoples—their histories, values, and cultures—and to specifically recognize the significance of their hair.

ATMOSPHERE

PROMPTS

- How does this text reflect the identities and lived experiences of the characters?

- How does it reflect your identities and lived experiences?

- In what ways does this book convey and bring you joy?

PATHWAYS

- Setting: Readers can notice the beauty and power of Native/Indigenous identities and values across time and space.

- Perspective: Readers learn about Native/Indigenous values, specifically the significance of hair, from the heart and mind of the character.
- Figurative Language/Imagery: Through the story, the author includes several messages and metaphors beginning with the words "Our ancestors say." Discuss each of these—their meaning and insights into the importance of hair.
- Mood/Tone: The author and illustrator demonstrate a deep reverence for the beauty, values, and significance of Native/Indigenous ways of being in the world.
- Themes: identity, self-expression, tradition, cultural values, connectedness, reclamation

ACTIVISM

PROMPTS

- What commitments will you make to learn more about Native/Indigenous Peoples?
- In addition to cultural genocide, forced assimilation, and White supremacy, what other issues does this text raise?

PATHWAYS

- Seek out Native/Indigenous authors of fiction and nonfiction and commit to reading their work; watch documentaries and series such as *Warrior Women* and *Reservation Dogs* that are created by and center Native/Indigenous Peoples.
- In the author's note, Carole Lindstrom writes, "I understand that, to my grandmother, long hair was taught to be a sign of 'wildness' and 'savageness.' For her not to be seen that way, she had to keep her hair short. And her daughter's hair. And her granddaughter's hair."

  - Establishing affinity groups in schools can create spaces for BIPOC students and White students to address the impact of racism and White supremacy in their lives in ways that are safe and affirming.
  - There is necessary work that BIPOC must do within themselves and within their communities to confront and disrupt the harmful ideas and beliefs they have internalized as a result of racism and White privilege.
  - White people who are antiracist can be co-conspirators by confronting and disrupting harmful, negative messages about BIPOC with White people.

ACCOUNTABILITY

PROMPTS

- How can this book influence your thinking and actions now and in the future?
- How will you remain alert for the ways your particular identities help you to understand a text and the world?

PATHWAYS

- Reflect on ways this text makes a difference to your heart and in your life. Consider commitments you'll make to care for people and communities.

- This text is an invitation for me to think deeply and possibly differently about

_____ and to apply this in my life (when/how)

_____.

Reflection and Accountability for Antiracist Educators:

This text is an invitation for me to think deeply and possibly differently as a reader

_____ and challenges me to make radical changes in my personal and

(in what ways?)

professional life _____.

(in what ways?)

In *Dancing the Tinikling,* written by Bobbie Peyton and illustrated by Diobelle Cerna, Jojo learns to dance the tinikling and about the ways he and his family maintain their Filipino cultural, community, and collective practices while navigating life in the United States.

Students may enjoy watching the traditional tinikling dance performed.

Watch Filipino college students combine traditional tinikling with Hip Hop.

About the Creators

Learn more about author Bobbie Peyton here: www.bobbiepeyton.com and about the illustrator here: www.astound.us/diobelle-cerna.

Six Critical Lenses

Prompts are provided to nurture students' thinking as they read in partnerships, groups, or independently.

Pathways capture the details and ideas that students may notice and think about as they read and respond to the text, and they can be used as guidance for educators to teach into.

AFFIRMATION

PROMPTS

- What are you learning about Jojo?
- What are you learning about Lola?
- What does this book help you to begin to understand about Filipino culture, values, and traditions?

PATHWAYS

- Jojo watches his Lola and others dance the tinikling.
- He continues to try dancing the tinikling until he's able to do it.
- Lola teaches the tinikling to others, and she dances Hip Hop.
- Jojo and Lola navigate "between two worlds"—Filipino culture and life in the United States.
- Jojo and Lola maintain their Filipino culture by speaking Tagalog at home, eating lumpia, and dancing the tinikling.

AWARENESS

PROMPTS

Colonization is a term to describe the actions and processes of a dominant group using violent force to seize control of land and Indigenous/Native Peoples and their resources. Colonizers also attempt to strip away the culture (language, traditions, values) of the people they colonize and impose their own culture and ways of life.

- Spaniards colonized the Philippine Islands in the 1500s. Considering this definition of colonization, why is it important for Lola to teach people to dance the tinikling?

- Why is it important that Jojo learns to dance the tinikling?

PATHWAYS

- Perhaps Lola teaches the tinikling to introduce it to Filipino Americans and others so that the dance is known and remembered.

- The tinikling dance is important to Lola because it is an expression of Filipino identity, it takes tremendous skill to perform, and it's fun.

- It's important for Jojo to learn to dance the tinikling because it is a part of his Filipino heritage, and it is a way for him to honor his ancestors and to carry on the tradition. It also makes his Lola very happy and it makes him happy and proud to learn the dance.

AUTHORSHIP

PROMPTS

- Who are the creators of this text?

- How do their identities influence this work?

- What is their motivation for creating this text?

PATHWAYS

- Author Bobbie Peyton was born in the Philippines and moved to the United States when she was a baby.

- The illustrator, Diobello Cerna, is Filipino and lives and works in the Philippines (astound.us/diobelle-cerna).

- In the author's note, Peyton writes, "The tinikling dance roots us to our Filipino culture and strengthens our identity as Filipino Americans." She is speaking directly to Filipino Americans, and writing this book is a way to honor and strengthen Filipino culture.

ATMOSPHERE

PROMPTS

- How does this text reflect the identities and lived experiences of the characters?

- How does it reflect your identities and lived experiences?

- In what ways does this book convey and bring you joy?

PATHWAYS

- Setting: Characters navigate life and culture in the United States while holding on to their Filipino culture.

- Perspective: The story offers cross-cultural understandings and ways of being.

- Figurative Language/Imagery: Discuss the significance of the idiom "dancing between two worlds" in this text.

- Mood/Tone: The book shows joyful embracing and dedication to dancing the tinikling.

- Themes: culture, tradition, pride, joy, preservation

ACTIVISM

PROMPTS

- The author writes, "Through the creation of the tinikling dance, Filipinos transferred an act of cruelty into a graceful and festive dance that probably evolved as a form of resistance from Filipino farmers toward their Spanish colonizers."

  - How might you learn more about the tinikling dance as a form of resistance?

  - How might you learn about more ways Filipinos resist in order to honor and maintain their culture?

  - In what ways can you resist the impact of colonization (e.g., systemic racism, loss of languages, cultures, environmental issues)?

PATHWAYS

- Ideas include:

  - learning about the history of the tinikling and learning to dance the tinikling by watching online tutorials,

  - researching and reading about the Philippines before colonization and after, and

  - learning about Filipino culture and activists such as Larry Itliong.

PROMPTS

- How can this book influence your thinking and actions now and in the future?
- How will you remain alert for the ways your particular identities help you to understand a text and the world?

PATHWAYS

- Reflect on ways this text makes a difference to your heart and in your life. Consider commitments you'll make to care for people and communities.
- This text is an invitation for me to think deeply and possibly differently about

  _____ and to apply this in my life (when/how)

  _____.

Reflection and Accountability for Antiracist Educators:

This text is an invitation for me to think deeply and possibly differently as a reader

_____ and challenges me to make radical changes in my personal and
    (in what ways?)

professional life _____.
        (in what ways?)

Plátanos Are Love

In ***Plátanos Are Love***, written by Alyssa Reynosso-Morris and illustrated by Mariyah Rahman, Esme enjoys spending time cooking with her Abuela and learning about the cultural traditions, history, and stories connected to her identity.

Check out this special read-aloud by the author.

About the Creators

Visit the author's website, www.alyssaauthor.com, and the illustrator's website, www.mariyahrahman.com, to learn more about the creators of this book.

SIX CRITICAL LENSES

Prompts are provided to nurture students' thinking as they read in partnerships, groups, or independently.

Pathways capture the details and ideas that students may notice and think about as they read and respond to the text, and they can be used as guidance for educators to teach into.

AFFIRMATION

PROMPTS

- What are you learning about Esme and Abuela?

- What are you learning about ways their cultural identities shape their lives?

- What brings them joy?

PATHWAYS

- Esme and Abuela enjoy spending time together.

- They speak Spanish and English.

- Plátanos are a part of their history and identity. ("Los plátanos son la comida of our ancestors." "Siempre recuerda, plátanos are part of our history.")

- They take pride and find joy in doing things the way their ancestors did. This is a way to maintain family connections.

- The characters enjoy the many ways to cook plátanos.

AWARENESS

PROMPTS

Oppression is the unjust treatment and excessive use of power against individuals and groups of people. Abuela says recipes for plátanos have been passed down in their family in secret because "our ancestors weren't allowed to leer, escribir, o dibujar. . . ."

- What does this story help you to understand about ways reading has been denied to groups of people?

- Why have people denied others the freedom to read?

- How does this influence people's lives today?

PATHWAYS

- Reading has been denied to Black people who were enslaved in the United States.

- Reading helps us to learn information and to learn about ourselves and the world around us.

- Denying people the freedom to read is a way to control others, to keep them from learning, dreaming, and pursuing freedom.

- Black people who have been denied the freedom to read in the past were resilient. They taught themselves secretly. They used their minds to preserve their culture. ("That's why Abuela knows every receta by heart.")

AUTHORSHIP

PROMPTS

- Who are the creators of this text?

- How do their identities influence this work?

- What is their motivation for creating this text?

PATHWAYS

- The author shares that she is "a queer Afro-Latinx Dominican and Puerto Rican writer, mother, and community organizer."

- The illustrator shares that she "was born and raised in Trinidad and Tobago."

- Both creators bring their Caribbean identities to this text.

- The author includes recipes that connect to her cultural identity. Readers may be inspired to try making and eating these dishes.

ATMOSPHERE

PROMPTS

- How does this text reflect the identities and lived experiences of the characters? How does it reflect your identities and lived experiences?

- In what ways does this book convey and bring you joy?

PATHWAYS

- Setting: Esme enjoys learning about her culture—her history and ancestors—through the stories and traditions Abuela shares.

- Perspective: Abuela shows Esme how food, history, and traditions are important parts of their identity.

- Figurative Language/Imagery: Discuss the metaphors in this book such as "Plátanos are love." "Abuela says they feed us in more ways than one." Discuss the ways plátanos feed Esme and her family.

- Mood/Tone: This story is warm and vibrant, demonstrating love of food and family.

- Themes: identity, family, traditions, culture

ACTIVISM

PROMPTS

- How does this story help you to think about the importance of cultural traditions?

- What does this story help you to understand about the power of preserving family traditions and stories?

PATHWAYS

- For many people, cultural traditions are ways to connect with their ancestors—to honor them and to keep the memory of them close.

- Storytelling about our cultural identities helps us stay connected to our heritage. It helps us to preserve our past, present, and future.

ACCOUNTABILITY

PROMPTS

- How can this book influence your thinking and actions now and in the future?

- How will you remain alert for the ways your particular identities help you to understand a text and the world?

- Reflect on ways this text makes a difference to your heart and in your life. Consider commitments you'll make to care for people and communities.

- This text is an invitation for me to think deeply and possibly differently about

_____ and to apply this in my life (when/how)

_____.

Reflection and Accountability for Antiracist Educators:

This text is an invitation for me to think deeply and possibly differently as a reader

_____ and challenges me to make radical changes in my personal and
(in what ways?)

professional life _____.
(in what ways?)

In *My Bindi,* written by Gita Varadarajan and illustrated by Archana Sreenivasan, it's time for Divya to choose her bindi, but she is worried about the reactions of her peers at school. Divya discovers the significance of wearing a bindi that is grounded in her cultural identity.

Hear from the author about the importance of identity, books that serve as mirrors, and books she's writing next.

About the Creators

Learn more about the author and illustrator by visiting their websites: www.gitavaradarajan.com and www.archanasreenivasan.com.

SIX CRITICAL LENSES

Prompts are provided to nurture students' thinking as they read in partnerships, groups, or independently.

Pathways capture the details and ideas that students may notice and think about as they read and respond to the text, and they can be used as guidance for educators to teach into.

AFFIRMATION

PROMPTS

- What are you learning about Divya?
- What is Divya learning about wearing a bindi—its power, purpose, and connection to her identity?

PATHWAYS

- Divya admires her mother and the bindi she wears every day.
- Divya is curious about why her mother wears a bindi.
- Divya learns that wearing a bindi is part of her identity as Hindu.
- Divya is worried that her peers will make fun of her if she wears a bindi to school.
- Divya thinks bindis are beautiful.
- When she picks out and wears a bindi, she feels shy and then proud.

PROMPTS

Cultural assimilation is the expectation that groups of people living in and new to a country adopt the culture, values, and social behaviors of the dominant majority in that country. People are expected to give up or hide parts of their culture, such as language, clothing, food, religions, and traditions, that the dominant majority does not speak, use, or practice.

- What role does assimilation play in how Divya feels about wearing a bindi?

- What patterns around race and religion can be noticed about who is encouraged to assimilate and who is encouraged to maintain their culture?

PATHWAYS

- Because no one else in her class wears a bindi, Divya is afraid her peers will laugh at her, call her names, and physically remove it from her. Divya worries that being different in this way will be seen as bad.

- In American society, White people are encouraged to maintain their culture. Most books published are written by White people and are about White people. Television shows, series, and movies overwhelmingly feature White people. Textbooks and curriculum taught in school typically teach about White people. White mainstream English is prioritized.

- Whiteness and Christianity are upheld as the norm. Anyone who isn't White or Christian is encouraged to try to exist as close to this norm as possible.

AUTHORSHIP

PROMPTS

- Who are the creators of this text?

- How do their identities influence this work?

- What is their motivation for creating this text?

PATHWAYS

- The endnote shares that the author, Gita Varadarajan, was born and raised in India and that the illustrator, Archana Sreenivasan, lives in India.

- In the illustrator's note, Sreenivasan shares that she grew up as Hindu but resisted bindis and traditional Indian clothes, and it was much later that she began to reconnect with her roots, a journey that, she explains, continues.

- Gita Varadarajan writes in the author's note, "I wrote this story to give every little Hindu girl the courage to embrace her culture and traditions."

ATMOSPHERE

PROMPTS

- How does this text reflect the identities and lived experiences of the characters?

- How does it reflect your identities and lived experiences?

- In what ways does this book convey and bring you joy?

PATHWAYS

- Setting: Divya navigates between how she feels about her culture at home and her fears about sharing parts of her identity at school.

- Perspective: Divya discovers the beauty, power, and purpose of the bindi and that of her Hindu identity.

- Figurative Language/Imagery: Discuss the significance of the recurred lines: "I see a shining star. My mother's joy. My father's pride. And then I see something else. She's different from all the rest, not quite like anyone else with a glimmering dot on her forehead. I see me."

- Mood/Tone: Discuss Divya's journey of self-discovery—from apprehension to empowerment—that sets the mood and tone.

- Themes: identity, self-discovery, self-love

ACTIVISM

PROMPTS

- What are the dangers of assimilationist thinking? Who benefits and who is harmed?

- How can you work to resist assimilationist ideas?

- How will you embrace your full authentic self? How can you encourage others as well?

PATHWAYS

- Assimilationist thinking robs people of their identity—their culture, history, and self-esteem.

- Assimilationist thinking robs everyone from learning about each other, important perspectives, points of view, innovative ideas, and so on.

- Assimilation supports White supremacy by creating a hierarchy in society where White people are at the top and everyone else is considered beneath them.

- Resist assimilationist thinking by nurturing relationships with a wide variety of people and by being genuinely interested in learning about various ways of knowing and being in the world.

- To be our full authentic selves, surround ourselves with those who love us completely, by being brave and expressing ourselves, by identifying the things we love about ourselves, and by not comparing ourselves to anyone else.

PROMPTS

- How can this book influence your thinking and actions now and in the future?

- How will you remain alert for the ways your particular identities help you to understand a text and the world?

PATHWAYS

- Reflect on ways this text makes a difference to your heart and in your life. Consider commitments you'll make to care for people and communities.

- This text is an invitation for me to think deeply and possibly differently about

_____ and to apply this in my life (when/how)

_____ .

Reflection and Accountability for Antiracist Educators:

This text is an invitation for me to think deeply and possibly differently as a reader

_____ and challenges me to make radical changes in my personal and
   (in what ways?)

professional life _____ .
                      (in what ways?)

Luli and the Language of Tea, written by Andrea Wang and illustrated by Hyewon Yum, is the story of Luli, who yearns for community and connection in her classroom of students who speak various languages. Luli has an idea for bringing her peers together that stems from cultural and community practices that will enable the class to communicate across languages.

Learn more about the creators in this interview.

About the Creators

Learn more about Andrea Wang and Hyewon Yum at their websites:

- www.andreaywang.com
- hyewon-yum.squarespace.com

SIX CRITICAL LENSES

Prompts are provided to nurture students' thinking as they read in partnerships, groups, or independently.

Pathways capture the details and ideas that students may notice and think about as they read and respond to the text, and they can be used as guidance for educators to teach into.

AFFIRMATION

PROMPTS

- What are we learning about Luli?
- What are you learning about parts of Luli's identity?

PATHWAYS

- Luli is smart and wants to make friends.
- Part of Luli's identity is that she speaks Chinese, she likes tea, she likes to share, and she's learning to speak English.

AWARENESS

PROMPTS

Language is more than about how we communicate with one another. It is an important part of our identity. It is deeply connected to our cultural backgrounds, family, beliefs, and places we're from. **Multilingualism** is the use of more than one language by an individual or group of people.

- Why is it important for people to nurture the various languages they speak?

- Why is it important to speak multiple languages?

- Even though language is an important part of who we each are, why do you think some people have been forced to speak one language?

- How might we instead encourage multilingualism and work to preserve rather than erase the languages people speak?

PATHWAYS

- Language is an important part of people's identity.

- Language is about more than communicating; it preserves the values, customs, and traditions that matter to people.

- Speaking multiple languages is a skill that opens up the world. A person who is multilingual can connect and form bonds with many groups of people and expand their access to diverse cultures, ideas, and perspectives.

- Colonization, White domination, and White supremacy have resulted in groups of people being disconnected from their native and cultural languages.

- We can encourage multilingualism by appreciating the beauty of all languages, understanding the cultural value of languages, and recognizing that becoming a citizen of the world means communicating in various languages in order to exchange ideas and learn alongside one another.

AUTHORSHIP

PROMPTS

- Who are the creators of this text?

- How do their identities influence this work?

- What is their motivation for creating this text?

PATHWAYS

- In the author's note, Andrea Wang shares that she learned that the word for tea is similar in over 200 languages. Because tea is important to her identity as the child of Chinese immigrants, she thought about the ways tea could bring together people who speak various languages.

- The author's motivation for writing this book is to honor the languages spoken around the world, to show similarities between them, and to show how people can come together as a multilingual community.

- In an interview, Hyewon Yum shares that she took classes to learn to speak English when she first came to the United States. Although she was an adult learner, she shares, "We felt so happy whenever we found something in common despite our language barrier or age differences. I thought about all those friends and the moments we had in that ESL class while drawing. And Miss Hirokane is modeled after my dear friend Makiko." (Read the interview here: qrs.ly/x9frdwy).

ATMOSPHERE

PROMPTS

- How does this text reflect the identities and lived experiences of the characters?

- How does it reflect your identities and lived experiences?

- In what ways does this book convey and bring you joy?

PATHWAYS

- Setting: In the English as a Second Language (ESL) classroom, children were silent and playing alone.

- Perspective: Language and tea can bring people together across racial and cultural identities.

- Figurative Language/Imagery: Practice saying *tea* in the various languages demonstrated in the book.

  ○ Discuss the last sentence of the story: "Luli's teapot was empty, but her heart was full."

  ○ Identify and learn about the countries the children in the story are from.

- Mood/Tone: Togetherness and connection fill us with joy.

- Themes: friendship, community, diversity, immigrant experiences

ACTIVISM

PROMPTS

- What does this book help you to understand about the experiences of some immigrants in the United States?

- How can you work to make sure your peers, specifically those who may not speak English, feel included?

PATHWAYS

- It's not easy to learn to speak another language.

- It can be lonely when people are brought together.

- We can learn words and phrases to speak with peers; we can learn to speak more than one language; we can find ways to play and spend time together.

ACCOUNTABILITY

PROMPTS

- How can this book influence your thinking and actions now and in the future?

- How will you remain alert for the ways your particular identities help you to understand a text and the world?

- Reflect on ways this text makes a difference to your heart and in your life. Consider commitments you'll make to care for people and communities.

- This text is an invitation for me to think deeply and possibly differently about

  _____ and to apply this in my life (when/how)

  _____.

Reflection and Accountability for Antiracist Educators:

This text is an invitation for me to think deeply and possibly differently as a reader

_____ and challenges me to make radical changes in my personal and

(in what ways?)

professional life _____.

(in what ways?)

In ***Amy Wu and the Perfect Bao,*** written by Kat Zhang and illustrated by Charlene Chua, Amy loves to eat bao. As she learns the cultural and community practice of making and eating bao, Amy longs to create bao that looks perfect just like the ones her mother, father, and grandma make.

Watch this interview of the author.

About the Creators

To learn more about Kat Zhang and this story, visit her website at www.katzhangwriter.com. Learn more about Charlene Chau and her illustrations by exploring her website at www.charlenechua.com.

Six Critical Lenses

Prompts are provided to nurture students' thinking as they read in partnerships, groups, or independently.

Pathways capture the details and ideas that students may notice and think about as they read and respond to the text, and they can be used as guidance for educators to teach into.

AFFIRMATION

PROMPTS

- What are you learning about Amy Wu?
- What makes her feel proud?
- What are you learning about making and eating bao as part of Chinese cultural identity?

PATHWAYS

- Amy feels confident and proud about the many things she can do.
- Amy doesn't give up when a task is challenging.
- Cooperation is important to Amy's family. Everyone pitches in to make bao.
- Making bao brings the whole family together.

- Amy has ingenuity and agency—she comes up with a way to make her own version of the perfect bao.
- Amy redefines "perfect." She discovers for herself that even the "not-so-perfect" bao tastes good.

AWARENESS

PROMPTS

Perfectionism is the wish for everything to be perfect and can cause the belief that nothing is ever good enough.

- What are you noticing about Amy's idea of what perfect means?
- What are you noticing about how Amy's ideas about perfection make her feel about herself?
- Have you observed or felt expectations around perfectionism?

PATHWAYS

- When we compare ourselves to others, we can lose sight of all that makes us unique.
- Perfectionism: When there's only one right way, this hinders creativity and ingenuity.
- Sometimes people feel ashamed when they believe they don't measure up to expectations they have for themselves or those others set for them.

AUTHORSHIP

PROMPTS

- Who are the creators of this text?
- How do their identities influence this work?
- What is their motivation for creating this text?

PATHWAYS

- In the author's note at the beginning of the book, Kat Zhang shares that she grew up in a Mandarin-speaking family and teaches readers how to say *bao zi* and how to pronounce the Americanized version, "bao."
- Kat Zhang shares in an interview that this story is based on her own experience as a child making bao with her parents, who wanted her to experience and share in cultural experiences from China (qrs.ly/8kfrdx0).
- One reason for creating this text is to disrupt perfectionism.
- The author provides a recipe for bao at the end of the story to preserve how to make authentic food from her culture and share it with the world.

ATMOSPHERE

PROMPTS

- How does this text reflect the identities and lived experiences of the characters?

- How does it reflect your identities and lived experiences?

- In what ways does this book convey and bring you joy?

PATHWAYS

- Setting: The story takes place in Amy's home. Home is a place where Amy develops confidence in who she is, is surrounded by people she loves, and can tackle challenges.

   - "Amy can do a lot of things. She can brush her teeth. She can tie her shoe. She can even do both at once . . . sort of."

- Perspective: Through Amy's experience of making bao, readers discover that the word *perfect* can be limiting.

   - "But there's one thing Amy cannot, cannot do. She cannot make THE PERFECT BAO."

   - "Maybe Amy just can't make a **perfect bao**."

- Figurative Language/Imagery: Invite students to notice the author's use of larger font size, capital letters, and bolded words across the story and to discuss the significance and intention.

   - Notice the size of the text of the first sentence in the book: "Amy can do a lot of things."

   - Also, notice words and phrases such as **too much, not enough, fall apart, cannot,** THE PERFECT BAO, **perfect bao.**

- Mood/Tone: The main character feels pressure to be perfect at making bao. When things do not work out based on her expectations, Amy is discouraged. She feels disappointment in herself.

   - ". . . **she's going to make the world's most perfect bao.**"

   - "Maybe Amy just can't make a **perfect bao**."

- Themes: self-acceptance, determination, ingenuity

ACTIVISM

PROMPTS

- Discuss perfectionism and how it causes harm.

PATHWAYS

- When being perfect is the goal, this leads to disconnection from one another (competition, resentment, lack of appreciation of our own gifts and talents).

- The word *perfect* can and should mean more than just one right way. Redefining perfect in this way removes comparison and leads to reconnection with ourselves and others.

- The need to "prove oneself" and to excel can lead to individuals feeling shame. Instead, we can focus on the learning process, reflect on any mistakes as learning opportunities, and recognize that mistakes can sometimes lead to something positive.

ACCOUNTABILITY

PROMPTS

- How can this book influence your thinking and actions now and in the future?
- How will you remain alert for the ways your particular identities help you to understand a text and the world?

PATHWAYS

- Reflect on ways this text makes a difference to your heart and in your life. Consider commitments you'll make to care for people and communities.
- This text is an invitation for me to think deeply and possibly differently about

_____ and to apply this in my life (when/how)

_____.

Reflection and Accountability for Antiracist Educators:

This text is an invitation for me to think deeply and possibly differently as a reader

_____ and challenges me to make radical changes in my personal and
   (in what ways?)

professional life _____.
               (in what ways?)

CHAPTER FOUR

Shatter Silences Around Racism

Although dandelions are often perceived as lawn killers, the relationship between dandelions and grass is quite the contrary. During their lifetime, dandelions aerate soil and reduce erosion. They pull calcium and other nutrients from deep within the soil and fertilize the grass.

On the first day of my 17th year teaching in a predominantly White school district, I parked my car and walked toward the middle school/high school complex in anticipation of greeting my sixth-grade students. The brightness of the sun along with the feeling of excitement and promise were abruptly eclipsed. Music blared from the front of the building. A large crowd of teenagers dressed in school colors sang loudly. What at first appeared to be a sea of green-and-white-clad students celebrating the start of their senior year quickly became a mob of White teenagers chanting the "N" word to the explicit lyrics of the song that was playing. Administrators from the district circulated among the crowd. But the chanting continued, louder than the music itself. I entered the complex from a side door, shaking.

I sank into the chair at my desk in my classroom trying to process what I'd just witnessed. There were several tasks I needed to do before my students arrived. Put out new, glittery pencils I'd purchased for them. Leave my first literary gift of the year on top of each desk—the poem "Quilt" by Janet Wong photocopied on purple paper and trimmed, ready to be glued to the inside of my students' readers' notebooks. Its message one that I'd hoped would become a metaphor for how we'd work together and care for each other that year.

Our family
is a quilt
of odd remnants
patched together
in a strange pattern,
threads fraying,
fabric wearing thin –
but made to keep
its warmth
even in bitter cold.

I wanted to wait by the door of our classroom, ready to greet each student with a wide smile and a warm hello. But instead, I sat at my desk trembling.

I thought about Black students in the district who would be navigating a large group of their White peers shouting a racial slur into the morning air. I quickly composed an email to administrators about what I'd experienced that morning and included the lyrics along with the racial epithet that students were chanting. I explained how shocked, unsafe, and disappointed I felt and my fear for Black students experiencing this.

The superintendent of the district, a White man, emailed back. He thanked me for expressing my "thoughts and concerns." He wrote that the song was "inappropriate and not a behavior we want to condone." He continued. "While we cannot go back in time, we can use the experience as awful as it may have been for you, to have our students understand the impact of the spoken word. I would even suggest (if you are interested) that you meet with some senior leaders to share the experience so they can begin to understand."

Take a moment to reflect on this experience and the response by the superintendent in the district. What do you notice? What do you wonder?

Reflect

- What can be noticed about the response from the educator with the most power in this school district?

- How might this leader have responded differently?

- What role does race play in his response?

- What might we wonder about the teaching that had occurred or was missing in this district that contributed to this moment?

- Whose responsibility is it to address racism?

There are several ways in which this leader's response was problematic. It was not deemed important by the superintendent who was outside that morning to stop the actions of the seniors. When I reported this event, it was not deemed important enough for the superintendent to ask about my well-being or to leave his office, located in the same building I taught in, to check on me—one of few Black teachers in the district. It was not deemed important by the superintendent to call a meeting with the principal of the high school, to notify teachers and parents about this experience, or to discuss with the students themselves the impact of their actions. In fact, it was suggested that *I* speak with the students to let them know how this made *me* feel. Essentially, I was being told that it was *my* job alone to address the racism I was also expected to navigate.

About 100 students stood on the steps of their high school building chanting the N-word on the first day of their senior year. There they were, at the threshold of their adult lives where they would go out into the world, some as college students and some into the workforce. Many of these students had sat in seats in my classroom, a space where we'd discussed racism. I felt the deep shame of failure. But the burden of that shame was not mine alone to carry, regardless of the superintendent's dismissal and suggestion. Too often it is expected that those who are experiencing marginalization and oppression are the ones expected to redress this. In this instance, the White superintendent, White teachers, and White students who witnessed it were silent; it is not enough to say after the fact that you disagree or that something is "horrible." The onus to address racism rests on the shoulders of all educators, and it's important that a proactive approach is taken. My colleagues and I, no matter what we'd taught, had most certainly failed in the most important work—teaching in ways that develop and activate students' critical consciousness. Teaching in ways that help students affirm one another's humanity.

Reading instruction is a powerful space in which to shatter silences about racism. Educators can intentionally use teaching approaches that help raise students' racial consciousness. As a result, students will develop the ability to recognize and analyze racism beyond isolated incidents to instead recognize how racism is entrenched within structures, institutions, and systems of the nation. Our teaching approaches can help students deeply understand that racism isn't just a past condition but a contemporary—right now—thriving one. And racism isn't only about individual acts of hate or the use of a racial slur as the high school students chanted repeatedly; racism functions systemically such as the superintendent's refusal to address this incident and educators' reluctance to explicitly teach about race and racism.

When educators instruct in ways to develop students' racial consciousness, students show up differently in the world and are better positioned to disrupt racism in their own lives. Just imagine if the high school students from my district had consistent access to books, ongoing discussions, and intentional instruction that helped them to talk and think about racism? How might they have shown up differently on that first day of school? Would that incident have even occurred?

Every book is about race whether race is explicit in the text or it isn't.

Every book is about race whether race is explicit in the text or it isn't. In *Playing in the Dark: Whiteness and the Literary Imagination* (1992), Toni Morrison explores the ways assumptions of racial language are embedded in literature despite its claims to be "humanistic" (pp. xii–xiii). American literature, she maintains, is not neutral. "The world does not become raceless or will not become unracialized by assertion. The act of enforcing racelessness in literary discourse is itself a racial act" (p. 46). Because race (as well as all social identities such as gender, dis/ability, sexual orientation, religion, etc.) is not neutral, but in fact a social construction that shapes our lives, authors and the texts they write are not neutral. Denial of this proliferates implicit understandings in the minds of readers that White is literature's default. Matthew Salesses's observations around the teaching of fiction writing offers clear examples of this as well as implications for reading instruction. In *Craft in the Real World: Rethinking Fiction Writing and Workshopping,* Salesses (2021) notes, "To name or not name a character's race is a matter of craft. To consider a character to be white unless stated otherwise is a matter of craft" (p. xiv). Antiracist reading instruction helps readers understand that every author's identity, experiences, and perspectives are imbued with race, which informs the ways in which they write and that every reader's identity, experiences, and perspectives are imbued with race, which informs the ways in which they read.

Race-neutral and White-as-default stances around literature drive book selections, curriculum, and teaching. Tricia Ebarvia, Lorena Germán, Dr. Kimberly Parker, and Julia Torres believe that "no curricular or instructional decision is a neutral one" (#DisruptTexts, n.d.). As cofounders of DisruptTexts, part of their mission is to help educators recognize that the texts included, those omitted, and the teaching around these texts can harm all students, especially BIPOC students. The kinds of books we make available in our classrooms lets students know whether the possibilities for their lives are limitless or limited. When White characters are the only characters students read about, without uttering a single word, we speak loudly and clearly about whose lives matter and whose doesn't.

Further, when Black and Brown characters are represented as stereotypes, the message to students is that they should accept these portrayals and believe them. Dr. Ebony Elizabeth Thomas (2019), author of *The Dark Fantastic: Race and the Imagination From Harry Potter to the Hunger Games,* names books that are misrepresentations and distortions of BIPOC and their lives "racialized mirrors, windows, and doors" (p. 7). Historically, there have been tremendous racialized disparities in children's literature—and that continues today. Thomas theorizes about this imagination gap and asserts that this issue is more extensive than just a lack of diversity in children's and young adult literature. "The problem extends far beyond the mere lack of representation of characters of color in children's publishing and media. Often, the characters of color who do appear on the page or screen are stereotypes or caricatures. Marginalization has been a persistent problem in literature for children and adolescents throughout history" (p. 7). Thomas also spotlights the racist trope of disposability of Black bodies in literature. It isn't only in mainstream horror movies where often it can be noticed that Black characters are first to die. This trope is established in literature, specifically within the genres of fantasy and science fiction such as *The Hunger Games.* With this understanding, then, discussions about race and racism should occur frequently in classrooms, as we nurture radical imagination within our students with books that position Black and Brown characters and people in various contexts and circumstances.

Think about some of the books that are at the core of your curriculum—whole class books, book club books, and read-alouds. How are these books about race whether this is made explicit in the book or not? What is the teaching that happens to support students' development of their racial consciousness? Or, does your teaching silence race and racism? I've filled in some examples in the following chart, but I challenge you to use this chart framework to examine the books in your curriculum—and interrogate, especially, those that are favorites or "canon." (Find a full-page blank chart in the Appendix to use for this exercise.)

EVERY BOOK IS ABOUT RACE				
TITLE & AUTHOR	What are the *hidden* rules students learn about race and racism?	What are the *clear* rules students learn about race and racism?	What is the *explicit* teaching about race and racism that's needed?	How can race and racism be *silenced* in teaching?
Because of Winn-Dixie by Kate DiCamillo	White is the default; anything else is the other.	Blackness is "different" and "problematic."	The normalization of White identity in texts.	Avoiding discussions about an author's use of characterization and racist ideas in a text.
Jabari Jumps by Gaia Cornwall	It's okay to dismiss, omit, and erase the impact of racism and White supremacy in the lives of Black people.	White authors get to tell stories about Black characters without addressing the fullness of Black characters' lives.	To erase the historical sociopolitical conditions that impact the lives of Black people is misrepresentation.	Avoiding discussions about the ways who tells the story matters and how race informs storytelling.
Books in your classroom library:				

I've chosen two books that readily come to mind when I think about both hidden and clear rules readers learn about race and racism as they engage these texts: *Because of Winn-Dixie* by Kate DiCamillo and *Jabari Jumps* by Gaia Cornwall. These award-winning books are beloved by teachers and young readers. And although race is central in these texts, I've noticed how conversations about race and racism are silenced in classrooms where they are used in curriculum.

During professional development experiences, my colleagues and I have helped participants explore the book *Because of Winn-Dixie* as an example of ways texts are not race-neutral and are in fact about race even when they aren't marketed in this way. Teachers analyzed DiCamillo's (2000) characterization of the one character of color in this story, a Black older woman named Gloria Dump. DiCamillo uses several problematic racial tropes across the book. Here are some things we discovered during this analysis:

- Not only does Gloria have a demeaning last name, but she is also depicted as an alcoholic who all of the White children in the community call a witch and are afraid of even though she is rarely seen.

- Gloria's skin color is described in the story. Such naming and describing of skin color does not occur for any other character in the book. The assumption here is that the readers of *Because of Winn-Dixie* are White. Signifying Blackness in this White context normalizes Whiteness. What lets readers know for sure that White is the default racial identity of all of the characters is descriptions of Blackness—the other.

- A combination of "The Black Best Friend" and "Magical Negro" tropes is also utilized. These tropes occur when Black characters are constructed as the comforting, helpful friend to the White protagonist. A wise, good-hearted, Black person is present in a text to pull a White person out of a crisis. Cerise Glenn and Landra Cunningham (2009) note key characteristics of the Magical Negro trope, including "(a) using magical and spiritual gifts for the White character, (b) assuming primarily service roles, (c) exhibiting folk wisdom as opposed to intellectual cognition, (d) possessing limited role outside of magical/spiritual guide, and (e) displaying an inability to use his or her powers to help himself or herself" (p. 9). Gloria's identity and purpose are boiled down to her servitude for Opal, the young, White protagonist, despite Gloria's capacity, needs, wants, and interests.

- DiCamillo also employs a White Savior trope. Opal befriends Gloria, which assures the community and readers that Black people aren't scary. Because of Gloria's failing eyesight, Opal reads aloud to her. The book that is recommended to

Opal by the local librarian is *Gone With the Wind*—a book that romanticizes the Civil War, slavery, and the Reconstruction Era and is filled with racist and stereotypical language, practices, characterization, and imagery. Opal "helps" by reading aloud a racist book to Gloria, a Black woman, who enjoys the story, according to DiCamillo's portrayal of this experience. This paradoxical pattern in literature is exposed in *Playing in the Dark: Whiteness and the Literary Imagination*. Toni Morrison (1992) observes, "Encoded or explicit, indirect or overt, the linguistic responses to an Africanist presence complicate texts, sometimes contradicting them entirely" and that White writer's response to Blackness "often provides a subtext" that "sabotages" the purported intentions of the text (p. 66).

For many readers, *Because of Winn-Dixie* is simply a beautiful story about a young girl and a dog and how new friendships help her find happiness. But when we shatter silences around race and racism, there is much more operating within this text.

A 20th anniversary edition of *Because of Winn-Dixie* was published in 2020. DiCamillo removed *Gone With the Wind* and replaced it with *David Copperfield*. While many may see this as an attempt to repair harm, many others recognize this text change alone doesn't acknowledge the harmful ways race is portrayed throughout the story. In this anniversary edition, DiCamillo (2000) writes,

> When I wrote this story more than twenty years ago, I gave Opal and Gloria Dump a classic novel of the South to share: *Gone with the Wind*. But when I reread *Because of Winn-Dixie* in preparation for this anniversary edition, I found it painful to see Opal and Gloria Dump sitting together, side by side, reading from a book that I cannot in good conscience recommend to my readers. I am grateful for this chance to give Opal and Gloria Dump a different book to share—a book that, while it is not perfect, does not diminish either one's humanity.

Scholar, educator, and activist Dr. Debbie Reese (2021) notes that neither DiCamillo nor Ann Patchett who wrote an introduction for the anniversary edition names racism when discussing the problematic choices made in the writing of *Because of Winn-Dixie*. Dr. Reese (2021) observes,

> It is interesting to read and think about DiCamillo and Patchett's words about *Gone with the Wind*. Neither one says it is racist. That last paragraph from Patchett about millions who have read *Because of Winn-Dixie* exudes warmth but it also excludes children who were yanked right out of the story

when they got to chapter 9 and learn about Gloria. That is where we learn about her, that her last name is Dump, and that the neighborhood kids call her a witch. People will argue that by the end of the book, readers love Gloria. They probably do, but the weight of coming to that point is on the shoulders of Black children.

Kate DiCamillo fans may be tempted to think that perhaps things have just gone awry with *Because of Winn-Dixie*. I challenge you to look at *Tiger Rising* and to consider how racial tropes exist in this text as well, particularly with DiCamillo's characterization of the one Black character in the book, Willie May. It can be tempting to cast aside everything you've just read and to instead hold on dearly to texts that are beloved to you. I urge you to reconsider. Antiracist teaching calls on us to not look away—to recognize and analyze harmful tropes and stereotypes in books and to consider the hidden and clear rules students learn about race and racism as they read. Antiracist teaching requires us to explicitly teach about race and racism. Antiracist teaching challenges us to move differently in the world rather than perpetuating ideas and practices that are psychologically violent to students.

Nostalgia for books we've read and loved can prevent us from seeing the problematic ideologies used to construct them. Tricia Ebarvia (2023) conveys that "we cannot ignore that our tendency toward nostalgia may also have particularly harmful implications for students of color and other marginalized groups. We can see the nostalgia bias clearly when thinking about text selection. No doubt that the stories that we're exposed to during childhood can leave an indelible mark on our hearts and minds. From fairy tales to picture books, these stories tend to stick with us" (p. 22). My former affinity for Dr. Seuss books is an example. I remember reading and loving *Cat in the Hat* and then reading this book as well as other Dr. Seuss books to my daughter, unconscious of the ways the author regularly used racist imagery in his work (Grady, 2021). A part of *Stamped (For Kids): Racism, Antiracism, and You* (Cherry-Paul et al., 2021) that young readers ask me the most about is where I share, in addition to Dr. Seuss, several examples of stories and movies that include racial stereotypes and have "racist ideas baked right into them." I explain, "This matters because words matter. And stories are powerful. The images on the page and screen become the images in our minds, shaping the ways we see ourselves and think about people" (p. 64). This is why the work of antiracism is so vitally important. It helps us to gain the ability to perceive what previously had been unrecognizable to us.

> *This is why the work of antiracism is so vitally important. It helps us to gain the ability to perceive what previously had been unrecognizable to us.*

Race is so clearly central in *Because of Winn-Dixie,* an award-winning, beloved text read by millions of children and centered in many reading curricula. Yet, discussions about race and racism in connection with this text are often silenced.

Unlike the overt ways racism shows up and is silenced in *Because of Winn-Dixie, Jabari Jumps* (2017) by Gaia Cornwall is an example of silencing through the omission of race. In *Jabari Jumps,* the young Black protagonist goes to a local swimming pool and is afraid to jump off the diving board. Gaia Cornwall is the author and illustrator who creates Black characters in this story, although she is not Black. Further, Cornwall does not address the historical context of Black people and swimming in the United States—history that continues to impact the lives of Black people today. Historically, Black people were kept out of public swimming pools around the country (Martin, 2008). This racist history continues to shape Black people's relationship with water. In 2017, the USA Swimming Foundation shared that 64% of Black children have "no/ low swimming ability" (USA Swimming, 2017). A deadly consequence of the nation's historical racist policies and practices is that Black children drown at rates that are significantly higher than that of White children (CDC, 2022). My father's experiences as a child are representative of this. Growing up in the segregated South, children in his community could only swim in creeks and lakes, areas that were mostly unsupervised. One day, his childhood friend drowned. As a result of living with this trauma for decades, my father protected his own children the best way he could—by keeping us away from water. My brother and I are living, breathing examples of the statistics on Black adults who do not know how to swim. I've broken this cycle of racial trauma with my own daughter, who attended swimming classes with her father as a baby and later swam competitively with a swim team. Another aspect of institutional racism that has contributed to these statistics on Black people and swimming is access to protective swimming caps for natural hair. Until 2022 at the Olympic level, the Federation Internationale de Natation (FINA), the world's governing body for aquatic sports, banned the use of protective swim caps, imposing additional barriers for Black swimmers (Diaz, 2022). To exclude the history of Black people in the United States and public pools in a story about Black characters and swimming is an attempt to erase the experience and impact of structural racism and White supremacy.

In response to readers' question, "How did you come up with the story?" Cornwall shares that the story was inspired by her life when she was a kid (qrs.ly/ylfrdx3). She explains that she loved swimming and remembers being really afraid of climbing up on the diving board. So the question is, for what purpose are the characters in *Jabari Jumps* Black? Particularly when she does not include the racial history of swimming in the story or even in an author's note. You may be thinking that perhaps Cornwall does not know this history. Perhaps she doesn't. I argue that she has a responsibility to know when portraying Black people in her work. For many readers, on the surface, *Jabari Jumps* is just a sweet story about a little boy overcoming his fears. But when we look more closely and through the lens of race, it's challenging to understand why this author tells this story using Black characters other than to possibly occupy space in "diverse" book collections.

I want to be clear. Although I've discussed these two titles in ways I hope will activate educators' racial consciousness, I do not believe in book banning. Instead, with greater awareness, books can be used as tools to talk about race, to critique racist ideas, and to help young readers recognize when they show up in the world around them. Think about a book you're using right now with students in a unit or as a read-aloud. What happens when you intentionally apply the lens of race to this text? What does this reveal? If it is filled with problematic ideas and tropes, how can you teach in ways that do not reinforce racism? Grade-level teachers can make it part of their practice to form study groups around texts used for whole-class teaching as well as conduct analyses of texts in their book room. Often, books are taught as whole-class novels, and this teaching goes unchallenged simply because a school has class sets of these texts. When teachers work together to critically evaluate texts, change is more attainable.

In *Developing a Liberatory Consciousness,* Dr. Barbara J. Love (2010) recalls a student in a class examining oppressions who declared that he could no longer just watch movies and laugh along. This student, Dr. Love explained, was now operating from what she calls a "waking position" where he was consciously aware of the ways texts were instilling values into his consciousness that he would otherwise reject if he were "consciously paying attention" (p. 602).

> *Book challenges, censorship, and banning are efforts to silence racism as well as LGBTQIA+ identities and prevent young people from living their lives from a "waking position" (Love, 2010).*

Book challenges, censorship, and banning are efforts to silence racism as well as LGBTQIA+ identities and prevent young people from living their lives from a "waking position." These efforts are persistent precisely because perpetrators understand that books have the power to inform, educate, and activate compassion and empathy within students. To those invested in upholding iniquity, reading freely is a threat. But the reality is that students are always learning something about race as they read, even in books that are not explicitly about the lived experiences of BIPOC. The scholarship of Toni Morrison, Dr. Ebony Elizabeth Thomas, Matthew Salesses,

Dr. Debbie Reese, #DisruptTexts, myself, and others illuminates this in the following ways:

- Whenever an author only takes the time to describe the skin color of characters of color but not of White characters, students are learning that Whiteness is the norm and everything else is "other."

- Whenever an author positions characters of color as victims and White characters as heroes, students are learning to accept this power dynamic rather than to disrupt the concept of White saviorism.

- Whenever an author relegates characters of color to minor characters who simply exist to support the aspirations of the major character who is White, students are taught to exclusively see Black and Brown people as subordinate and White people as dominant.

- Whenever students are reading books all year that do not include characters of color at all, students are learning that the lives and experiences of White people should be prioritized while the lives and experiences of Black and Brown people are inconsequential.

- Whenever students read books by White authors that depict BIPOC in ways that are misrepresentative and distortions of who they are, students are socialized into racism and are learning to accept harmful stereotypes.

- Whenever students read books by White authors who dismiss, downplay, or completely erase historical, sociopolitical racist conditions, students are learning that the longevity and magnitude of racism isn't significant and doesn't matter in the lives of Black and Brown people today.

Like dandelions, conversations about race are often misunderstood. They are frequently avoided in classrooms around the country because they are seen as divisive. The steady rash of book banning policies and laws furthers such avoidance. However, even in states where such policies do not exist, teaching that explicitly addresses racism can be silenced. When educators avoid such discussions, it is possible they believe their role is to be neutral, and they view teaching about race as political. They are right. To teach about race and racism is political. To *not* teach about race and racism is also political. Intertwined within the fabric of schooling are values, beliefs, and cultural norms that are passed on to students. Educator and philosopher Paulo Freire (2000) reminds us that schooling is a political and moral practice that influences the knowledge students acquire, what they believe, and how they act. When educators do not see their work as political, students miss opportunities to deconstruct racist ideas that surround them and can instead perpetuate them.

It is critical that educators cultivate brave and psychologically safe spaces for students to read about and discuss race and racism. This begins by centering Black and Brown students in these conversations—protecting their hearts, and safeguarding their spirits and self-esteem. In the educator's guide for *The 1619 Project: Born on the Water,* abolitionist educator and author Aeriale Johnson emphasizes the importance of mitigating harm to Black students. Johnson asserts, "Our own personal biases, internalized racism, and ignorance of historical truths show up in our interactions with children and our teaching moves when we choose not to reckon with prejudices, wrestle with any cognitive dissonance we experience, and unlearn false information. Having a trustworthy teacher who is willing to be vulnerable and learn in tandem with students is critical to their real and perceived safety in a classroom community" (p. 6) (qrs.ly/n5frdx8).

Additional resources to support educators in this work are provided in the introduction of this book.

The superintendent of my former school district was right about one thing. In his email to me, he referenced a well-known, anonymous quote stating he understood that "once a stone is tossed or a word is spoken, it cannot be taken back." The actions of the seniors that day could never be undone. But what could happen is a radical reimagining of teaching where the work of equity and antiracism is the foundation from which all curriculum emerges. What could happen is breaking the shell of silence about race. What could happen is proactive, intentional work in reading instruction by educators who disrupt what Subini Ancy Annamma, Darrell D. Jackson, and Deb Morrison (2017) conceptualize as color-evasive ideologies. Utilizing the six critical lenses helps students navigate the most challenging terrains. When educators lean into and facilitate conversations about race, they shatter the shell of silence, making it possible for antiracist actions to transform not only classrooms or the front steps of a school but also all aspects of students' lives.

> *Dandelions are fast growers and have long life spans. One dandelion plant can live for years. Dandelions are survivors that bloom not only in lawns but also in unexpected places such as cracks in the cement.*

SHATTER SILENCES
AROUND RACISM: PROMPTS AND PATHWAYS

Facilitating conversations about race and racism requires that you plan to mitigate harm to those in your care who are most impacted by racism—BIPOC students. Ongoing reflection on your own racial identity and racial socialization along with interrogating biases is necessary, critical work. To avoid doing this often results in causing more harm to Black and Brown students. Please refer to resources shared in Chapter 1 that can support you in this work.

There is a tendency for teachers and students to say that oppression, specifically racism, happened or happens because of the racial identity of the individual or group being oppressed (e.g., "This happened because they're Black."). This leads students, especially BIPOC students, to believe that there's something wrong with being Black, Latinx, Asian American, Indigenous, and so on. It is important to shift such language so that students understand that racial oppression occurs because of racist ideas—that Black and Brown skin is not the problem, White supremacy is.

BOOKS FEATURED IN THIS CHAPTER

Unspeakable: The Tulsa Race Massacre, by Carole Boston Weatherford and illustrated by Floyd Cooper	Page 168
When We Say Black Lives Matter, written and illustrated by Maxine Beneba Clarke	Page 172
The 1619 Project: Born on the Water, by Nikole Hannah-Jones and Renée Watson and illustrated by Nikkolas Smith	Page 176
Build a House, by Rhiannon Giddens and illustrated by Monica Mikai	Page 181
We Are Still Here! Native American Truths Everyone Should Know, by Traci Sorell and illustrated by Frané Lessac	Page 185

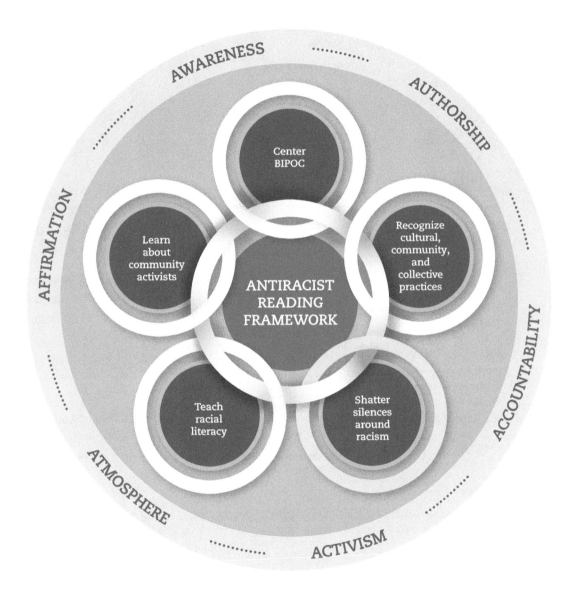

AWARENESS

AUTHORSHIP

AFFIRMATION

ACCOUNTABILITY

ATMOSPHERE

ACTIVISM

Center
BIPOC

Recognize
cultural,
community,
and
collective
practices

Learn
about
community
activists

ANTIRACIST
READING
FRAMEWORK

Teach
racial
literacy

Shatter
silences
around
racism

Unspeakable: The Tulsa Race Massacre, written by Carole Boston Weatherford and illustrated by Floyd Cooper, is the story of the thriving, African American town of Greenwood and the Tulsa Race Massacre, one of the worst incidents of racial violence in the United States.

About the Creators

Learn more about Carole Boston Weatherford and her work at her website: www.cbweatherford.com.

Download the free educator's guide for *Unspeakable*.

Watch this video of Floyd Cooper, who shares his personal connection to the Tulsa Race Massacre.

SIX CRITICAL LENSES

Prompts are provided to nurture students' thinking as they read in partnerships, groups, or independently.

Pathways capture the details and ideas that students may notice and think about as they read and respond to the text, and they can be used as guidance for educators to teach into.

AFFIRMATION

PROMPTS

- What are you learning about the Black community of Greenwood?
- What are you learning about the town of Greenwood?

PATHWAYS

- Black people resisted racism by leaving the segregated South and resisted racism by creating their own community in the West.
- Black people started their own businesses and systems—restaurants, shops, libraries, news, education, and so on.
- Black people built homes, created economic opportunities, established fair laws and policies, and supported each other in ways that helped their community thrive.
- There was unity, pride, and a strong sense of community in Greenwood.

PROMPTS

White supremacy is about the ways White people overwhelmingly control power and material resources in society and can hold conscious as well as unconscious ideas of superiority. White supremacy has existed since White colonizers arrived in what became the United States of America and has been used to justify the genocide of Native Americans as well as hundreds of years of chattel slavery.

Historian and author Carol Anderson explains that "white rage," White Americans' hostility toward advancements and achievements of African Americans, is evident across the history of the United States, including today.

- How was Greenwood a symbol of resistance against Whiteness?
- How was the Tulsa Race Massacre a result of White supremacy?

PATHWAYS

- White womanhood was used as a weapon to perpetuate violence against Black people in Greenwood. Additional examples past (e.g., Emmett Till) and present (e.g., Christian Cooper) demonstrate that across history, White women have been complicit in systems of oppression that result in violence against Black men.
- The town of Greenwood was known as Black Wall Street with more than 200 Black-owned businesses in this thriving community of employment, wealth, and success. White people's response to Greenwood's success was rage, hatred, and violence.

AUTHORSHIP

PROMPTS

- Who are the creators of this text?
- How do their identities influence this work?
- What is their motivation for creating this text?

PATHWAYS

- The endnote explains that Carole Boston Weatherford's work "spans the slavery and segregation eras" and that she mines "the past for family stories, fading traditions, and forgotten struggles." In her author's note, Weatherford shares that she has personally experienced racist backlash against a family member.
- Weatherford recognizes that the Tulsa Race Massacre is a part of U.S. history that has been suppressed.
- Floyd Cooper was born and raised in Tulsa, Oklahoma, where he heard about the Tulsa Race Massacre from his grandfather, who is a survivor.
- Creating this book is a way to make sure the history of Greenwood and the tragedy of the Tulsa Race Massacre is not forgotten.

ATMOSPHERE

- How does this text reflect the identities and lived experiences of the characters/people?

- How does it reflect your identities and lived experiences?

- In what ways does this book convey and bring you joy?

PATHWAYS

- Setting: The illustrator helps readers to visualize the thriving, successful African American town of Greenwood.

- Perspective: The text provides the experiences of Black people living in Greenwood—their dreams, successes, and joys—who were terrorized by White people during the massacre.

- Figurative Language/Imagery: Discuss Weatherford's use of "Once upon a time . . ." to develop this story; discuss the significance and various meanings of the title of this book: *Unspeakable*.

- Mood/Tone: The story pays tribute to the humanity of Black people and their struggle against racism, and it is a call to action for racial justice.

- Theme: resistance, resilience, reconciliation

ACTIVISM

PROMPTS

Reconciliation is the process of making amends and repairing a relationship that has been damaged.

- What will it mean for the United States to truly reconcile with its past?

- How does this story help you to think about what can be done to help heal the scars of racism and to interrupt racism today?

PATHWAYS

- The nation has done very little to acknowledge and apologize for the harm racism has caused African Americans.

- Reconciliation is not possible if racism is denied, dismissed, and downplayed.

- Black people continue to fight for the nation to take enforced actions to prevent continued racism.

- Reconciliation Park is a place not only to remember the past, particularly the victims of the massacre, but also to consider the responsibility of each of us to forge a better future.

- Committing to antiracist actions and ideas and taking action against unequal treatment of anyone based on their racial identity can bring the nation closer to achieving racial justice.

PROMPTS

- How can this book influence your thinking and actions now and in the future?

- How will you remain alert for the ways your particular identities help you to understand a text and the world?

PATHWAYS

- Reflect on ways this text makes a difference to your heart and in your life. Consider commitments you'll make to care for people and communities.

- This text is an invitation for me to think deeply and possibly differently about

_____ and to apply this in my life (when/how)

_____.

Reflection and Accountability for Antiracist Educators:

This text is an invitation for me to think deeply and possibly differently as a reader

_____ and challenges me to make radical changes in my personal and
    (in what ways?)

professional life _____.
            (in what ways?)

When We Say Black Lives Matter

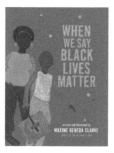

When We Say Black Lives Matter, written and illustrated by Maxine Beneba Clarke, is the story of parents explaining the mantra that is Black Lives Matter to their child throughout their life—both the joys of being Black as well as the hardships caused by racism.

Learn more about Maxine Beneba Clarke and listen to her discuss the writing, art, and her hopes for this book in these interviews.

About the Creator

Learn more about Maxine Beneba Clarke and listen to her discuss the writing, art, and her hopes for this book in the interviews linked to the QR codes.

Six Critical Lenses

Prompts are provided to nurture students' thinking as they read in partnerships, groups, or independently.

Pathways capture the details and ideas that students may notice and think about as they read and respond to the text, and they can be used as guidance for educators to teach into.

AFFIRMATION

PROMPTS

- What are you learning from this story about ways Black parents work to make sure their children feel loved?
- What are you learning from this story about the beauty and joys of Black Lives?
- In what ways does Black Lives Matter work as a mantra to communicate love, pride, and hope?

PATHWAYS

- Black parents let their children know that Black people are "wonderful-strong," and they deserve respect and to feel joy.
- Black people are resilient and brave; their ancestors guide them.
- Black Lives Matter is a constant reminder that Black people are beautiful, brilliant, and worthy of protection and love.

PROMPTS

- How does Black Lives Matter work as a mantra to call out racism?

- What are you learning about ways Black people resist racism?

- In what ways is "All Lives Matter" NOT a harmless or inclusive response to Black Lives Matter but, in fact, a problematic response?

PATHWAYS

- The mantra Black Lives Matter is about remembering racism of the past as well as recognizing racism today.

- Black people have resisted racism by working together as a collective—speaking out against it, marching, and creating movements such as the Civil Rights Movement and the Black Lives Matter Movement.

- Black people resist racism by not allowing it to take away their joy and by continually working together to fight for freedom.

- "All Lives Matter" has been a response by some White people as well as some people of color who refuse to acknowledge the ways Black people have and continue to be treated. It dismisses the data that show the ways Black people are harmed most in institutions such as policing, health care, and education. The mantra Black Lives Matter does not suggest that "only" Black Lives Matter. When Black lives matter in the United States and Black people are not mistreated, we move closer toward the idea that "all" lives matter in the United States.

AUTHORSHIP

PROMPTS

- Who are the creators of this text?
- How do their identities influence this work?
- What is their motivation for creating this text?

PATHWAYS

- In an interview, Maxine Beneba Clarke shares that her parents were Black British migrants and that her family was the only African diaspora family in much of the area of Sydney, Australia, where she grew up.

- Her identity as a Black woman and experiences in the world influence this story and her motivation for writing it.

- Maxine Beneba Clarke explains that *When We Say Black Lives Matters* was written after the killing of George Floyd in 2020.

- As she watched Black Lives Matter protests happening all over the world, in places where she has family, she thought about Black children trying to make sense of this.

ATMOSPHERE

PROMPTS

- How does this text reflect the identities and lived experiences of the characters/people?

- How does it reflect your identities and lived experiences?

- In what ways does this book convey and bring you joy?

PATHWAYS

- Setting: Parents help their child to know their beauty and worth from infancy to adulthood.

- Perspective: The story acknowledges the beauty of Black identity as well as the anguish caused to Black people because of racism.

- Figurative Language/Imagery: Invite readers to notice the depth of meaning in the mantra Black Lives Matter. Invite readers to notice the rhythm and cadence of the writing as well as the vibrancy of the art. Discuss this line from the story: "We're saying trouble still stalks to this day, that we've seen it monster in the shadows and must all help drive it away."

- Mood/Tone: This story demonstrates the beauty, joys, hopes, and anguish of Black people.

- Theme: equity, Black resistance and resilience

ACTIVISM

PROMPTS

- What is Black Lives Matter a call to do?

- What is the "monster in the shadows"?

- What can you do to show you believe that Black Lives Matter?

PATHWAYS

- Black Lives Matter is a call to acknowledge the brilliance and importance of Black people and the ways Black people continue to be harmed by racism.

- The "monster in the shadows" is racism—the prejudice, discrimination, and marginalization that has been happening to Black people because of racist ideas about skin color.

- I can learn more about the history of Black people by reading books and watching television shows and movies that center Blackness. I can name racism when I see it happening. I can say Black Lives Matter to help others realize this.

ACCOUNTABILITY

PROMPTS

- How can this book influence your thinking and actions now and in the future?

- How will you remain alert for the ways your particular identities help you to understand a text and the world?

- Reflect on ways this text makes a difference to your heart and in your life. Consider commitments you'll make to care for people and communities.

- This text is an invitation for me to think deeply and possibly differently about

_____ and to apply this in my life (when/how)

_____.

Reflection and Accountability for Antiracist Educators:

This text is an invitation for me to think deeply and possibly differently as a reader

_____ and challenges me to make radical changes in my personal and
(in what ways?)

professional life _____.
(in what ways?)

The 1619 Project: Born on the Water

The 1619 Project: Born on the Water, written by Nikole Hannah-Jones and Renée Watson and illustrated by Nikkolas Smith, is an origin story specifically for Black children. It helps Black children and all children understand the freedom and joys of Black people in Africa prior to enslavement, the tragedies of enslavement in the United States, and the ways Black people resist racism and continue to fight for their freedom and for the promise of democracy.

About the Creators

Learn more about the creators by visiting their websites:

- www.nikolehannahjones.com
- www.reneewatson.net
- www.nikkolas.com

Six Critical Lenses

Prompts are provided to nurture students' thinking as they read in partnerships, groups, or independently.

Pathways capture the details and ideas that students may notice and think about as they read and respond to the text, and they can be used as guidance for educators to teach into.

AFFIRMATION

PROMPTS

- What are you learning about the cultural identity and history of Black people in the Kingdom of Ndongo in West Central Africa?
- What are some of the knowledge and joys of the Ndongo people?
- What does this book help you to understand about Black people before enslavement in the United States, and why is this important?
- How does this book help you to understand the resilience of Black people?

Access the educator's guide developed by educator Aeriale Johnson for more ways to teach with *Born on the Water*. Review this guide for directions on ways to mitigate harm when teaching *Born on the Water* and talking about racism."

Read an NPR interview with the authors.

Watch Renée Watson discuss the book and its importance in the world in this YouTube video.

PATHWAYS

- There are rich, cultural identities of Black people in Africa.

- The Ndongo people had their own language and were smart and skilled in science, math, agriculture, music, dance, and more.

- The Ndongo people were not idle; they took care of their community, celebrated, and loved each other.

- This book makes it clear that Black history does not begin with slavery. It is important to know this so that the history of Black people is not erased or limited only to oppression.

- Enslavement did not take away the resolve of Black people to live, to hope, to love, to survive, and to continue to fight for freedom.

AWARENESS

PROMPTS

- What is your understanding about the horrors of slavery?

- How does this book help you to understand the ways Black people resisted enslavement and racism?

- How does this book help you to think about what the United States owes Black people?

PATHWAYS

- When Black people were stolen and enslaved, they lost all that they were forced to leave behind—their families, their ways of life, their possessions, their freedom.

- Black people were treated cruelly and many did not survive being on the treacherous ships that brought them across the ocean.

- Black people continued to be treated inhumanely by White people who forced them to work all day, beat them, and separated them from their children.

- Black people fought enslavers, remembered their traditions, and passed them on to their children.

- Black people built the country, survived enslavement, and have made significant contributions to all aspects of the United States.

- The United States would not be what it is today without the sacrifice, brilliance, and greatness of Black people.

AUTHORSHIP

- Who are the creators of this text?

- How do their identities influence this work?

- What is their motivation for creating this text?

PATHWAYS

- Nikole Hannah-Jones is a Pulitzer Prize–winning journalist who has worked to spotlight racial injustice. On her website, she shares that she first became interested in journalism in high school when she wrote for her school newspaper about students like herself who were "bused across town as part of a voluntary school desegregation program." She is the creator of the 1619 Project on the transatlantic slave trade and its legacy in the United States.

- Renée Watson is an award-winning children's book author. On her website, she shares, "Many of her books are inspired by her experiences growing up as a Black girl in the Pacific Northwest. Her poetry and fiction center around the experiences of Black girls and explore themes of home, identity, body image, and the intersections of race, class, and gender."

- In the authors' note, Nikole Hannah-Jones and Renée Watson share that the purpose of this book is to "show that Black Americans have their own proud origin story, one that did not begin in slavery, in struggle, and in strife but that bridges the gap between Africa and the United States of America."

ATMOSPHERE

PROMPTS

- How does this text reflect the identities and lived experiences of the characters/people?

- How does it reflect your identities and lived experiences?

- In what ways does this book convey and bring you joy?

PATHWAYS

- Setting: This book shares the history and lives of Black people before, during, and after enslavement.

- Perspective: An origin story is provided that helps Black children understand who they are and where they come from.

- Figurative Language/Imagery:

  o Invite students to discuss why the authors chose poetry to create this book.

  o Discuss the line "Ours is no immigration story" that is repeated in this book.

- Discuss the image of the White Lion ship and why the creators chose not to include words on these two pages.

- Discuss the significance and meaning of the title *The 1619 Project: Born on the Water* and what the illustrations convey.

- Mood/Tone: This book reveals the joys, brilliance, and histories of Black people as well as the cruelty and tragedies of enslavement.

- Theme: origins, resistance, and resilience of Black people; horrors of slavery

ACTIVISM

PROMPTS

- How does this book help you understand the importance of using the word **enslaved** rather than **slave** when discussing what happened to Black people in 1619?

- What actions can you take to center the full humanity of Black people in ways that amplify their joy and lift the weight of shame?

PATHWAYS

- Words matter. The word *enslaved* helps us understand what was done to Black people. The word *slave* is an attempt to describe who Black people are, removing the fullness of their humanity. This is an important distinction.

- It's important to care about the words we use and to use words with care because we find freedom and liberation in language.

- We can center the humanity of Black people by continuing to learn their histories prior to 1619, learning about African countries and people, and learning about the significant contributions Black people have made and continue to make in the United States.

- We can remove the weight of shame by learning about the pride and joys of Black people, recognizing the tremendous work they've done to survive, as well as the truth about enslavement and understanding what it will take to reconcile the harms that have been done.

ACCOUNTABILITY

PROMPTS

- How can this book influence your thinking and actions now and in the future?

- How will you remain alert for the ways your particular identities help you to understand a text and the world?

- Reflect on ways this text makes a difference to your heart and in your life. Consider commitments you'll make to care for people and communities

- This text is an invitation for me to think deeply and possibly differently about

_____ and to apply this in my life (when/how)

_____.

Reflection and Accountability for Antiracist Educators:

This text is an invitation for me to think deeply and possibly differently as a reader

_____ and challenges me to make radical changes in my personal and

    (in what ways?)

professional life _____.

        (in what ways?)

Build a House

Build a House, written by Rhiannon Giddens and illustrated by Monica Mikai, traces the experiences of Black people in the United States from enslavement to emancipation, spotlighting the cycle of White supremacy, racism, as well as Black resilience and resistance.

About the Creators

Visit Rhiannon Giddens's website (www.rhiannon giddens.com) and Monica Mikai's website (www.monica mikai.com) to learn more about their work.

Watch this online interview on The Black Creators Series to learn more about Rhiannon Giddens and *Build a House*.

Access the Teaching Tips for *Build a House*.

SIX CRITICAL LENSES

Prompts are provided to nurture students' thinking as they read in partnerships, groups, or independently.

Pathways capture the details and ideas that students may notice and think about as they read and respond to the text, and they can be used as guidance for educators to teach into.

AFFIRMATION

PROMPTS

- What are you learning about the resilience and ingenuity of Black people?

- In what ways were Black people critical to the foundation of the United States?

PATHWAYS

- Black people were enslaved not only because they were forced to provide free labor; they were enslaved because of the knowledge they possessed.

- Black minds and Black genius were used to build and cultivate the land.

PROMPTS

White supremacy does not only refer to White supremacist hate groups. It describes a political, economic, and cultural system where White people overwhelmingly control power, oversee material resources, and hold conscious and unconscious ideas of White superiority and entitlement.

- Who is "you" in this story?

- In what ways does this story and illustrations demonstrate various forms of White supremacy?

PATHWAYS

- The "you" in this story refers to White people who enslaved Black people. The "you" also addresses people today who continue to perpetuate racism.

- In the United States, slavery existed and racism persists because of White supremacy. Some examples of White supremacy in the book:

  - Forced labor

  - Burning of the house

  - Forced language

  - Cultural appropriation (e.g., music)

AUTHORSHIP

PROMPTS

- Who are the creators of this text?

- How do their identities influence this work?

- What is their motivation for creating this text?

PATHWAYS

- In an interview, Rhiannon Giddens identifies as Black, biracial who grew up in the U.S. South (qrs.ly/5cfrdxc). She also discusses her work as a musician and shares that *Build a House* is also a song. In the author's note, Giddens writes, "I am proud to be a banjo-playing descendant of the Afro-Carolinians who, against all the odds, made a culture and built a home and survived, so I could thrive."

- In a video about her life and work on *Build a House*, Monica Mikai discusses how she processed her family's lineage and connection to slavery as a student and uses her art to tell the story of trauma and resistance (qrs.ly/whfrdxh).

- The author challenges readers to think about the ways we "make our family and our home, no matter where we are . . . no matter what."

ATMOSPHERE

PROMPTS

- How does this text reflect the identities and lived experiences of the characters/people?

- How does it reflect your identities and lived experiences?

- In what ways does this book convey and bring you joy?

PATHWAYS

- Setting: Readers learn about the ways Black people cultivated and constructed the United States and had to migrate in order to find safety.

- Perspective: Readers learn about the trauma Black people experienced during and after enslavement and the ways they resisted, built community, and reclaimed joy.

- Figurative Language/Imagery: The illustrator uses symbolism throughout the story. Consider the significance of the cottonwood tree seeds/plant the little girl carries, the mother's water bucket, the mule, and the instruments and the ideas they represent.

- Mood/Tone: The words and illustrations demonstrate inner strength, determination, and survival.

- Theme: resilience, hope, family, resistance

ACTIVISM

PROMPTS

Access the QR code at the end of the book to listen to Rhiannon Giddens and Yo-Yo Ma perform *"Build a House."*

- What does the song invite you to feel and do?

- What does the book invite you to feel and do?

- How does *Build a House* help you to think about the importance of preserving the stories of those who are marginalized and whose lived experiences can be silenced?

- How will you plan to access and learn from these stories?

- Consider how Black creators use their musical brilliance as a form of activism and seek out songs that demonstrate this (e.g., What meaning and message do Black creators share about humanity?).

PATHWAYS

- Preserving the stories of those who are too often silenced matters.

- We can seek out and listen to these stories in books and interviews in order to have a clearer understanding of each other's experiences and of the world around us.

- Across history, music and stories have filled people with a sense of determination, hope, and the importance of caring for one another.

PROMPTS

- How can this book influence your thinking and actions now and in the future?

- How will you remain alert for the ways your particular identities help you to understand a text and the world?

PATHWAYS

- Reflect on ways this text makes a difference to your heart and in your life. Consider commitments you'll make to care for people and communities.

- This text is an invitation for me to think deeply and possibly differently about

  _____ and to apply this in my life (when/how)

  _____.

Reflection and Accountability for Antiracist Educators:

This text is an invitation for me to think deeply and possibly differently as a reader

_____ and challenges me to make radical changes in my personal and
    (in what ways?)

professional life _____.
              (in what ways?)

In *We Are Still Here! Native American Truths Everyone Should Know*, written by Traci Sorell and illustrated by Frané Lessac, 12 Native American children present 12 historical and contemporary ideas, events, policies, and laws on Indigenous Peoples' Day at school. The children's presentations demonstrate the impact of White supremacy and racism on the lives of Native Peoples as well as the advocacy and activism of Native Peoples to hold the United States accountable for redressing harm.

About the Creators

Learn more about the creators by visiting their websites at www.tracisorell.com and www.franelessac.com.

Listen to Traci Sorell discuss why she wrote this book in this YouTube interview.

There are important distinctions and nuances around the words *Indigenous, Native American, American Indian, tribe,* and *nation.* In my discussion of texts, I use the language and terminology the author uses. It's important to listen for who people tell us they are and to teach children to listen as well and to respect what they are learning. Learn more here about the impact of words and using accurate terms: qrs.ly/cufrdvt.

SIX CRITICAL LENSES

Prompts are provided to nurture students' thinking as they read in partnerships, groups, or independently.

Pathways capture the details and ideas that students may notice and think about as they read and respond to the text, and they can be used as guidance for educators to teach into.

AFFIRMATION

PROMPTS

- What are you understanding about what it means to be Indigenous?
- What are you learning about resistance and resilience of Native Peoples?
- In what ways does the sentence "We are still here!" function as a mantra for Native Nations?

- Indigenous Peoples are the original inhabitants of what is now known as North America. Indigenous Peoples existed before colonizers from Europe arrived and Indigenous Peoples still exist.

- Native Peoples have resisted colonization by holding onto their culture—knowledge, language, traditions, and so on—through activism and legal action to protect Native Peoples.

- By declaring "We are still here," Native Nations remind each other of their survival, their pride, and their love for one another.

AWARENESS

PROMPTS

- What are you learning about the impact of colonization and White supremacy on Native Peoples?

- What are you learning about ways the U.S. government has harmed Native Peoples?

- In what ways have Native Peoples pushed the United States to repair harm?

PATHWAYS

- White, European colonizers made treaties with Native Nations and then broke them.

- U.S. leaders worked to strip away Native People's cultures (language, religion) and replace it with White culture. White people removed Native children from their families and forced them to attend boarding schools.

- White people removed Native Peoples from their land and took the land and resources for themselves.

- Native Peoples engage in activism to hold the United States accountable for redressing harm and to advocate for the collective in ways that ensure their survival.

AUTHORSHIP

PROMPTS

- Who are the creators of this text?

- How do their identities influence this work?

- What is their motivation for creating this text?

PATHWAYS

- Traci Sorell shares that she was born and raised in the Cherokee Nation and has worked for Native advocacy groups.

- Frané Lessac shares that she grew up in New Jersey and now lives in Australia and that she researched extensively to create the illustrations for this book.

- In the author's note, Traci Sorell shares, "Everything in this book is a fundamental part of the United States' history, as well as its present, and should be known by everyone living in this country."

ATMOSPHERE

PROMPTS

- How does this text reflect the identities and lived experiences of the characters/people?
- How does it reflect your identities and lived experiences?
- In what ways does this book convey and bring you joy?

PATHWAYS

- Setting: Presentations are shared on Indigenous Peoples' Day about historical and contemporary ideas, actions, policies, and laws that impact the lives of Native Peoples.
- Perspective: Truths about U.S. history have been hidden and erased that all people of this country should know.
- Figurative Language/Imagery: Discuss the recurred sentence "We are still here!" as a mantra that declares Native people's survival.
- Mood/Tone: Truths are illuminated about colonization, assimilation, and continued efforts at attempted erasure of Native Peoples.
- Theme: resistance, resilience, self-determination, historical accuracy

ACTIVISM

PROMPTS

Indigenous Peoples' Day

"Though many continue to call it Columbus Day, the National Congress of American Indians (NCAI) again proudly joins the growing number of tribal nations, states, counties, cities, and school districts that are instead celebrating the second Monday of October as Indigenous Peoples Day. In so doing, we honor the enduring social, cultural, and political survivance of tribal nations that authored the original story of America" (National Congress of American Indians, qrs.ly/zwfrdxt).

"On Indigenous Peoples' Day, we honor the perseverance and courage of Indigenous peoples, show our gratitude for the myriad contributions they have made to our world, and renew our commitment to respect Tribal sovereignty and self-determination" (A Proclamation—The White House, qrs.ly/6ufre11).

- How does this book help you to understand the significance of Indigenous Peoples' Day?
- How does this book help you to understand the ways Native Peoples have and continue to engage in protecting their culture and the environment?

PATHWAYS

- Continuing to acknowledge Columbus Day is to dismiss the destruction and genocide of Native Peoples by White, European colonizers.

- Indigenous Peoples' Day is one way of centering and honoring Native Peoples.

- Native and Indigenous activism has occurred since colonizers arrived and continues today.

- This book shows that Native Peoples have always advocated for their sovereignty and the protection of their culture.

- Activism continues and has helped to revive Native languages, increase economic opportunities, protect the environment, and so on.

ACCOUNTABILITY

PROMPTS

- How can this book influence your thinking and actions now and in the future?

- How will you remain alert for the ways your particular identities help you to understand a text and the world?

PATHWAYS

- Reflect on ways this text makes a difference to your heart and in your life. Consider commitments you'll make to care for people and communities.

- This text is an invitation for me to think deeply and possibly differently about

_____ and to apply this in my life (when/how)

_____.

Reflection and Accountability for Antiracist Educators:

This text is an invitation for me to think deeply and possibly differently as a reader

_____ and challenges me to make radical changes in my personal and
(in what ways?)

professional life _____.
                    (in what ways?)

CHAPTER FIVE

Help Students **Acquire Racial Literacy**

Part of the perennial family, dandelions survive the winter and flower in spring, returning again and again, year after year. They are notoriously challenging to remove.

In 2023, I presented at a national conference in Chicago, Illinois. I decided to embark on a short excursion and take the Chicago Riverboat Architecture Tour. On the way there, a memorial (Photo 5.1) framing the concrete overpass to the river caught my attention.

■ Photo 5.1 Memorial in Chicago

A memorial in Chicago that reads: "In Honor of Louis Jolliet & Pere Jacques Marquette | the First White Men to Pass Through the Chicago River in 1673 | This tablet is placed by the Illinois Society of the Colonial Dames of America, Under the auspices of the Chicago Historical Society, 1925."

The memorial pays tribute to Louis Jolliet and Père Jacques Marquette with the words, "The first white men to pass through the Chicago River in 1673." Numerous monuments have been erected honoring White explorers and colonizers across many cities in the United States. But this was the first time I'd seen one that so blatantly and literally stated its intent—to honor White men.

Perpendicular to this monument was a mural (Photo 5.2) created by local Ojibwe artist Andrea Carlson.

You are on Potawatomi Land. I read the words again and again and hoped to learn more about this on the tour, particularly about the two conflicting messages at this water-front. I didn't. The tour erased Indigenous Peoples' existence as well as Black ingenuity that contributed greatly to the construction of the city and simply glorified colonizers and White architects and businessmen. Later, I did some research on my own.

I learned that eight months prior to my visit, the *Chicago Tribune* reported that a task force recommended the removal of the Jacques Marquette–Louis Jolliet Memorial because it "reinforces stereotypes about American Indians and glorifies a complicated

■ Photo 5.2   Mural from Bridge

Mural that reads "YOU ARE ON POTAWATOMI LAND." Overlooking the mural from Dusable Bridge/Michigan Avenue. (Photo/Courtesy of Andrea Carlson.)
Native News Online (2021)

and painful history of Western expansion" (Pratt & Yin, 2022). The Chicago Monuments Project released a report recommending a series of new public memorials across Chicago along with the removal of several statues, including one of Christopher Columbus, that were flagged for honoring White supremacy or disrespecting Indigenous Peoples. I also learned that the mural was installed in 2021, and the plan was for it to be on display for at least two years. The tension between the two contrasting narratives about the history of Chicago raises several questions that are also not limited just to this city. Among them are:

Read more about this mural and its artist, Andrea Carlson.

- Whose stories and experiences are etched in stone?

- Whose are painted on canvas and are later added to the landscape temporarily?

Since the 2020 murder of George Floyd in Minneapolis by a White police officer, there has been a concerted effort by officials and activists across many cities to remove statutes that glorify White men who have caused irreparable harm to BIPOC communities. The Southern Poverty Law Center reports that 168 Confederate monuments and symbols around the country have been removed (Southern Poverty Law Center, n.d.). A group of protestors in St. Paul, Minnesota, led by a Native activist, tore down the 10-foot statue of Christopher Columbus outside the state capitol (Pfosi, 2020). A marble statue of Columbus was torn down by protestors in Baltimore and tossed into the city's Inner Harbor (Treisman, 2020). And in Chicago, two statues of Columbus were removed in acknowledgment of the genocide and exploitation of Native Peoples in the United States ("Christopher Columbus," 2020). But this has not occurred without backlash from those who believe such monuments deserve to remain in place. In 2021, a judge reversed the city of Philadelphia's decision to remove a statue of Columbus. In his ruling, Common Pleas Court judge Paula Patrick wrote, "It is baffling to this court as to how the city of Philadelphia wants to remove the statue without any legal basis. The city's entire argument and case is devoid of any legal foundation" (Associated Press, 2021). We must remember that White rage in response to the removal of White supremacist monuments, statues, and symbols was on display prior to the killing of Mr. Floyd. In 2017, the nation and the world saw hundreds of White nationalists in Charlottesville, Virginia. In response to the news of plans to remove a Confederate statue, violence erupted (Elliott, 2022). And we must also remember and uplift the beautiful resistance of Black people. Like Bree Newsome, who 10 days after a White supremacist killed eight Black parishioners and the pastor of their church in 2015 in Charleston, North Carolina, drove to South Carolina, scaled the flagpole outside the state capitol, and removed the Confederate battle flag that flew there (Joiner, 2017).

While some monuments have been removed and sometimes replaced with more honorable historical figures, many students, particularly BIPOC students, attend schools every day that are named after White colonizers and oppressors whose problematic histories are circumvented or hidden (Mitchell, 2020; Smith, 2022). When these schools claim equity as an important value, this is educational gaslighting at its finest. Failing to teach the truth about the individuals whose names are etched in stone across school buildings reinforces inequality and upholds White supremacy. Such reinforcement continues in curriculum and instruction that fails to fully illuminate people and events, past and present.

Consider what you've learned in your K–12 schooling about the following people and events and what facilitated that learning. What strategies were taught to help you to decode issues related to race and understand racism as structural and systemic rather than individual and isolated acts of hate? (There is a blank, reproducible version of the chart in the Appendix; use this to write in your responses.)

K–12 REFLECTIONS
Think about your K–12 schooling. When, how, and what did you learn about the following people and events? What were you also learning about race and racism?

Christopher Columbus, 1492	The arrival of the first Africans in Virginia, 1619	Founding Fathers and the Constitutional Convention, 1787	1819 Civilization Fund Act
The Emancipation Proclamation, 1863	The first Memorial Day Commemoration organized by freed enslaved people on May 1, 1865	Juneteenth, June 19, 1865	Carlisle Indian Industrial School, 1879–1918
1882 Exclusion Act	Tulsa Race Massacre, 1921	Internment of Japanese Americans, 1942–1946	Civil Rights Movement, 1954–1968
The murder of Emmett Till, 1955	Dolores Huerta, 1962	Malcolm X, 1963	The Black Panther Party, 1966
The Brown Berets, 1967	American Indian Movement and Wounded Knee, 1968–1973	Marsha P. Johnson, 1969	JoAnn Tall, 1993

Many of the people and events in this chart were not taught or discussed during my elementary, middle, and high school experiences. For those that were taught, race was often downplayed, and my peers and I were not provided with the language and skills to discuss racism or to understand how racism functions structurally, systemically, and across institutions. It was my parents and family members who taught me about Black history and who took me to places where I could further my learning. Additional learning happened in my adulthood through my own reading and studies. In my work today with educators, it is not uncommon for teachers to share that they were adults when they'd learned about many of the people and events listed. Some were learning about them at the very moment of our discussion. This is significant because when access to the fullness of history is limited, so too is the ability to understand and discuss issues related to race and racism in the present. This pattern is then perpetuated in classrooms and curriculum today.

> *Racial literacy makes it possible for students to analyze the connection between past and contemporary issues.*

At the top of Dr. Yolanda Sealey-Ruiz's (2021) Racial Literacy Development model is interruption—our ability to "interrupt racism and inequality at personal and systemic levels" (p. 8). This, Sealey-Ruiz asserts, requires educators to intentionally "engage the critical readings of texts" about race and racism in order to acquire "language to discuss, problematize, and refute racial stereotypes and racist hierarchical systems in society and in their schools" (pp. 4–5). As mentioned in Chapter 2, Dr. Sealey-Ruiz emphasizes the urgency of this work for BIPOC to reject narratives that paint them as inferior and to resist a victim stance and for White people to adopt an antiracist stance that includes acknowledging and affirming the brilliance, contributions, and resistance of people of color. This doesn't happen when entire people and events are silenced across the curriculum. Teaching students to be racially literate requires students having access to information, ideas, and teaching that help them to acquire language to recognize, analyze, and discuss race and racism, skills I didn't have as a young student. The work of building racial literacy in students includes helping them develop an awareness for injustices related to identity as well as supporting their vocabulary and skills to have thoughtful, productive conversations. Racial literacy makes it possible for students to bridge connections between past and contemporary issues.

Consider again your elementary, middle, and high school experiences as well as your teaching today. How inclusive and accurate were the books, curriculum, and instruction that teach students about history? How inclusive are they now?

Reflect

In books and teaching about history . . .

- Who and what benefits from erasure?

- Why do narrow, oversimplistic, incomplete, and, too often, inaccurate narratives exist?

- What is lost when limited narratives about history prevail?

- What is gained when narratives are widened and sharpened to reveal truthful representations of people and events?

Without racial literacy, we muddle through events and issues not having an accurate understanding of race and the various ways racism exists. When educators are unequipped and ill-prepared, they tread lightly or avoid altogether topics that cause them discomfort. Students then are unable to access instruction that helps them develop tools to transform society. France Winndance Twine (2004) designates the following components of racial literacy. Think about which aspects are addressed in reading instruction and the books that lend themselves to such teachings. (A reproducible version of this chart appears in the Appendix, too.)

Racial Literacy Development and Reading Instruction

COMPONENTS OF RACIAL LITERACY To be racially literate is to . . .	BOOK (TITLE/AUTHOR) Which books help me address one or more of the components of racial literacy?	TEACHING How does my instruction help students to become racially literate?
Recognize race as a contemporary problem		
Understand race as a construct		
Acknowledge intersectionality		
Identify Whiteness and White supremacy		
Develop language and lenses to discuss race and racism		
Acquire the ability to decode racism		

Just imagine the antiracist possibilities of teaching racial literacy with books that support this work. The possibilities and advantages are noted by Price-Dennis and Sealey-Ruiz (2021):

> As applied to teaching and learning in schools, racial literacy is the ability of students to identify, in professionally published and student-generated texts, concepts related to race and racism, and exercise their skills in discussing the complexity of these topics. For example, they investigate how race and racism manifest in the lives of the characters they read about and they are able to make comparisons to their own lives. Students who have this skill are able to discuss the constructions and implications of race, specifically American racism in constructive and forward-thinking ways. (p. 14)

Further, "Those who practice racial literacy have a strong historical knowledge of past events and can make connections to current events" (Price-Dennis & Sealey-Ruiz, 2021, p. 25). In other words, racially literate students can access the truth about race and racism, analyze the world around them, imagine how things can be otherwise, and apply their knowledge as tools of change.

When we teach about the Carlisle Indian Industrial School, students are positioned to understand assimilationism and the ways governmental leaders continue to create policies and laws to oppress and exclude Indigenous Peoples.

When we teach about Emmet Till, then the murders of Trayvon Martin, Michael Brown, Sandra Bland, Breonna Taylor, George Floyd, and others by the police, students recognize this not as a few isolated events by a few bad apples but instead as part of a long legacy of state-sanctioned killings of Black people and systemic racism.

When we teach about Marsha P. Johnson and Stonewall, students are better equipped to discuss LGBTQ+ rights today and the continued fight for equality, specifically how this impacts the Black and Brown transgender community.

When we teach about the Exclusion Act that blocked Chinese workers from legally entering the United States and prevented Chinese immigrants already living there from becoming citizens, after their essential role in building the Transcontinental Railroad, students can recognize the longevity of anti-Asian hatred in this country. They will understand that the violence toward Asian Americans and Pacific Islanders occurring during the COVID-19 pandemic is not new and unprecedented. Students can put into context the sentiments that led to the U.S. internment of Japanese

Americans during World War II. And while people around the world immigrate to the United States every year from everywhere, students are able to notice racial patterns when the borders have been closed to large groups of people. They can put into perspective current U.S. immigration policies that have resulted in the detention, caging, and separation of child migrants and their families at the U.S.–Mexican border, yet admitting more than 271,000 Ukrainian refugees since the Russian invasion of Ukraine began in 2022 (Ainsley, 2023).

When we teach students about JoAnn Tall and her fierce environmental advocacy and work to protect the lands and improve the lives of the Lakota People, then Greta Thunberg does not become the sole face for such advocacy, and students are positioned to learn about the long legacy of Indigenous activism as well as the lives and work of young environmentalists such as Xiuhtezcatl Martinez, Autumn Peltier, and Aslan Tudor.

When we teach racial literacy, students are able to see how relevant the past is to their lives today. They see and understand the connection between the Insurrection at the U.S. Capitol of January 6, 2021 and book banning. Rather than viewing these events and issues as isolated and incidental, racism is recognized as endemic.

As educators, we can acknowledge that facilitating conversations about race and racism can be uncomfortable. But we must also recognize that collectively, we remain stuck when we lean away from the discomfort rather than confront it and work to dismantle inequity in all of its forms. Students need more than just phonemic awareness to read books and to, as Paulo Freire (2000) asserts, read the world. Racial literacy is an essential life skill, one that remains with students and can be applied in all aspects of their lives. Leaning into the six critical lenses during reading instruction helps students develop racial literacy—the collective capacity they'll need to understand how racism functions institutionally as well as the substantial and continuous work that is needed to dismantle it.

Once their roots are firmly established in the landscape, dandelions are difficult to destroy. They take their rightful place in the environment and belong.

HELP STUDENTS ACQUIRE RACIAL LITERACY: PROMPTS AND PATHWAYS

Facilitating conversations about race and racism requires that you plan to mitigate harm to those in your care who are most impacted by racism—BIPOC students. Ongoing reflection on your own racial identity and racial socialization along with interrogating biases is necessary, critical work. To avoid doing this often results in causing more harm to Black and Brown students. Please refer to resources shared in Chapter 1 that can support you in this work.

There is a tendency for teachers and students to say that oppression, specifically racism, happened or happens because of the racial identity of the individual or group being oppressed. (e.g., "This happened because they're Black."). This leads students, especially BIPOC students, to believe that there's something wrong with being Black, Latinx, Asian American, Indigenous, and so on. It is important to shift such language so that students understand that racial oppression occurs because of racist ideas—that Black and Brown skin is not the problem, White supremacy is.

BOOKS FEATURED IN THIS CHAPTER

Stamped (For Kids): Racism, Antiracism, and You, by Sonja Cherry-Paul, Ibram X. Kendi, and Jason Reynolds and illustrated by Rachelle Baker	Page 200
Skin Again, by bell hooks and illustrated by Chris Raschka	Page 204
The Antiracist Kid: A Book About Identity, Justice, and Activism, by Tiffany Jewell and illustrated by Nicole Miles	Page 207
Our Skin: A First Conversation About Race, by Megan Madison, Jessica Ralli, and illustrated by Isabel Roxas	Page 211
Where Are You From? by Yamile Saied Méndez and illustrated by Jaime Kim	Page 215

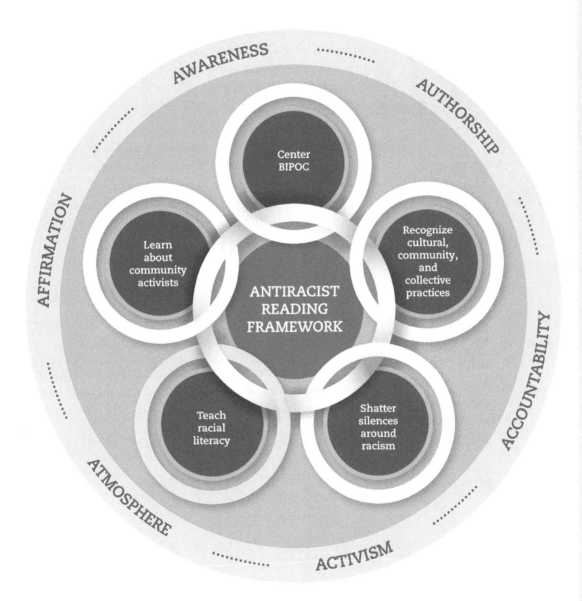

The framework wheel shows, at its center, ANTIRACIST READING FRAMEWORK, surrounded by six linked circles: Center BIPOC; Recognize cultural, community, and collective practices; Shatter silences around racism; Teach racial literacy; Learn about community activists. The outer ring is labeled: AWARENESS, AUTHORSHIP, ACCOUNTABILITY, ACTIVISM, ATMOSPHERE, AFFIRMATION.

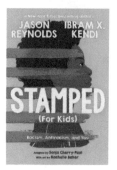

In ***Stamped (For Kids): Racism, Antiracism, and You,*** written by Sonja Cherry-Paul, Ibram X. Kendi, and Jason Reynolds and illustrated by Rachelle Baker, the history of race and racism in the United States is explained. The authors provide key language to analyze historical and contemporary people, events, policies, and laws to help young readers learn the ways racist ideas impact the lives of Black and Brown people and how antiracist ideas lead us toward liberation.

About the Creators

Learn more about the authors by visiting their websites: www.sonjacherrypaul.com, www.jasonwritesbooks.com, and www.ibramxkendi.com. Learn more about the illustrator Rachelle Baker at www.rachellebakerdraws.com.

Use the free educator's guide to further support classroom instruction.

Learn more about using *Stamped (For Kids)* to have discussions about race.

SIX CRITICAL LENSES

Prompts are provided to nurture students' thinking as they read in partnerships, groups, or independently.

Pathways capture the details and ideas that students may notice and think about as they read and respond to the text, and they can be used as guidance for educators to teach into.

AFFIRMATION

PROMPTS

- What are you learning about Black freedom fighters, writers, artists, and activists and their work to liberate the collective?

- What are you learning about the ways antiracist ideas bring people and movements together?

- What are you learning about the resistance and resilience of Black people?

- Frederick Douglass, Phillis Wheatley, Sojourner Truth, Ida B. Wells, Langston Hughes, Audre Lorde, Dr. Martin Luther King Jr., Malcolm X, Angela Davis, Alicia Garza, Patrisse Cullors, and Opal Tometi are examples of Black people who worked on behalf of the collective and those who continue the work of using words, art, and collective actions to fight for the liberation of Black people.

- Antiracist ideas bring people and movements together to fight for racial justice, such as the Greensboro sit-in, the Civil Rights Movement, the Black Panther Party for Self-Defense, and the Black Lives Matter Movement.

- Black people have always resisted racist ideas and have fought bravely for equality. Black people have endured the horrors of enslavement, segregation, and continued racism and continue to survive within a racist society.

AWARENESS

PROMPTS

Segregationist: "One who expresses the idea that one racial group is permanently inferior and supports policy that keeps groups separate" (p. 155).

Assimilationist: "One who expresses the racist idea that a racial group is culturally or behaviorally interior, believing that a racial group can be changed for the better by acting like another racial group" (p. 151).

Antiracist: "One who expresses the idea that racial groups are equal and who supports policy that reduces racial inequity" (p. 151).

- What are you learning about words that can be used to analyze and understand people and their ideas across history and even today?

- What are you learning about the ways people become tied to racist ideas?

- What are you learning about ways to disrupt racist ideas?

PATHWAYS

- The words *segregationist, assimilationist,* and *antiracist* help me to recognize social, political, and economic conditions created to oppress Black and Brown people and the untangling of policies, laws, and practices that antiracists have and continue to accomplish.

- Racist ideas are embedded in many books, movies, and words shared by politicians, leaders, and more.

- When racist ideas are not thought about critically, interrogated, and interrupted, people can believe them and become tied to them. Antiracists work to disrupt racist ideas.

AUTHORSHIP

PROMPTS

- Who are the creators of this text?

- How do their identities influence this work?

- What is their motivation for creating this text?

PATHWAYS

- Sonja Cherry-Paul, who adapted *Stamped (For Kids),* is a former educator and antiracist scholar. During author visits, she shares this with students: "It should not be lost on readers that a Black woman adapted *Stamped for Kids* and the myriad ways this matters. I amplified the role and work of Black women in the ongoing pursuit for Black liberation. This was deliberate and intentional, not at all accidental or coincidental, as I thought deeply about widening and sharpening understandings about history."

- In an interview (2021), Cherry-Paul explains part of her motivation for adapting *Stamped (For Kids)* and how it helps young readers move beyond an understanding of racism as name-calling and recognize larger issues at work. "What we need to do is shift to systems to help kids understand that there is a legacy of systems treating people unfairly, and giving them examples of that across time so that they can understand how we got here." (Interview found here: qrs.ly/nefrdyj).

ATMOSPHERE

PROMPTS

- How does this text reflect the identities and lived experiences of the characters/people?

- How does it reflect your identities and lived experiences?

- In what ways does this book convey and bring you joy?

PATHWAYS

- Setting: Readers are able to look across history at how anti-Blackness and racist ideas developed.

- Perspective: The authors reveal truths that are often omitted from discussions and texts about enslavement and racism.

- Figurative Language/Imagery: Discuss the metaphor used across the book: "Rope can be used to tie, pull, hold, and lift. How do people become tied to racist and antiracist ideas? Who are the people pulling at each end? How do racist ideas hold people down? How do antiracist ideas lift people up? How did things get so tangled in the first place? And who are the people working to unravel this mess?" (pp. 3–4)

- Mood/Tone: Truth and hope bolstered by intentions, commitment, and actions can lead us toward an antiracist future.

- Theme: antiracism, truth, hope

PROMPTS

- How does this book help you to recognize antiracists and their work for racial justice?

- How does this book inspire you to work for racial justice?

PATHWAYS

- Recognize antiracists by their actions—the words they say and the work they do in their communities, and how their work benefits those who are most harmed by racism.

- Work for racial justice by believing the world can be good and that people can change. Keep talking about race and learning about racism. Learn from antiracists in books and in the community and apply what is learned.

ACCOUNTABILITY

PROMPTS

- How can this book influence your thinking and actions now and in the future?

- How will you remain alert for the ways your particular identities help you to understand a text and the world?

PATHWAYS

- Reflect on ways this text makes a difference to your heart and in your life. Consider commitments you'll make to care for people and communities.

- This text is an invitation for me to think deeply and possibly differently about

  _____ and to apply this in my life (when/how)

  _____.

Reflection and Accountability for Antiracist Educators:

This text is an invitation for me to think deeply and possibly differently as a reader

_____ and challenges me to make radical changes in my personal and
(in what ways?)

professional life _____.
(in what ways?)

Skin Again, written by bell hooks and illustrated by Chris Raschka, invites students to recognize both the beauty of skin color and its limitations for truly knowing the heart and mind of a person. hooks provides young readers with an initial understanding of race, conceived notions made around racial identity, and the importance of and its insufficiency valuing people for who they really are.

About the Creators

Learn more about bell hooks and Chris Raschka by reading the articles linked in the QR codes.

bell hooks's last interview

Chris Raschka: The Habits of an Artist

Six Critical Lenses

Prompts are provided to nurture students' thinking as they read in partnerships, groups, or independently.

Pathways capture the details and ideas that students may notice and think about as they read and respond to the text, and they can be used as guidance for educators to teach into.

AFFIRMATION

PROMPTS

- What are you learning about skin color?
- What makes you, you?

PATHWAYS

- Skin is a covering.
- Everyone's skin color is special and unique.
- Skin color is one part of a person's identity.
- The things that make me who I am include the people I love, the things I love to do, all of the stories inside me, and the ways I imagine myself.

AWARENESS

PROMPTS

- What are you learning about ways people try to tell what someone is like based only on their skin color?
- What are you learning about how we truly come to know one another?

PATHWAYS

- Sometimes people think they can know what a person is like based on the color of their skin, but this isn't true.
- When we talk, listen, and care about a person, we get to know who they really are on the inside.

AUTHORSHIP

PROMPTS

- Who are the creators of this text?
- How do their identities influence this work?
- What is their motivation for creating this text?

PATHWAYS

- In an interview, bell hooks describes herself as a Black woman and feminist who was raised in Kentucky. She has written numerous books on race, gender, and identity.
- Chris Raschka is an artist who lives and creates in New York City.
- These creators have created several books together for children.

ATMOSPHERE

PROMPTS

- How does this text reflect the identities and lived experiences of the characters/people?
- How does it reflect your identities and lived experiences?
- In what ways does this book convey and bring you joy?

PATHWAYS

- Setting: This nonfiction book provides an initial exploration of skin color, race, and identity.
- Perspective: Readers learn that skin color is only one small part of a person's identity.
- Figurative Language/Imagery: Invite students to discuss this line from the book and what it means to them: "You have got to come inside and open your heart way wide."

- Mood/Tone: An encouraging call to look at what's inside, not just what's outside, in order to value and appreciate one another.
- Theme: identity, skin color, race

ACTIVISM

PROMPTS

- How can you appreciate people for who they are?
- How can "coming close" be a way to take action against judging people based on skin color?

PATHWAYS

- People can appreciate each other for who they are by learning their stories and finding out what a person is like on the inside.
- hooks says, "Coming close and letting go of who you might think I am." This can help people to resist racist ideas and judgments based on skin color and see people as real and human, and love them for who they are.

ACCOUNTABILITY

PROMPTS

- How can this book influence your thinking and actions now and in the future?
- How will you remain alert for the ways your particular identities help you to understand a text and the world?

PATHWAYS

- Reflect on ways this text makes a difference to your heart and in your life. Consider commitments you'll make to care for people and communities.
- This text is an invitation for me to think deeply and possibly differently about

  _____ and to apply this in my life (when/how)

  _____.

Reflection and Accountability for Antiracist Educators:

This text is an invitation for me to think deeply and possibly differently as a reader

_____ and challenges me to make radical changes in my personal and
      (in what ways?)

professional life _____.
        (in what ways?)

The Antiracist Kid: A Book About Identity, Justice, and Activism, written by Tiffany Jewell and illustrated by Nicole Miles, helps readers understand key vocabulary and ideas to build racial literacy and become antiracist.

About the Creators

Learn more about the creators by visiting their websites at www.tiffanymjewell.com and www.nicolemillo.com.

SIX CRITICAL LENSES

Prompts are provided to nurture students' thinking as they read in partnerships, groups, or independently.

Pathways capture the details and ideas that students may notice and think about as they read and respond to the text, and they can be used as guidance for educators to teach into.

AFFIRMATION

PROMPTS

- What are you learning about the various parts of your identity?
- What are you learning about similarities and differences of people?
- How does this book strengthen your ability to talk about differences?

PATHWAYS

- We each have various personal and social identities that make up who we are.
- Genetically, people are much more similar than different. Our differences make us unique.
- Understanding words such as *race, ethnicity, stereotype,* and the various parts that make up people's identities helps me have more tools to talk about identity in antiracist ways.

AWARENESS

PROMPTS

- What are you learning about meanings and differences of words like *fairness* and *justice, equality* and *equity?* Why does this matter?

- What are you learning about power—who has it and how it is used?

- What are you learning about oppression?

PATHWAYS

- Words like *fairness* and *equality* are about people being treated the same. *Justice* and *equity* are about people getting what they need to thrive.

- Everyone has power, but people of the dominant culture have much more than others. Having more power means having more control and privileges in society. This imbalance of power can cause beliefs that some people are superior or inferior. Inaccurate and unjust ideas about race and gender as well as other identities are used to support beliefs about superiority and inferiority.

- There are various forms of oppression such as colonization, ableism, heterosexism, racism, and so on. People can experience oppression in intersectional ways across many institutions (such as health care, policing, education, etc.).

AUTHORSHIP

PROMPTS

- Who are the creators of this text?

- How do their identities influence this work?

- What is their motivation for creating this text?

PATHWAYS

- In the letter to the reader, Tiffany Jewell shares that she is "a teacher, mama, and antiracist adult" and a "Black, biracial, cisgender woman and a Person of the Global Majority."

- Nicole Miles shares that she is from The Bahamas and currently lives in the United Kingdom.

- Tiffany Jewell shares that she has written this book to help readers understand what antiracism is.

- Her hope is readers "help to make this an antiracist world."

ATMOSPHERE

PROMPTS

- How does this text reflect the identities and lived experiences of the characters/people?

- How does it reflect your identities and lived experiences?

- In what ways does this book convey and bring you joy?

- Setting: This book provides readers with language and ways of analyzing the world that are antiracist.

- Perspective: Readers have agency to work toward an antiracist future by learning about identity, justice, and activism and applying this knowledge in their daily lives.

- Figurative Language/Imagery: Invite readers to consider what they're learning and how this informs their ideas about what it means to be antiracist.

- Mood/Tone: This book offers readers tools to understand themselves, their communities, and ways to dismantle injustices.

- Theme: agency, antiracism, identity, justice, activism

ACTIVISM

PROMPTS

- How does this book help you to understand ways to advocate for yourself and others?

- How does this book help you to understand what activism is and ways to be an activist in your daily life?

PATHWAYS

- I can advocate for myself by believing in my own self-worth, speaking up about words and actions that are harmful when I can, asking for help, and understanding that I will make mistakes and can take responsibility for them.

- Activism is the way people take action against injustice. There are many ways to be an activist: writing to leaders about laws that should be changed or that are needed, deciding where to spend money in order to support People of the Global Majority and not supporting people who discriminate, and working with peers and the community to address injustice.

ACCOUNTABILITY

PROMPTS

- How can this book influence your thinking and actions now and in the future?

- How will you remain alert for the ways your particular identities help you to understand a text and the world?

PATHWAYS

- Reflect on ways this text makes a difference to your heart and in your life. Consider commitments you'll make to care for people and communities.

- This text is an invitation for me to think deeply and possibly differently about

  _____ and to apply this in my life (when/how)

  _____.

Reflection and Accountability for Antiracist Educators:

This text is an invitation for me to think deeply and possibly differently as a reader

_____ and challenges me to make radical changes in my personal and
   (in what ways?)

professional life _____.
                       (in what ways?)

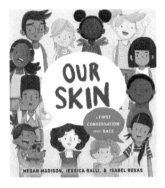

Our Skin: A First Conversation About Race, written by Megan Madison, Jessica Ralli, and illustrated by Isabel Roxas, debunks the myth that young children do not notice skin color, demystifies how people get their color, and provides language and definitions of race and racism.

About the Creators

Learn more about the creators by visiting their website at www.firstconversations.com.

SIX CRITICAL LENSES

Prompts are provided to nurture students' thinking as they read in partnerships, groups, or independently.

Pathways capture the details and ideas that students may notice and think about as they read and respond to the text, and they can be used as guidance for educators to teach into.

Review the educator's guide for additional resources to support conversations about race and racism.

Learn more about the creators by accessing this discussion.

AFFIRMATION

PROMPTS

- What are you learning about the uniqueness of skin color?
- What are you learning about how we all get our color?
- What do you admire about your skin color?

PATHWAYS

- People in the same family can have different skin colors.
- Everyone's skin color is beautiful and different.
- Skin color comes from melanin that makes our skin colors range from dark to light.

AWARENESS

PROMPTS

- What are you understanding about the word *race*—its history and its purpose?

- What are you understanding about the word *racism*—how it happens and how it makes people feel?

- How do the words *race* and *racism* relate to skin color?

- What is you understanding about how people can use skin color to make unfair judgments about each other?

PATHWAYS

- Race was made up in order for White people to believe they were better than everyone else.

- Race isn't real, but racism is.

- Racism means that White people are treated better.

- Racism gives White people more power than anyone else.

- Examples of racism include hurtful words said to people, harmful ideas about people, and unfair actions done to people.

- Racism is always hurtful, harmful, unfair, and wrong.

AUTHORSHIP

PROMPTS

- Who are the creators of this text?

- How do their identities influence this work?

- What is their motivation for creating this text?

PATHWAYS

- Megan Madison shares that she "loves being a Black queer woman and she dreams of justice." She is a former preschool teacher.

- Jessica Ralli is also a former preschool teacher. She shares, "As a white, cisgender mom of two young white children—having intentional conversations around race, white privilege, gender, body liberation and consent has been as essential as potty training and bedtime stories."

- Isabel Roxas is an illustrator and author and shares, "She was born in the Philippines, raised on luscious mangoes, old wives' tales, and monsoon rains."

- Megan Madison and Jessica Ralli discuss the ways their identities and backgrounds inspired them to write a book that was clear and powerful for young readers learning about race.

ATMOSPHERE

PROMPTS

- How does this text reflect the identities and lived experiences of the characters/people?

- How does it reflect your identities and lived experiences?

- In what ways does this book convey and bring you joy?

PATHWAYS

- Setting: This book demonstrates the various ways racism works in our lives.

- Perspective: Children can see skin color and the ways race and racism impact their lives.

- Figurative Language/Imagery: Invite students to discuss this part of the text and what they've noticed in their lives: "Just by looking at someone, we can't tell who they are on the inside. But sometimes people try to anyway."

- Mood/Tone: This book can help students acquire knowledge about skin color, race, and racism in order to determine how they can imagine a more just and antiracist world.

- Themes: skin color, race, racism, racial justice

ACTIVISM

PROMPTS

- How does this book help you to imagine a racially just world?

- What actions can you take to help achieve this vision?

PATHWAYS

- A racially just world is one where BIPOC have the power and resources to thrive.

- A racially just world is one where White people do not have power over BIPOC and are not treated better than BIPOC just because they're White.

- Achieving the vision of a racially just world includes:
  - Appreciating and respecting all people
  - Interrupting racist ideas when they are shared
  - Caring about unfairness happening to people based on race and doing whatever can be done to change this

ACCOUNTABILITY

PROMPTS

- How can this book influence your thinking and actions now and in the future?

- How will you remain alert for the ways your particular identities help you to understand a text and the world?

- Reflect on ways this text makes a difference to your heart and in your life. Consider commitments you'll make to care for people and communities.

- This text is an invitation for me to think deeply and possibly differently about

  _____ and to apply this in my life (when/how)

  _____.

Reflection and Accountability for Antiracist Educators:

This text is an invitation for me to think deeply and possibly differently as a reader

_____ and challenges me to make radical changes in my personal and
    (in what ways?)

professional life _____.
               (in what ways?)

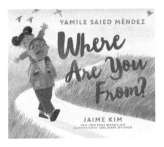

Where Are You From? written by Yamile Saied Méndez and illustrated Jaime Kim, is the story of a little girl who is questioned about her identity based on her appearance. Her grandfather provides her with tools to recognize the question *Where are you from?* as racially coded language, counter assumptions made about her identity, and strengthen her sense of self.

About the Creators

Learn about Yamile Saied Méndez by visiting her website: www.yamilemendez.com.

And learn more about Jaime Kim by visiting her website: www.jaimekim.com.

View a video of a read-aloud of *Where Are You From?* by the author.

Six Critical Lenses

Prompts are provided to nurture students' thinking as they read in partnerships, groups, or independently.

Pathways capture the details and ideas that students may notice and think about as they read and respond to the text, and they can be used as guidance for educators to teach into.

AFFIRMATION

PROMPTS

Your identity is all of the things that make you, you. This includes skin color, hair texture, languages spoken, race, ethnicity, nationality, gender, religion, dis/ability, who we love, things we like to do, and more.

- What does the little girl learn about her identity from her Abuelo?

- How does Abuelo make her feel?

PATHWAYS

- Abuelo tells her about the places, people, experiences, and histories that are part of her identity (e.g., the Pampas, gaucho, the environment, ancestors who were enslaved, Abuelo's heart).

PROMPTS

Microaggressions are direct or indirect discriminatory statements or actions that intentionally or unintentionally target individuals or groups of people who are marginalized.

- On the surface, asking someone where they're from can seem like a question that isn't harmful. What are you learning about how this question made the main character feel?

- How can this question be a microaggression?

PATHWAYS

- The question "Where are you from?" makes the main character feel confused, frustrated, doubtful, sad, excluded, and so on.

- The question can be a microaggression when assumptions are made based on a person's appearance that they don't "belong" or aren't from a specific place.

- Assumptions made about a person's identity (e.g., skin color, hair texture, facial features, languages spoken, etc.) are used to inform their ideas about who belongs and who doesn't.

AUTHORSHIP

PROMPTS

- Who are the creators of this text?

- How do their identities influence this work?

- What is their motivation for creating this text?

PATHWAYS

- On her website, the author shares that she was born and raised in Argentina but has lived in Utah for most of her life and she taught herself English: "Yamile Méndez hopes that readers will see themselves reflected in her characters or the situations they go through. She also hopes that if readers come from different backgrounds, they may gain a new perspective on the world through her writing."

- The illustrator shares on her website that she was born in South Korea and moved to the United States when she was 18: "Her favorite things are the sun, the moon, the sky and stars—which is why they always creep into her artwork."

- In an interview, Méndez discusses the power of writing, particularly for marginalized communities. She shares, "Writing is a revolutionary act in itself, especially for members of marginalized communities who have sometimes been incorrectly labeled 'voiceless' through the years. We have a voice, and traditionally marginalized authors have been writing for a long time. The stories they created paved the way for me, and authors like me, to tell our stories today. Not only stories of resistance and oppression, but also of joy and fulfillment, of victory and love—which are revolutionary concepts, too. The mind can change when exposed to different ideas and worldviews, and as an author, I recognize the power and responsibility I have to be as authentic as possible in every word attributed to me" (Jackson, 2020).

ATMOSPHERE

PROMPTS

- How does this text reflect the identities and lived experiences of the characters/people?

- How does it reflect your identities and lived experiences?

- In what ways does this book convey and bring you joy?

PATHWAYS

- Setting: Readers learn the various places, including school, where children like the main character are forced to navigate questions about their identity, as well as the importance of family and community.

- Perspective: The main character's feelings of doubt, confusion, frustration, and later, because of Abuelo, pride about her identity are shown across the story.

- Figurative Language/Imagery: Discuss the power and purpose of all of the ways Abuelo answers the question "Where am I from?" with metaphors about the main character's identity.

- Mood/Tone: The mood of the main character shifts from frustration, confusion, and doubt to self-assuredness, pride, and love.

- Theme: identity, culture, family, love

ACTIVISM

PROMPTS

- How does this story inspire you to think differently about asking "Where are you from?"

- How can you recognize the importance of identity to everyone?

PATHWAYS

- Rather than making assumptions about a person's identity and asking someone where they're from, we can focus on being a friend, waiting until people decide to share parts of their identity, and listening to who they tell us they are.

- Our identities shape how we view, navigate, and are treated in the world. We can learn about people and their identities and experiences. We can respect each other's uniqueness.

PROMPTS

- How can this book influence your thinking and actions now and in the future?
- How will you remain alert for the ways your particular identities help you to understand a text and the world?

PATHWAYS

- Reflect on ways this text makes a difference to your heart and in your life. Consider commitments you'll make to care for people and communities.
- This text is an invitation for me to think deeply and possibly differently about

  _____ and to apply this in my life (when/how)

  _____.

Reflection and Accountability for Antiracist Educators:

This text is an invitation for me to think deeply and possibly differently as a reader

_____ and challenges me to make radical changes in my personal and
       (in what ways?)

professional life _____.
                    (in what ways?)

CHAPTER SIX

Learn About Community Activists

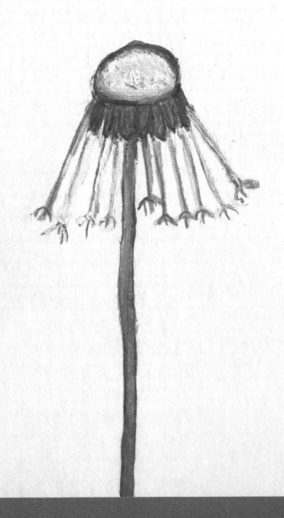

"But dandelions were what she chiefly saw. Yellow jewels for everyday studding the patched green dress of her backyard. She liked their demure prettiness second to their everydayness; for in that latter quality she thought she saw a picture of herself, and it was comforting to find that what was common could also be a flower."

—Gwendolyn Brooks, *Maud Martha*, 1993 (1953), p. 2

Where I'm From by Sonja Cherry-Paul

I'm from the Projects
from shared terraces on every floor
and benches in front of buildings
where neighbors sit all summer long.
From up North and down South
Aunt Mary's Everything Room
where strips of colorful cloth become new quilts
for my bed.
I'm from government cheese
from black outs and block parties with tables full of food
Run DMC, Donna Summer, The O'Jays, and Earth Wind and Fire
blasting from speakers taller than me.
I'm from open hydrants for spraying and drinking
cooling off in the summer heat
From handball, double dutch, and tag
From red light greenlight 1, 2, 3
and bottle tops packed with clay
playing skully until sunset.
I'm from pizza slices
So big they require both hands
Big enough to eat with Samantha and Valerie
washed down with strawberry soda.
I'm from community centers
Halloween parties and Black history events
Food drives, coat drives, and sign-ups for basketball tournaments
I'm from volunteering for change —
youth programming, political campaigns, neighborhood improvement
Power from and to the people
Hope, strength, and love abound

Growing up, examples of activism were always around me. The summer breakfast program at a local school cafeteria. Empty lots filled with garbage and glass turned into community gardens. Fathers and uncles creating and coaching softball leagues to keep young boys out of gangs. Block parties organized to bring the community together for the purposes of fun, disseminating information about issues and events, and strengthening bonds between neighbors. My mother joining the PTA and using that platform to help parents resist the school's "English only" policy and practice that stripped children of their language and identity. Throughout my childhood, my neighbors and parents demonstrated that the responsibility to make change was theirs and that such change should benefit the community, particularly those who were most disenfranchised.

Like many students, I also learned a few things about activism and activists in school. Books featuring historical figures such as Dr. Martin Luther King Jr., Rosa Parks, as well as young activists today such as Malala Yousafzai and Marley Dias and others can be found in many classroom and school libraries. But there can also be limitations: Curriculum and books can present whitewashed versions of activists and issues. When learning about Dr. King and the Civil Rights Movement, for example, children can be taught in ways that cause them to believe that segregation and racism are relics of the past. Curriculum and teachings about activists have proliferated the lone-hero narrative, removing individuals and achievements from the collective work of many. Further, certain activists such as Angela Davis, Malcolm X, and the Black Panther Party can be misrepresented or erased from the historical landscape.

The current landscape of book censorship and banning creates additional challenges to teaching and learning about activists and activism. Books that provide inclusive perspectives that expose White supremacy are seen as threats, rather than White supremacy itself. *Ruby Bridges Goes to School: My True Story* by Ruby Bridges (2009) is one example. Moms of Liberty, a parent group working to block students' access to books about historical events and racism, targeted this book, objecting to parts of the writing (e.g., "large crowd of angry white people who didn't want Black children in a white school") and claiming that the end of the story fails to offer "redemption." In 1960, when Ruby Bridges walked past the large group of angry White people that waited for her each morning on her way to school, could she imagine that decades later a whole new generation of angry White people would be trying to suppress her story? And what sort of redemption would the truthful telling of Ruby Bridges's story offer this angry mob of White people? Students' understanding of the world and themselves is obstructed when their access is limited only to perspectives that are incomplete and even false about people and their lived experiences.

Think about your own curriculum and instruction. What is the teaching that helps students develop ideas about activism—ways they, along with their communities, can make observations about issues and the collective work of change-making? (A reproducible version of this chart is available in the Appendix.)

CONSIDERING CURRICULUM, BOOKS, AND ACTIVISM	
Who are the activists your students learn about and under what circumstances?	
Which activists are silenced? Why? For what purpose?	
What understandings do your students have about activism? What has facilitated these understandings?	

As teachers of reading, our instruction has the power to help students understand that activism is about working for the good of the collective and advocating for those who are underrepresented, disenfranchised, and oppressed. Activists amplify the voices of those who are marginalized and work alongside them to fight for change. In order for students to develop such understandings, educators must see themselves as activists whose work is about much more than teaching students to decode words. Our work is about teaching in ways that confront the issues impacting our students' daily lives. This critical love, as theorized by Dr. Yolanda Sealey-Ruiz (2021), is an "ethical commitment" requiring us to connect with the communities we serve, understanding their concerns, their values, and the work they're doing each day to bring about change. There are many examples of this kind of commitment in students' communities that educators should know about and make accessible to students.

Like Kamal Bell, who observed food scarcity in his community as a child. Bell noticed the interconnectedness of race and economic status resulting in communities being deprived of healthy food. Today, Bell leads Sankofa Farms, a multifaceted agricultural entity where he mentors African American boys and young men and works to create sustainable food sources for people of color in rural and urban areas he grew up in. (Learn more here: qrs.ly/ohfrdyp)

Like Priya Vulchi and Winona Guo (2018), who realized they had almost finished high school without ever having any real, substantive conversations about race and racism in their school. Vulchi and Guo decided to defer their college admissions and travel to each of the 50 states of the nation to collect stories about race and intersectionality. Vulchi and Guo include these stories along with research on the importance of racial literacy in their book, *Tell Me Who You Are*. (Learn more here: qrs.ly/ntfrdyt)

Like Edha Gupta (2021) and Christina Ellis, two high school seniors in York County, Pennsylvania, who took sustained action against their school's board after banning a list of hundreds of books and resources. Gupta and Ellis organized and led daily protests with their peers, informing their community about their concerns. They wrote letters to the editor of their local paper, activated social media, and drew national attention and the support of prominent activists such as Bernice King, the daughter of Rev. Dr. Martin Luther King Jr. Their persistence and pressure led the board to reverse its decision. (Learn more here: qrs.ly/jgfrdyx)

There is much that can be learned from the work of these young activists about anti-racism, activism, and liberation.

Reflect

As you think about activists and activism . . .

- What are some of the social issues and concerns facing the school community you serve?

- Who is harmed and who benefits by these issues? How?

- Who are the people/groups working to improve conditions for those who are most impacted by these issues?

- What does their work entail? What strategies and tools do they use in their work?

- How can you include the work of these activists in your teaching?

Ladson-Billings (2017) positions the work of critical consciousness as the "'so what' factor" (p. 145) that links what students learn in school to what matters in their lives beyond school. She notes the following:

> Projects like "saving the rainforest," "recycling," or "animal rights" may emerge because the teacher has a deep passion for them. However, racial profiling, mass incarceration, or inequity in suspension may be impacting students directly. These more politically volatile topics are ones that teachers may want to hold at arm's length. But failure to engage them is exactly why students do not trust schools to be places that deal honestly and forthrightly with the issues of their lives. (p. 146)

Antiracist teaching raises students' sociopolitical consciousness and helps them to question, challenge, and confront the *right now* issues they are experiencing and concerned about. I am reminded of Yvonne, a third-grade teacher working in New York City, who describes herself as an antiracist educator and activist who is "careful not to let her teaching become static and detached from the lived experiences of the children in her classroom." In an article for *Education Leadership* (Cherry-Paul, 2023), I wrote about this teacher-activist. Yvonne shared, "I'm a firm believer that the work we do in a unit or in a curriculum doesn't just stay in school—it needs to transfer to their real lives. . . . We're in the business of building humans who can do more than just what we assign them in the classroom." Antiracist teaching branches out beyond classrooms and schools and into communities, transforming students' lives.

Reading instruction that engages students in learning about people who work to improve their communities can help students understand that activists are not just the names of famous people written about in books; activists are all around them. Using the six critical lenses, students come to realize that activism is about planting seeds of hope and the sustained actions that lead to transformation. Students are empowered to see themselves as activists who work in community with others around them toward justice for their neighborhoods, schools, and themselves.

Dandelion seeds are sensitive to wind direction and respond differently. Some fly north. Others fly south, east, west, or a direction in between. This selective dispersal is deliberate. Such resistance helps dandelions avoid all of their seeds flying in the same direction, resulting in a wider distribution of seeds across a landscape.

LEARN ABOUT COMMUNITY ACTIVISTS: PROMPTS AND PATHWAYS

Facilitating conversations about race and racism requires that you plan to mitigate harm to those in your care who are most impacted by racism—BIPOC students. Ongoing reflection on your own racial identity and racial socialization along with interrogating biases is necessary, critical work. To avoid doing this often results in causing more harm to Black and Brown students. Please refer to resources shared in Chapter 1 that can support you in this work.

There is a tendency for teachers and students to say that oppression, specifically racism, happened or happens because of the racial identity of the individual or group being oppressed. (e.g., "This happened because they're Black."). This leads students, especially BIPOC students, to believe that there's something wrong with being Black, Latinx, Asian American, Indigenous, and so on. It is important to shift such language so that students understand that racial oppression occurs because of racist ideas—that Black and Brown skin is not the problem, White supremacy is.

BOOKS FEATURED IN THIS CHAPTER

We Have a Dream: Meet 30 Young Indigenous People and People of Color Protecting the Planet, by Dr. Mya-Rose Craig and illustrated by Sabrena Khadija	Page 228
Autumn Peltier, Water Warrior, by Carole Lindstrom and illustrated by Bridget George	Page 232
Resistance: My Story of Activism, by Frantzy Luzincourt	Page 236
Young Water Protectors . . . A Story About Standing Rock, by Aslan Tudor and Kelly Tudor	Page 240
The Light She Feels Inside, by Gwendolyn Wallace and illustrated by Olivia Duchess	Page 244
More Than Peach: Changing the World . . . One Crayon at a Time! by Bellen Woodard and illustrated by Fanny Liem	Page 248

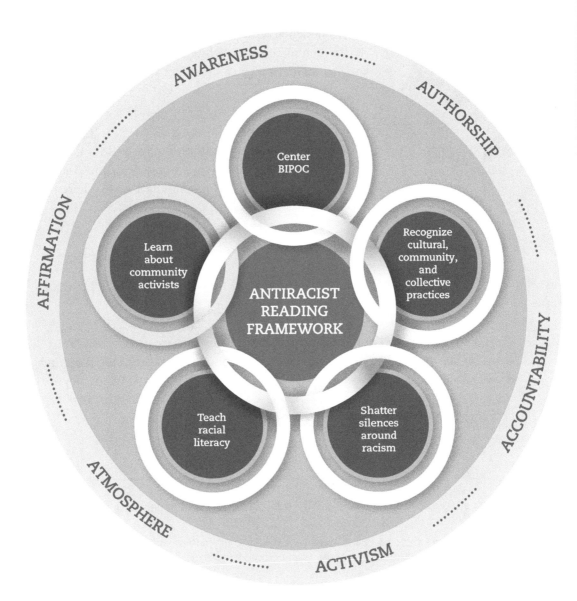

In *We Have A Dream: Meet 30 Young Indigenous People and People of Color Protecting the Planet,* written by Dr. Mya-Rose Craig and illustrated by Sabrena Khadija, readers learn about the work of young environmental activists who are disproportionately impacted by environmental injustice while simultaneously working to improve conditions in their communities and in the world.

Watch and listen to the author discuss her motivation for writing this book.

About the Creators

Learn more about the author, Dr. Mya-Rose Craig, aka Birdgirl, at her website: www.birdgirluk.com. And learn more about the illustrator, Sabrena Khadija, here: www .sabrenakhadija.com.

There are important distinctions and nuances around the words *Indigenous, Native American, American Indian, tribe,* and *nation.* In my discussion of texts, I use the language and terminology the author uses. It's important to listen for who people tell us they are and to teach children to listen as well and to respect what they are learning. Learn more here about the impact of words and using accurate terms: qrs.ly/cufrdvt.

SIX CRITICAL LENSES

Prompts are provided to nurture students' thinking as they read in partnerships, groups, or independently.

Pathways capture the details and ideas that students may notice and think about as they read and respond to the text, and they can be used as guidance for educators to teach into.

AFFIRMATION

PROMPTS

- What are you learning about Indigenous People and people of color who are activists in the environmental movement?

- In what ways do their racial/ethnic/cultural identities influence their activism?

- There are many Indigenous People and people of color around the world who are environmental activists.

- Their racial/ethnic/cultural identities inform the work they do as activists by understanding the specific issues that impact their communities.

- As insiders who are from and live in the places they work, activists are able to use expertise, methods, and strategies that are specific to their communities.

AWARENESS

PROMPTS

Environmental injustice and *environmental racism* are terms used to describe the ways communities of color and the poor are disproportionately exposed to and impacted by environmental hazards.

Dr. May-Rose Craig shares, "Indigenous People and People of Color are disproportionately affected by climate change. And yet they are underrepresented within the environmental movement."

- Greta Thunberg, a Swedish environmental activist, has become the most prominently recognized person in the environmental movement. How does racism show up in the environmental movement?

- What are you learning about various issues environmental activists are working to challenge and change?

PATHWAYS

- Although Indigenous Peoples and communities of color experience environmental racism the most, they are recognized the least in the environmental movement.

- Greta Thunberg is White and most visible in the environmental movement, even though there are many Indigenous People and people of color who are doing important work in the environmental movement and have been activists long before Thunberg's recognition.

- Lack of recognition of Indigenous Peoples and communities of color in the environmental movement is racism; it's a way to diminish and erase their work and contributions.

- A focus solely on Greta Thunberg takes attention and resources away from communities of color who need them most.

- There are numerous issues that environmental activists work to challenge and change such as rising sea levels, reducing waste, protecting Indigenous land, eliminating deforestation, and more.

- These issues are distinct and interconnected.

AUTHORSHIP

PROMPTS

- Who are the creators of this text?

- How do their identities influence this work?

- What is their motivation for creating this text?

PATHWAYS

- Dr. Mya-Rose Craig shares that she is "a British Bangladeshi naturalist, environmentalist, and campaigner for equal rights."

- Sabrena Khadija shares that she is "a Sierra Leonean American illustrator" and a "Black creative" who "takes a lot of pride in creating work that helps others feel seen and inspired not only to see beauty within themselves but to recognize and acknowledge that of others."

- Dr. Maya-Rose Craig shares part of her purpose for writing this book, stating, "I believe that to protect the environment is to leverage the input and contributions of as many people as possible. But it's not for me to speak for others. The time has come for people to speak for themselves."

ATMOSPHERE

PROMPTS

- How does this text reflect the identities and lived experiences of the characters/people?

- How does it reflect your identities and lived experiences?

- In what ways does this book convey and bring you joy?

PATHWAYS

- Setting: Readers learn about 30 Indigenous People and People of Color environmental activists from around the world.

- Perspective: The advocacy and activism of Indigenous People and People of color has been minimized and invisibilized.

- Figurative Language/Imagery: Dr. Mya Rose-Craig and each of the activists in this book share their dreams. Invite students to discuss their dreams for the environment.

- Mood/Tone: This book provides empowering portraits that introduce and discuss each activist, their work, and their dream.

- Theme: activism, environmental movement, environmental injustice

ACTIVISM

PROMPTS

Dr. Mya-Rose Craig extends an invitation to readers to "cultivate your own dream" and offers several suggestions to get started.

- What are you learning about activism as you read this book?

- How might you join in the effort to protect the environment?

PATHWAYS

- Activism is strong when it emerges from the communities activists are from.

- Activists think about their expertise and strengths and apply them as they work to protect their communities and the environment.

- Joining the effort to protect the environment can happen by learning about environmental issues, connecting with activists in the community, teaching the community and others about ways to help, and so on.

ACCOUNTABILITY

PROMPTS

- How can this book influence your thinking and actions now and in the future?

- How will you remain alert for the ways your particular identities help you to understand a text and the world?

PATHWAYS

- Reflect on ways this text makes a difference to your heart and in your life. Consider commitments you'll make to care for people and communities.

- This text is an invitation for me to think deeply and possibly differently about

_____ and to apply this in my life (when/how)

_____.

Reflection and Accountability for Antiracist Educators:

This text is an invitation for me to think deeply and possibly differently as a reader

_____ and challenges me to make radical changes in my personal and
   (in what ways?)

professional life _____.
       (in what ways?)

Autumn Peltier, Water Warrier

In ***Autumn Peltier, Water Warrior,*** written by Carole Lindstrom and illustrated by Bridget George, readers learn about the ways Indigenous women have always cared and worked to protect water for future generations. Readers learn about the activism of Grandma Josephine and her great-niece, Autumn Peltier, who give voice to water and work tirelessly to keep it clean and safe.

About the Creators

Learn more about Carole Lindstrom and Bridget George by visiting their websites: www.carolelindstrom.com and www.bridgetgeorge.com.

Read this short interview with both creators.

There are important distinctions and nuances around the words *Indigenous, Native American, American Indian, tribe,* and *nation.* In my discussion of texts, I use the language and terminology the author uses. It's important to listen for who people tell us they are and to teach children to listen as well and to respect what they are learning. Learn more here about the impact of words and using accurate terms: qrs.ly/cufrdvt.

Listen to Autumn Peltier discuss her water advocacy.

SIX CRITICAL LENSES

Prompts are provided to nurture students' thinking as they read in partnerships, groups, or independently.

Pathways capture the details and ideas that students may notice and think about as they read and respond to the text, and they can be used as guidance for educators and caregivers to teach into.

AFFIRMATION

PROMPTS

- What are you learning about Josephine Mandamin and Autumn Peltier?

- What are you learning about Anishinaabe women's knowledge about and relationship to water?

- Josephine Mandamin was known as Grandma Josephine and was a respected elder who fiercely protected water.
- Grandmother Josephine taught younger generations about Indigenous ways, including the importance of caring for and protecting water.
- Autumn Peltier is Grandmother Josephine's great niece, who continues the work of advocating for water.
- Anishinaabe women have cared for and continue to protect water and view water as sacred.
- Josephine Mandamin (Grandmother Josephine) was an Anishinaabe Indigenous Rights activist.
- Autumn Peltier is an Anishinaabe Indigenous water advocate and Indigenous Rights activist.

AWARENESS

PROMPTS

The name **water protectors** comes from Indigenous activists working on behalf of the protection of water all over the world. In the foreword, Autumn Peltier shares, "In our culture, we look at water as a living being, and we're taught to treat it with the same respect we would show another human."

Seven generations is described in the glossary of this text as an Indigenous belief and way of life that guides decisions and actions made in one's current life to secure future generations.

- What are you learning about the importance of water and its protection?
- How does knowing about seven generations support your understanding of the fierce advocacy by Indigenous activists to protect the environment?

PATHWAYS

- Water is life!
- Water sustains the life of many organisms—plants, animals, as well as human beings.
- If water isn't protected, animals, plants, and humans can become sick.
- Indigenous activists work hard to protect the environment now so that future generations can thrive.

AUTHORSHIP

PROMPTS

- Who are the creators of this text?
- How do their identities influence this work?
- What is their motivation for creating this text?

PATHWAYS

- Carole Lindstrom shares that she is "Anishinaabe/Métis and a proud member of the Turtle Mountain Band of Ojibwe Indians."

- Bridget George shares that she "was raised on the Anishinaabe nation of Kettle and Stony Point and belongs to the Bear Clan."

- In an interview, Carole Lindstrom shares that her work as an author has made her hopeful about the future and that young readers' responses to her work "gives me so much faith in the next generations."

ATMOSPHERE

PROMPTS

- How does this text reflect the identities and lived experiences of the characters/people?

- How does it reflect your identities and lived experiences?

- In what ways does this book convey and bring you joy?

PATHWAYS

- Setting: Readers learn how water is neglected and the importance of protecting it.

- Perspective: The Anishinaabe women have always cared for water and worked to protect it for generations to come.

- Figurative Language/Imagery: Invite students to discuss the beauty and significance of the author's personification of water. Because water does not have a human voice, the author uses her voice and shares how activists such as Grandmother Josephine and Autumn Pelteir use their voices to call attention to its needs.

- Mood/Tone: The beauty and power of water is demonstrated alongside the urgency to care for it.

- Theme: water, protection, activism, Indigenous activists

ACTIVISM

PROMPTS

- How might the environment be impacted if everyone asked themselves how their actions will affect future generations?

- What are you learning about being an activist?

PATHWAYS

- The environment can be healthier if people think about their actions prior to doing things that hurt it.

- If people think about how what they do today will affect generations to come, they may be more cautious about their actions.

- Being an activist involves being knowledgeable about what you are working to protect or change.

- Being an activist means doing everything you can—informing others, speaking up for what is wrong, and working alongside others to make things better.

ACCOUNTABILITY

PROMPTS

- How can this book influence your thinking and actions now and in the future?

- How will you remain alert for the ways your particular identities help you to understand a text and the world?

PATHWAYS

- Reflect on ways this text makes a difference to your heart and in your life. Consider commitments you'll make to care for people and communities.

- This text is an invitation for me to think deeply and possibly differently about

_____ and to apply this in my life (when/how)

_____.

Reflection and Accountability for Antiracist Educators:

This text is an invitation for me to think deeply and possibly differently as a reader

_____ and challenges me to make radical changes in my personal and
    (in what ways?)

professional life _____.
        (in what ways?)

Resistance

Resistance: My Story of Activism, written by Frantzy Luzincourt, provides readers with the opportunity to listen and learn directly from Frantzy's experiences with injustice and his work to advance racial justice.

About the Creators

Learn about more activists and authors of books from the I, Witness series and access the free educators' guide in the QR code to support reading and teaching with these books.

Access the free
educators' guide.

SIX CRITICAL LENSES

Prompts are provided to nurture students' thinking as they read in partnerships, groups, or independently.

Pathways capture the details and ideas that students may notice and think about as they read and respond to the text, and they can be used as guidance for educators to teach into.

AFFIRMATION

PROMPTS

- What are you learning about Frantzy and how he sees the world?

- In what ways does Frantzy's neighborhood and community affirm his racial and cultural identity?

- Who and what in Frantzy's life influences and empowers him and in what ways?

PATHWAYS

- Frantzy founded his high school's first-ever Black student union.

- He attends the International Congress of Youth Voices to "learn about different perspectives, to grow and become more open-minded."

- His goal is to "become more strategic" in how he builds "relationships with activists and other people across the world."

- Frantzy identifies as a "first-generation American born to Haitian immigrants," and he loves his neighborhood that is made up of a diverse community of immigrants from Haiti and other Caribbean countries.

- Frantzy feels his neighborhood helps him to "maintain a connection" to his culture.

- Frantzy greatly admires and has the opportunity to introduce congressman and civil rights leader John Lewis.

AWARENESS

PROMPTS

The American Civil Liberties Union defines **racial profiling** as "the discriminatory practice by law enforcement officials of targeting individuals for suspicion of crime based on the individual's race, ethnicity, religion or national origin" (ACLU, 2005).

- How does the policy and practice of racial profiling by law enforcement influence the practices of business owners?

- How has racial profiling affected Frantzy, his brother, and his mother?

- How do you believe racial profiling affects the lives of Black and Brown people?

- Why is racial profiling dangerous?

PATHWAYS

- If racial profiling is sanctioned by the police who are sworn to uphold the law, then it can be considered appropriate to do by business owners and others in society.

- Frantzy and his brother were singled out based on stereotypes and assumptions made about Black people.

- Being racially profiled has caused trauma to Frantzy, his brother, and his mother that has lasted long after the event itself.

- When race-based assumptions are made about people and believed to be true, it influences how they are treated. This is discrimination and racism.

- Racial profiling causes physical and psychological harm to the individuals and groups targeted. Many people have lost their lives because of racial profiling.

- Racial profiling limits understandings about people and the world.

AUTHORSHIP

PROMPTS

- Who are the creators of this text?

- How do their identities influence this work?

- What is their motivation for creating this text?

- Frantzy Luzincourt shares his experiences growing up in Brooklyn, New York, in a Caribbean community with his parents who are Haitian immigrants.

- His identity as a Black man influences the writing of this text and his journey to becoming an activist.

- One goal of his work with this text is to educate people about anti-Blackness and the importance of activism in the fight for racial justice.

ATMOSPHERE

PROMPTS

- How does this text reflect the identities and lived experiences of the characters/people?

- How does it reflect your identities and lived experiences?

- In what ways does this book convey and bring you joy?

PATHWAYS

- Setting: The physical and emotional landscape of New York City is shown through the experiences of the author, a Black man, who navigates anti-Blackness and racism throughout his life.

- Perspective: Frantzy shares his lived experiences, which inform his views on activism.

- Figurative Language/Imagery: Invite students to discuss the title of this book, *Resistance*, and the ways resistance shows up both in the work of and response to activism.

- Mood/Tone: The urgent need for advocacy and change is revealed.

- Theme: action, chance, activism, accountability

ACTIVISM

PROMPTS

- What is the purpose of the Black student union?

- What can be noticed about the role of activism in Black student unions?

- Discuss the word *strategy*. What does it entail? How does this inform your understanding of the purpose and work of Strategy for Black Lives?

PATHWAYS

- Black student unions are safe, affirming spaces that help Black students thrive in school.

- Black student unions play an important role in schools and universities to educate and raise awareness about issues impacting Black students and communities and to take action to address inequities.

- Frantzy writes, "Why weren't we seeing structural or policy change? We knew we had to do something about this. We might not be able to solve the entire problem, but we were positive we could be part of the solution" (p. 54). Frantzy offers a vision of what structural and policy change looks like to end police brutality. His seven-point document of demands explains strategies to implement to accomplish this.

ACCOUNTABILITY

PROMPTS

- How can this book influence your thinking and actions now and in the future?
- How will you remain alert for the ways your particular identities help you to understand a text and the world?

PATHWAYS

- Reflect on ways this text makes a difference to your heart and in your life. Consider commitments you'll make to care for people and communities.

- This text is an invitation for me to think deeply and possibly differently about

_____ and to apply this in my life (when/how)

_____.

Reflection and Accountability for Antiracist Educators:

This text is an invitation for me to think deeply and possibly differently as a reader

_____ and challenges me to make radical changes in my personal and
    (in what ways?)

professional life _____.
        (in what ways?)

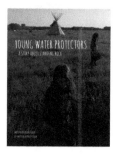

Young Water Protectors . . . A Story About Standing Rock, written by Aslan Tudor and Kelly Tudor, offers a firsthand account of Tudor's activism in North Dakota and the activism of many coming together in solidarity to protect the Standing Rock community.

About the Creators

Read the interview linked in the QR code to learn more about Aslan Tudor and Kelly Tudor and their experiences at Standing Rock.

Read this interview to learn more about Aslan Tudor and Kelly Tudor.

There are important distinctions and nuances around the words *Indigenous, Native American, American Indian, tribe,* and *nation.* In my discussion of texts, I use the language and terminology the author uses. It's important to listen for who people tell us they are and to teach children to listen as well and to respect what they are learning. Learn more here about the impact of words and using accurate terms: qrs.ly/cufrdvt.

SIX CRITICAL LENSES

Prompts are provided to nurture students' thinking as they read in partnerships, groups, or independently.

Pathways capture the details and ideas that students may notice and think about as they read and respond to the text, and they can be used as guidance for educators to teach into.

AFFIRMATION

PROMPTS

- What are you learning about Aslan and what's most important to him?
- What knowledge does Aslan share?

PATHWAYS

- Aslan cares about the land, which he calls "sacred."
- Aslan wants to prevent water from becoming polluted.

- He shares knowledge about the Lakota language, traditional prayers, and songs; geographic knowledge about North and South Dakota; historical knowledge about treaties and Native territories; environmental knowledge about water and pollution; and so on.

AWARENESS

PROMPTS

Oil spills from ships and pipes pollute the land, air, and water. When ships carrying oil leak or sink, pipelines break, or drilling errors occur, oil spills cause major problems to the environment. In 1989, 11 million gallons of oil spilled into the ocean from the Exxon *Valdez* oil tanker in Alaska. In 2010, 134 million gallons of oil spilled into the ocean when a drilling operation disaster happened in the Gulf of Mexico. It is incredibly difficult to clean up an oil spill from the water. Animals, plants, and human beings are harmed and killed when exposed to toxic and dangerous amounts of oil.

Initial proposals for the pipeline were for construction to occur across the Missouri River near Bismarck, North Dakota, until community members expressed their concerns that an oil spill could impact the drinking water. More than 85% of residents of Bismarck are White; more than 75% of residents at Standing Rock are Native. Visit the Standing Rock Sioux and Dakota Access Pipeline | Teacher Resource to learn more about the Dakota Access Pipeline: qrs.ly/hxfrdyz.

- What can be noticed about the role of race in this issue?

- Who benefits and who may be harmed by the decision to construct the pipeline at Standing Rock?

- How do Aslan and the protesters help raise awareness about the Dakota Access Pipeline and the concerns of the Standing Rock Sioux Tribe?

PATHWAYS

- The concerns of residents of Bismarck, North Dakota, who are mostly White, were heard and valued while the concerns of residents of Standing Rock were dismissed.

- The water supply and cultural resources of the Standing Rock Sioux Tribe are jeopardized if there is a leak in the pipeline.

- Aslan and protesters asked people from around the country and the world to come to Standing Rock in a display of support and unity. Protestors posted flags from their Native Nations, created signs and "messages of resistance," marched to the pipeline construction, and so on.

AUTHORSHIP

PROMPTS

- Who are the creators of this text?

- How do their identities influence this work?

- What is their motivation for creating this text?

PATHWAYS

- Aslan wrote this book when he was 10 years old. Kelly, his mother, helped Aslan share his story.

- The About the Author section shares that Aslan is a citizen of the Lipan Apache Tribe of Texas.

- His identity influences the writing of this book as well as Aslan's activism. "As Native Americans we want to protect the earth and water from getting polluted and harmed because these are sacred lands and waters to us. We want to keep our homelands from getting harmed."

ATMOSPHERE

PROMPTS

- How does this text reflect the identities and lived experiences of the characters/people?

- How does it reflect your identities and lived experiences?

- In what ways does this book convey and bring you joy?

PATHWAYS

- Setting: Readers learn about the Standing Rock Sioux Tribe and the Standing Rock Sioux Tribe Indian Reservation.

- Perspective: Aslan provides his insights into the protests during his time there in 2016.

- Figurative Language/Imagery: Discuss the significance of this metaphor: "In Kaota, Mni Wiconi means 'water is life.'"

- Mood/Tone: The urgency of the issue of protecting the water and cultural resources of the Standing Rock Sioux Tribe begins from the first page describing who a water protector is and why they're needed in the world.

- Theme: activism, solidarity, unity, resistance

ACTIVISM

PROMPTS

Environmental racism occurs as a result of the policies and practices of government and corporations that intentionally target BIPOC and low-income communities by exposing them to toxic and hazardous waste. Environmental justice occurs when all people are treated fairly and are involved meaningfully in the laws, regulations, policies, practices, norms, and values that work to create safe and sustainable communities.

- How does listening to the voices of BIPOC help broaden your understanding about the various ways racism functions in society?

- Who are the antiracists working to fight for communities affected by environmental racism?

- What strategies do activists use to fight for environmental justice?

- Racism is not just individual acts or words of hate; it is also the ways laws and policies create hazardous environments where BIPOC are most impacted.

- Aslan Tudor, Daphne Frias, Autumn Peltier, and other young activists of color are working at the intersection of environmental and racial justice. Learn more about them from these websites:

  - Daphne Frias: www.daphnefrias.com
  - Autumn Peltier: qrs.ly/o6frdz3
  - Leah Thomas, Jocelyn Longdon, Vic Barrett, Xiye Bastida, Kristy Drutman, Mikaela Loach, and Isra Hirsi: qrs.ly/iwfrdz8

- Activists use strategies such as writing articles and books, creating podcasts, speaking at environmental awareness events, using social media, creating campaigns and platforms, and more to fight for environmental justice.

ACCOUNTABILITY

PROMPTS

- How can this book influence your thinking and actions now and in the future?

- How will you remain alert for the ways your particular identities help you to understand a text and the world?

PATHWAYS

- Reflect on ways this text makes a difference to your heart and in your life. Consider commitments you'll make to care for people and communities.

- This text is an invitation for me to think deeply and possibly differently about

  _____ and to apply this in my life (when/how)

  _____.

Reflection and Accountability for Antiracist Educators:

This text is an invitation for me to think deeply and possibly differently as a reader

_____ and challenges me to make radical changes in my personal and
    (in what ways?)

professional life _____.
          (in what ways?)

The Light She Feels Inside, written by Gwendolyn Wallace and illustrated by Olivia Duchess, is the story of Maya, who feels the glow of pride and joy for the people she loves and her community. She feels very differently when she experiences and observes injustices. Learning about Black women activists empowers her to work for the changes she'd like to see in the world.

Read this article to learn about the author's purpose for writing this book.

About the Creators

Learn more about the creators by visiting their websites:

- www.gwendolynwallace.com

- www.oliviaduchess.com

SIX CRITICAL LENSES

Prompts are provided to nurture students' thinking as they read in partnerships, groups, or independently.

Pathways capture the details and ideas that students may notice and think about as they read and respond to the text, and they can be used as guidance for educators to teach into.

AFFIRMATION

PROMPTS

- What are you learning about Maya that makes her glow?

- What are you learning about the importance of the Maya learning about Black women activists before her?

- What gives Maya joy?

PATHWAYS

- Maya glows from the love she has for her family and community and when she feels safe.

- Learning about Black women activists soothes Maya and fills her with hope and pride. The Black women she learns about help her to see herself and protect her heart.

- Learning about her ancestors gives Maya joy. The librarian, Ms. Scott, gives Maya joy.

- Maya feels pride and joy in doing things the way her ancestors did—imagining a brighter future and working to make things better for her community.

The Equal Justice Initiative explains that racial profiling, assigning criminal suspicion to a person due to their race, extends from the long history of racialization of criminality in the United States and "relies on the same prejudices and stereotypes" of the past. "After slavery ended, the image of Black people as 'criminal' and 'dangerous' became pervasive as a justification for continued inequality and exploitation of Black people and has persisted since" (Equal Justice Initiative, 2014).

Gentrification is the process of change that occurs in a neighborhood to make it more appealing to people who have more money than those who already live there. As a result, rent prices increase and people from the community have to move out. This mostly impacts people of color in neighborhoods who are pushed out when white people move in.

PROMPTS

- What is Maya noticing in her community?

- What turns Maya's glow to a burn?

- What are you learning about the importance of Maya's emotions?

PATHWAYS

- Maya is noticing the specific hardships that her family and community are experiencing.

- Maya's glow turns to a burn as she notices economic challenges, environmental issues, bullying, racial profiling by the police, and gentrification.

- She's noticing injustices that are connected to racism such as racial profiling of her cousin by the police and gentrification, which will result in a tree she loves being removed in order to build fancy apartments.

- Maya's emotions are valid and not something she should fear. Her feelings of love and anger matter, and they can fuel her work toward a better future.

AUTHORSHIP

PROMPTS

- Who are the creators of this text?

- How do their identities influence this work?

- What is their motivation for creating this text?

PATHWAYS

- On her website, Gwendolyn Wallace writes that she is "a New York City–based researcher, storyteller, and children's literature author. Her work for both children and adults centers **Afrodiasporic** voices to explore the unfolding relationship between the spatial logics of colonialism and our bodyminds."

- Olivia Duchess shares in her bio at the end of the book that she is "an illustrator from and based in London."

- Gwendolyn Wallace shares in an interview that she didn't learn about the Black women activists she writes about until she was in high school but always noticed, even as a young child, the existence of racism. She shares, "While I felt scared about the enormity of the systems that harmed me, I felt incredibly grateful to be part of a long legacy of resistance, creativity, and care. I grieve for the person I could have been if I had learned this history earlier. I wrote my newest picture book, *The Light She Feels Inside,* in response to this mourning." (Read the interview here: qrs.ly/kjfrdza)

ATMOSPHERE

PROMPTS

- How does this text reflect the identities and lived experiences of the characters/people?

- How does it reflect your identities and lived experiences?

- In what ways does this book convey and bring you joy?

PATHWAYS

- Setting: Maya has strong emotions in the places she loves most—her home, school, and community.

- Perspective: All of Maya's emotions are a strength; they help her understand what's most important to her and what's worth working to improve or change. Learning about Black women activists helps her to see herself and understand the activism she wants to do.

- Figurative Language/Imagery: Invite students to discuss this part of the story: "She isn't sure what to do with all this glowing inside her. All she knows is that it's starting to feel too heavy to carry" and to consider their own glowing feelings and ways they honor them.

- Mood/Tone: Encouragement and empowerment by ancestors fill the pages of this book.

- Theme: activism, pride, connection, community

ACTIVISM

PROMPTS

- What are you learning from this story about ways to be an activist?

- What are you learning about ways you can be an activist in your own community?

PATHWAYS

- Activists learn about activists before them, such as Ida B. Wells, Nina Simone, Fannie Lou Hamer, Gwendolyn Brooks, Marsha P. Johnson, June Jordan, and the Combahee River Collective.

- Activists learn about activists in their own lives—their families and communities.

- Activists observe what's happening in the world around them—in their communities and beyond.
- Activists lean into and not away from their emotions and use them to work toward change.
- Activists teach others—family and friends—about the work of activism and activists.
- Activists work in community with others to make things better for everyone.

ACCOUNTABILITY

PROMPTS

- How can this book influence your thinking and actions now and in the future?
- How will you remain alert for the ways your particular identities help you to understand a text and the world?

PATHWAYS

- Reflect on ways this text makes a difference to your heart and in your life. Consider commitments you'll make to care for people and communities.
- This text is an invitation for me to think deeply and possibly differently about

_____ and to apply this in my life (when/how)

_____.

Reflection and Accountability for Antiracist Educators:

This text is an invitation for me to think deeply and possibly differently as a reader

_____ and challenges me to make radical changes in my personal and
    (in what ways?)

professional life _____.
        (in what ways?)

More Than Peach

In ***More Than Peach: Changing the World . . . One Crayon at a Time!*** written by Bellen Woodard and illustrated by Fanny Liem, Bellen's critical consciousness is raised as a result of language used to discuss skin color in her classroom. She is determined to help her peers and teachers make a shift in how they talk about crayons to be more inclusive of the wide variety of skin tones of human beings.

About the Creators

Learn more about the author, Bellen Woodard, and the More Than Peach Project online here: www.morethanpeach.com. And learn more about the illustrator, Fanny Liem, here: www.fannywen.com.

Six Critical Lenses

Prompts are provided to nurture students' thinking as they read in partnerships, groups, or independently.

Pathways capture the details and ideas that students may notice and think about as they read and respond to the text, and they can be used as guidance for educators to teach into.

AFFIRMATION

PROMPTS

- What are you learning about Bellen?
- What brings her joy?

PATHWAYS

- Bellen loves time with her family—her parents and her brothers.
- Bellen enjoys her friends
- Bellen feels that "school is a home away from home."
- Bellen is smart, observant, and an activist.

PROMPTS

The Merriam-Webster dictionary defines **socialization** as "the process beginning during childhood by which individuals acquire the values, habits, and attitudes of a society." Bellen Woodard shares that "the peach crayon was actually named 'flesh'" and "I found it pretty strange that there was just one crayon with that and that even today only one was being called 'the skin-color' crayon."

- How does this story help you to recognize ways children are socialized into racist ideas?

- What are you learning about what the "skin color" crayon means?

- Who is included? Who is excluded?

PATHWAYS

- Bellen's classmates didn't stop to think critically about what the "skin-color" crayon really means. And that although she found the language problematic, she would "always pass the peach crayon."

- The "skin-color" crayon suggests there's only one skin color.

- This includes anyone whose skin color resembles peach, which are people who have lighter skin colors. Using the peach crayon as "skin color" includes White people.

- This excludes anyone whose skin color does not resemble peach, which are people who have darker skin colors. Black people and those who have brown skin are excluded because the peach crayon does not represent their skin colors.

AUTHORSHIP

PROMPTS

- Who are the creators of this text?

- How do their identities influence this work?

- What is their motivation for creating this text?

PATHWAYS

- Bellen shares that she is the president of Bellen's More Than Peach Project.

- Fanny Liem shares that she was born and raised in Indonesia.

- Bellen shares that her goal for this book is "to make sure that absolutely no kid feels 'disincluded' in their spaces for simply being the human they're intended to be." She also shares her belief that every kid can be an activist, right now.

ATMOSPHERE

PROMPTS

- How does this text reflect the identities and lived experiences of the characters/people?

- How does it reflect your identities and lived experiences?

- In what ways does this book convey and bring you joy?

PATHWAYS

- Setting: Bellen feels joy, loved, and included when she's with her family and begins to notice ways she feels excluded at school.

- Perspective: Bellen works to bring attention to language and ideas she finds problematic and exclusive.

- Figurative Language/Imagery: Invite students to discuss these lines from the story and what it means to them.

  o "It's so important that your space is brilliant. Just like you."

  o ". . . we're more—much more than peach. We're each."

- Mood/Tone: This book conveys empowerment to transform spaces so they are inclusive and humane for everyone.

- Theme: skin color, exclusion, activism

ACTIVISM

PROMPTS

- What are you noticing about ways Bellen's activism is focused primarily on making change rather than receiving credit?

- Why is it important to acknowledge people for their work?

- What are you learning from this story about being an activist?

PATHWAYS

- Bellen is humble; she focuses on "Gently, knowingly, trying to change the language" in her classroom and school that is problematic.

- Bellen notices students and teachers begin to shift their language to be more inclusive around skin color.

- It's important to credit people for their work because it validates their efforts and makes them feel recognized.

- Activists help people become more conscious about problematic language and ideas.

- Activists, regardless of their age, think about what they want to change, consider how it will make things better, and work toward that goal.

- Activists work with others as a team and with their communities to achieve their goals.
- Applying the L.O.V.E. tips Bellen shares is a way to get started on the activism that can be done in schools and communities.

ACCOUNTABILITY

PROMPTS

- How can this book influence your thinking and actions now and in the future?
- How will you remain alert for the ways your particular identities help you to understand a text and the world?

PATHWAYS

- Reflect on ways this text makes a difference to your heart and in your life. Consider commitments you'll make to care for people and communities.
- This text is an invitation for me to think deeply and possibly differently about

_____ and to apply this in my life (when/how)

_____.

Reflection and Accountability for Antiracist Educators:

This text is an invitation for me to think deeply and possibly differently as a reader

_____ and challenges me to make radical changes in my personal and
　　　(in what ways?)

professional life _____.
　　　　　　　　　　(in what ways?)

CHAPTER SEVEN

Sustaining the Revolution

"*These and other inanimate things she saw and experienced. They were real to her. She knew them. They were the codes and touchstones of the world, capable of translation and possession. She owned the crack that made her stumble; she owned the clumps of dandelions whose white heads, last fall, she had blown away; whose yellow heads, this fall, she peered into. And owning them made her part of the world, and the world a part of her.*"

—Toni Morrison, *The Bluest Eye*, 1999 (1970), pp. 45–46

The first time I read *Maud Martha* by Gwendolyn Brooks and *The Bluest Eye* by Toni Morrison, I was a freshman in college. The protagonists in each book, Maud Martha and Pecola, navigate lives where Whiteness serves as the standard for beauty. Both books are an exploration of race, class, gender—the social, economic, and political factors that shape the identities and sense of self of Black girls and Black women.

As a young Black woman attending a predominantly White college, these characters challenged and changed me. Reading these books back then raised questions I continue to grapple with today such as: What conditions allow Black girls and Black women to push against power structures that threaten to break their spirits? How can we protect ourselves from the onslaught of dominant constructions of beauty that can cause internalized self-loathing? How do we heal our wounds and reclaim our self-worth?

There were about 5,000 students at my college, and about 100 students were BIPOC. I experienced racism constantly and didn't think I'd survive there past the first semester. What fortified me? Black and Brown students who became my family. The Black Student Union that was a haven for me and all students of color. And the courses that centered Black authors, Black history, and Black culture, which helped me to see myself as well as make sense of and interrogate my reality.

In a world that is too often ugly, cruel, and loveless toward Black people, Brooks and Morrison use dandelions as symbolic representations of hope. Dandelions are an invitation to focus on what others might miss, deem insignificant, and therefore ignore. Dandelions are a call to seek and know love even in the bleakest landscape by tapping into the deepest part of one's humanity. Maud Martha and Pecola are dandelions—unique, important, precious. Just as they are, they matter. Brooks (1992) writes, "To be cherished was the dearest wish of the heart of Maud Martha Brown" (p. 2). But Morrison (1970/1999) reminds us of what happens when we are planted in infertile ground. "This soil is bad for certain kinds of flowers. Certain seeds it will not bear, certain fruits it will not bear" (p. 204). Growth just isn't possible without love.

Antiracist teaching fertilizes the soil where children are planted and nurtures their souls, making it possible for them to thrive within schools and beyond them. It helps children recognize that it is racist ideas that are the weeds that threaten humanity—ugly, undesirable—and that who they are, exactly as they are, is beautiful. Like Maud Martha and Pecola, children look at dandelions and see beauty rather than weeds. Antiracist teaching disrupts dominant perspectives so that children know they are not insignificant, unwanted, and ignored; they are part of the world and the world is part of them. Antiracist teaching is radical love.

I have asked you to come with me along a journey of antiracist thinking and action in the teaching of reading. And by now, as you engage this last chapter, I imagine you may be feeling many things. You may be feeling exhilarated—ready to put into action many of the ideas about reading instruction you've encountered across these pages. You may be feeling overwhelmed as you reconsider and reimagine ways of teaching that you've practiced for quite some time. Perhaps you are anxious. In this national moment of misrepresentation and mischaracterization of critical

> As with any revolution, the work of fighting for change is not fleeting; it's enduring. And it will require us to approach teaching as activists who are committed to antiracism even in times of tension.

race theory, anti-CRT laws, book banning, and policies and laws designed to halt the work of equity and antiracism, you may be feeling defeated. Or you may be fearful of angry parents, board members, apathetic colleagues, and unsupportive administrators. Maybe you are simply exhausted. All of these feelings are valid. It is my hope that we transform our exhaustion into fuel and that this book contributes to the scholarship that reenergizes us in the fight for racial justice.

As with any revolution, the work of fighting for change is not fleeting; it's enduring. And it will require us to approach teaching as activists who are committed to antiracism even in times of tension. Even and especially amid the storm. In my work with educators around the country, particularly White educators, many explain that it isn't only their discomfort that keeps them from advancing the work of antiracism. It is also their fear. Fear of making a mistake. The truth is we will all make mistakes. In *Risk. Fail. Rise. A Teacher's Guide to Learning From Mistakes,* M. Colleen Cruz (2021) spotlights one of the biggest mistakes in the work of antiracism and equity—connecting mistakes to intention. Cruz asserts, "Our students and their families are most adversely impacted from our errors, intentional or not. As the maker of the mistake, the onus is on us to focus and acknowledge the impact" (p. 6). It's critical that we confront our mistakes rather than attempt to minimize or conceal them. "When we own impact," Cruz shares, we are communicating that the relationship we have with students and their families matters. How do we move forward from mistakes? "We hold ourselves accountable to the relationship" (p. 6). As we become consciously aware of this, we understand that the real risk in the work of antiracism is in doing nothing.

Throughout this book, I have provided a pathway for educators and students for antiracist teaching and learning in reading. I have demonstrated how to put ideas into action using several incredible children's books. But remember, this work is not about providing educators with a list of books. It is about providing educators with tools to see and do more with books in order to cultivate an antiracist reading stance. Because it is my hope that these tools will be utilized often and in a variety of circumstances, I suggest the following toolkits. These toolkits—one students can use to sustain an antiracist reading revolution in their own lives and one educators can use to continue nurturing young readers—can help to bring about liberatory practices in reading. Both toolkits, the **Student Toolkit of Critical Lenses for Antiracist Reading** and the **Educator Toolkit of Critical Lenses for Antiracist Reading Instruction,** provide opportunities for meaningful reflection around nurturing reading environments that radiate students' personal and cultural expressions. Each toolkit includes the six critical lenses in order to create a more fluid power dynamic between educators and students working in community together. (Find reproducible versions of these toolkits in the Appendix.)

STUDENT TOOLKIT OF CRITICAL LENSES FOR ANTIRACIST READING

Readers can use the **Student Toolkit of Critical Lenses for Antiracist Reading** individually to support their book selection choices and when reading independently. They can also use this toolkit during reading partnerships and book clubs to discuss patterns they're noticing about their reading—those they'd like to continue or break—and to reflect on what difference their reading is making to their hearts and in their lives.

This toolkit is not a checklist. It is a guide that feeds young readers' joy, brilliance, resilience, and resistance. They will read in ways that encourage them to commit to being learners, amplifiers of the voices of BIPOC, and builders of new strategies, structures, and systems, rather than succumbers to complacency and complicity. Such resistance will empower students to boldly call out oppression and radically reimagine how things can be changed. Resistance helps young readers to confront whitewashed versions of history and to develop the internal armor they'll need to remain steadfast in the work of antiracism. Resilience is fostered in students whenever they read for liberation, align themselves with the people who are engaged in the collective struggle for freedom, and remain alert by asking themselves, "What is the work we need to do next?"

STUDENT TOOLKIT OF CRITICAL LENSES FOR ANTIRACIST READING FOR OLDER READERS	
CRITICAL LENS	**GUIDING QUESTIONS**
Affirmation	• Does this book/text affirm the racial and cultural identities of characters of color/people without generalizing, stereotyping, or misrepresenting? • Are characters of color/BIPOC portrayed in ways that reflect the full range of their lived-experiences and humanity? • How does this book/text reflect and affirm my identities and lived experiences?
Awareness	• How does this book help me to think and talk about race and racism? • What opportunities does this book/text provide to analyze and interrogate systems of oppression? • In what ways does this book/text help me to develop ideas about disrupting inequities?
Authorship	• How many of the books/texts that I have access to are written by BIPOC authors? • In what ways do the identities of the author influence the book/text they've written? • If books are not written by BIPOC but are about BIPOC, what makes the author qualified to tell this story? Have they done so with authenticity and care?

(Continued)

(Continued)

STUDENT TOOLKIT OF CRITICAL LENSES FOR ANTIRACIST READING FOR OLDER READERS	
CRITICAL LENS	**GUIDING QUESTIONS**
Atmosphere	• Are the books/texts in my classroom relevant to my life today? • Do books/texts feature characters/people of color from various backgrounds, environments, settings? • How do the books/texts help me to understand the world around me?
Activism	• Which books/texts/authors/stories am I drawn to and why? • In what ways do the books/texts create opportunities for me to reflect, make connections, and think critically about my life and society? • What am I learning and possibly unlearning that helps me recognize what I will advocate for?
Accountability	• How am I being challenged and changed as a result of reading this book/text and discussing it with peers? • What about my own identities or the identities of others do I need to know more about? • What will I commit to doing that helps to advance the work of antiracism and equity?

STUDENT TOOLKIT OF CRITICAL LENSES FOR ANTIRACIST READING FOR YOUNGER READERS	
CRITICAL LENS	**GUIDING QUESTIONS**
Affirmation	• What makes the characters/people in this book feel happy, special, proud, loved? • What are you learning about the things that the characters/people in this book like to do? What ideas do they have about themselves, their families, their communities, and the world? • In what ways does the story feel like it's about your and your life?
Awareness	• What problems does this book help you to think more about? • How does this book help you to understand who is harmed most by these problems? • What ideas does this book share about ways to make things better?
Authorship	• How many books in my classroom are written by authors who share one or more of my identities? • Why might the author have written this book? • What can I notice about whether books about Black and Brown characters/people are written with care and respect?
Atmosphere	• Which books feel like they are about me and my life? • Are there lots of different kinds of stories about Black and Brown characters/people in my classroom? • What am I learning about my life and the world from characters/people in the books I'm reading?
Activism	• Which books and authors are my favorite to read? • How do these books challenge me and inspire me? • What do these books make me care about and want to change in the world?
Accountability	• What does talking about this book with my friends and teachers help me to understand about myself and others? • What about my identity and others do I want to learn more? • How will I work to make my life and the life of others more peaceful, joyful, and free?

EDUCATOR TOOLKIT OF CRITICAL LENSES FOR ANTIRACIST READING INSTRUCTION

The **Educator Toolkit of Critical Lenses for Antiracist Reading Instruction** guides educators in implementing liberatory practices as facilitators of antiracist reading instruction. To sustain an antiracist reading revolution within students involves a willingness, as librarian Shana Frazin recommends, examine books both individually and collectively. In doing so, educators can determine what is the story being told about individuals and groups of people simply by the books made available in the classroom. *Who is seen and validated? Who is missing? Which lived experiences are visible? Which are silenced?* Such examination and reflection can position educators to see more in the books in their classrooms and curriculums and also to teach in ways where students learn to ask these kinds of questions themselves as readers. Educator and author Tricia Ebarvia (2023) conveys the importance of students doing what she has named a "C-M-M analysis" as they read that helps them notice which characters, people, and perspectives are represented in a text (p. 247). Ebarvia invites students to ask themselves, "Who is centered? Who is marginalized? Who is missing?"

At a time when book censorship threatens students' access not to just books but also to knowledge, truth, validation, joy, safety, and ideas about freedom, it's critical that educators are intentional in the decisions they make about books and instruction. Equally important is intentionality about antiracist teaching during whole- and small-group instruction and reading conferences.

As you use this toolkit to guide your planning and teaching, consider how reading instruction helps to nurture and sustain students as readers as changemakers. Whether teaching students as they read independently, in partnerships, or in book clubs or groups, this toolkit supports educators in applying critical lenses to both evaluate books and guide antiracist reading instruction.

EDUCATOR TOOLKIT OF CRITICAL LENSES FOR ANTIRACIST READING INSTRUCTION		
CRITICAL LENS	**CONSIDERATIONS FOR BOOK SELECTION**	**IMPLEMENTATION**
Affirmation	• Are there a variety of books that affirm students' racial and cultural identities? • How are students' funds of knowledge (Moll, Amanti, Neff, & Gonzalez, 1992) reflected? • Which books validate the cultural and linguistic competencies of students and their communities?	Ask questions that invite students to think about their multiple identities. Utilize the scholarship of Dr. Rudine Sims Bishop (1990) and Dr. Gloria Ladson-Billings (1995). *In what ways might this book be a mirror, window, or both for you?*
Awareness	• Which books help students to recognize how the social, cultural, political, economic, and ecological systems they're embedded in can create and perpetuate inequity and injustice? • What opportunities do books provide for students to analyze and interrogate systems of oppression? • In what ways do books help students to develop ideas about disrupting inequities?	Ask questions that raise students' consciousness about the purpose and function of inequities. Utilize the scholarship of Dr. Barbara Love (2010). *In what ways are you feeling empowered to recognize and challenge injustice and work toward a better future?*
Authorship	• Does the library/curriculum reflect #ownvoice authors? • If books are not by #ownvoice authors, what makes the author qualified to tell this story? • In what ways does this book amplify the voices and experiences of underrepresented and historically excluded identities?	Ask questions that help students recognize the dedication of authors who write with cultural nuance that stems from being part of that culture. Utilize the scholarship of Dr. Sonja Cherry-Paul. *How do creators demonstrate the full range of humanity of characters/people/groups who have been marginalized? Are they doing this with authenticity and care?*

(Continued)

(Continued)

EDUCATOR TOOLKIT OF CRITICAL LENSES FOR ANTIRACIST READING INSTRUCTION		
CRITICAL LENS	**CONSIDERATIONS FOR BOOK SELECTION**	**IMPLEMENTATION**
Atmosphere	• Are there numerous ways students of color can see themselves reflected in books made accessible to them? • Are there a variety of genres, time periods, settings, contexts, and issues? • Does the library include books that feature characters/people of color from various backgrounds, identities, and environments?	Ask questions that invite students to consider the ways books are reflective of who they are as well as the world around them. Utilize the scholarship of DisruptTexts. *In what ways is this book relevant to you? How has it made a difference in your life?*
Activism	• Which books help students to develop racial literacy? • What opportunities do books provide for students to analyze and interrogate systems of oppression? • In what ways do books help students develop ideas about disrupting inequities?	Ask questions that invite students to consider how a book addresses antiracism. Utilize the scholarship of Dr. Yolanda Sealey-Ruiz (2021). *What opportunities for conversations around justice and equity does this book offer?*
Accountability	• Which books help students understand the meaning of solidarity and commitment? • In what ways do the books made accessible to students disrupt white saviorism and instead demonstrate the importance and value of working in community with BIPOC? • Which books are grounded in hope and love so that students understand the work of antiracism as sustained, ongoing actions?	Ask questions that invite students to consider ways they will advance the work of antiracism. Utilize the scholarship of Dr. Sonja Cherry-Paul (2024). *What will stay with you, inspire you, and inform how you move forward with intentionality and humility to create a racially just world?*

As you apply the six critical lenses to support book selection and implementation of antiracist teaching in reading instruction . . .

- What are you learning about your students and their reading identities?

- Which books/authors are students drawn to?

- How do the library and curriculum create opportunities for students to reflect, make connections, and think critically about being a reader?

- In what ways do the books you've made accessible increase students' confidence and foster their love of reading?

It is my hope that when utilized, these toolkits and the antiracist reading instruction and approaches they call for increase students' confidence and help to nurture a love of reading and an active antiracist stance. And I hope that educators are emboldened to provide access to books and teach in ways that empower students intellectually, culturally, socially, and politically.

Across this book, I have used dandelions as a symbol of antiracist teaching. Despite their beauty and various benefits to the natural environment and humanity, efforts to destroy dandelions are indefatigable. From spraying herbicides, to uprooting them, to smothering them underneath mulch in flower beds, attempts to eradicate dandelions are constant, yet often unsuccessful. Poet, educator, and philosopher Daisaku Ikeda offers insight into the resiliency of dandelions, how they manage to survive these threats, and what we can all learn from them. "*Why doesn't constant trampling defeat the dandelion? The key to its strength is its long and sturdy root, which extends deep into the earth. The same principle applies to people. The true victors in life are those who, enduring repeated challenges and setbacks, have sent the roots of their being to such a depth that nothing can shake them*" (Ikeda, 2005).

How do we nurture an antiracist reading revolution? We become dandelions who root our students and ourselves in an unshakable love that fortifies and endures.

Building the Movement for Human Liberation

In the United States and around the world, we can recognize the reciprocal relationship between hope and solidarity. We deepen our understanding of what abolitionist organizer and activist Mariame Kaba (2021) means by "hope is a discipline," and how to cultivate hope as a practice, to sustain a revolution. Hope and solidarity are inextricably linked. Hope is the heartbeat of solidarity.

As I finish writing this book, hope has felt elusive with war and ongoing violence raging in the Democratic Republic of Congo, Gaza, Sudan, Haiti, and Ukraine. I am a forever-student of activist, scholar, and author Angela Y. Davis, and her words and works remind me how mass movements and collective struggle makes it possible to confront a world filled with injustice. Davis (2016) challenges us to do the necessary work of building the movement for human liberation. And in doing so, she offers, "It is in collectivities that we find reservoirs of hope and optimism."[1] Yet, in these turbulent times, I find myself grappling with several questions.

How do we cultivate hope in order to sustain a revolution?

What are important patterns and connections we can draw from as sources of strength?

What are the pitfalls we must work to avoid?

When we are exhausted and feeling alone, how do we move forward?

Looking across movements for human liberation with these questions in mind, I am able to see hope and solidarity as a constant, a well we can dip into when fatigue weakens our collective struggle for freedom. Without this reservoir, the barriers we face are too great for any one of us to confront alone.

Take, for example, the longevity of solidarity between Black and Asian American and Pacific Islander communities.

In his 1867 speech titled "Composite Nation," abolitionist Frederick Douglass emphasized equality and human rights as he argued on behalf of Chinese immigration to America. He pointed out the hypocrisy of immigration policies, explaining that the rationale for restricting Chinese immigrants would have also justified banning immigrants from Europe. He declared,

> It is this great right that I assert for the Chinese and Japanese, and for all other varieties of men equally with yourselves, now and forever. I know of no rights of race superior to the rights of humanity, and when there is a supposed conflict between human and national rights, it is safe to go to the side of humanity.[2]

---

[1]https://www.haymarketbooks.org/books/780-freedom-is-a-constant-struggle
[2]https://www.loc.gov/resource/mss11879.22017/?sp=1&st=image&r=-1.221,0.252, 3.441,1.498,0

Black leaders such as Ida B. Wells and Bishop Henry M. Turner spoke out in support of the Filipino community during the Philippine–American War from 1899 to 1913. Turner called it an "unholy war of conquest."[3]

Later, Black leaders would again speak out against injustices during the Vietnam War. Malcolm X and Dr. Martin Luther King Jr. openly denounced it. Muhammad Ali was stripped of his boxing license because of his refusal to fight in the war and was threatened with imprisonment. When asked about his impending jail sentence, Ali disrupted the either/or binary that is firmly established in White supremacy culture. He said,

> It has been said that I have two alternatives. Either go to jail or go to the army. But I would like to say that there is another alternative. And that alternative is justice.[4]

Detroit philosopher and author Grace Lee Boggs devoted much of her life to activism and community building, which included working side by side with leaders of the Civil Rights and Black Power Movements. She was so rooted within these movements that the FBI closely monitored and maintained a thick file on her. She wrote,

> Civil and voting rights for blacks didn't come from the White House or from masses demonstrating in front of the White House. They came after the Montgomery Bus Boycott of 1955–56, the Freedom Rides in 1961, the Children's Crusade in Birmingham in 1963, the Mississippi Freedom Summer and Freedom Schools in 1964, and the Selma-to-Montgomery march in 1965.[5]

Boggs reminded the world that progress for civil rights and equality came only after hundreds of thousands of Black Americans and their supporters accepted the challenge and risks of making the changes they wanted to see in the world.

Activist Yuri Kochiyama spent years in an internment camp with her family and later joined the Civil Rights Movement, developed a close friendship with Malcolm X, and became an advocate for Black liberation. In a 1972 interview, she said, "I was heading in one direction, integration, and he was going in another, total liberation, and he

---

[3] http://fanhs-national.org/filam/1741-2/

[4] https://www.amnesty.org/en/latest/news/2016/06/muhammad-ali-the-worlds-greatest-conscientious-objector/

[5] https://www.ucpress.edu/book/9780520272590/the-next-american-revolution (2012, p. xiv)

opened my eyes. He opened my mind, like opening a door to a new world."[6] And, "He helped me to start thinking, studying, listening, and observing and seeing contradictions."[7]

In response to the 2016 killings of Philando Castille in Minnesota and Alton Sterling in Louisiana by police, Asian Americans created Letters for Black Lives: An Open Letter Project on anti-Blackness. Working in more than 40 languages, Asian Americans confront anti-Blackness in their communities and urge their elders to care about police brutality against Black Americans. This campaign intensified after the killings of Breonna Taylor and Ahmaud Arbery, as well as George Floyd in 2020. As anti-Black racism continues, so does this intergenerational, crowdsourced expression of love and solidarity.

Powerful alliances such as these as well as others have led to major advancements in the fight for racial justice and liberation. From studying this history, a clear pattern emerges—people recognizing the ways their circumstances are bound, their lived experiences intertwined, their struggles connected, coming together to work toward a common goal.

Amid the 2023 Israel–Hamas war, global examples of Jewish and Arab solidarity demonstrate an understanding that collective liberation is reliant upon unity. Working as a collective, people are raising their voices to end the death and violence. Thousands upon thousands of people. A global, earth-shaking, interracial, intergenerational understanding that solidarity is more than allyship. Solidarity is about recognizing our common humanity—how we choose to be in relationship with, and accountable to, each other.

Davis (2016) asserts, "Our histories never unfold in isolation. We cannot truly tell what we consider to be our own histories without knowing the other stories. And often we discover that those other stories are actually our own stories." In the United States and around the world, we can recognize the reciprocal relationship between hope and solidarity. We deepen our understanding of what abolitionist organizer and activist Mariame Kaba (2021) means by "hope is a discipline"[8] and how to cultivate hope as a practice, to sustain a revolution. Hope and solidarity are inextricably linked. Hope is the heartbeat of solidarity.

---

[6]https://aaww.org/celebrating-100-years-of-yuri-kochiyama/
[7]https://www.lacaaea.com/our-blog/aapi-contributions-meet-yuri-kochiyama
[8]https://www.haymarketbooks.org/books/1664-we-do-this-til-we-free-us

Solidarity helps us answer the question, "How do we cultivate hope?" We are able to understand hope as not simply a passive feeling or something to wish for but as an action underpinned by intentions, commitment, and accountability. Solidarity means we choose to see patterns rather than shield our eyes from them and maintain the status quo. Solidarity means we confront, challenge, and change ourselves, even and especially when the work is hard, fully understanding that the journey to justice is not simple or linear.

I'm often told about the resistance that creates obstacles for moving forward on the path toward justice and liberation. That the work that's necessary feels overwhelming and, at times, just too difficult. I'm asked by educators, "But what can I do? I'm just one person." At times, including while writing this book, I have wondered the same. The truth is I feel bone-weary more often than not. And so the most dangerous pitfall we must work to avoid is isolationism. Davis (2016) reminds us that we are each responsible for building the movement for human liberation. "It is essential to resist the depiction of history as the work of heroic individuals in order for people today to recognize their potential agency as a part of an ever-expanding community of struggle." None of us can do everything, but each of us can do something. Find your people. Form your squad. They may be in the same building as you. They may not be. Identify and seek out those who will hold space for you. Those who you'll turn to, who help you to release, reflect, and refuel.

There are many uncertainties about what lies ahead in the world, in our schools, and in our communities. There will be numerous obstacles and many difficult decisions to make. What I know for sure is that it's critical for us to determine that we are in solidarity with humanity. To steady our resolve for peace and freedom during turbulent times. To recognize that we nurture and maintain an unbreakable allegiance with our students and their families and to each other whenever we place aspirations above academics, collectivism over individualism, humanity over curriculum. To remember that solidarity means not only, help is here. Hope is here.

Appendix Contents

Appendix A: Antiracist Reading Framework (Chapter 1)

Appendix B: Recalling Reading Experiences in School (Chapter 2)

Appendix C: Historical and Sociocultural Understandings Chart (Chapter 3)

Appendix D: Every Book Is About Race! (Chapter 4)

Appendix E: What I Learned in K–12 Schooling (Chapter 5)

Appendix F: Racial Literacy Development and Reading Instruction (Chapter 5)

Appendix G: Considering Curriculum, Books, and Activism (Chapter 6)

Appendix H: Student Toolkit of Critical Lenses for Antiracist Reading for Older Readers (Chapter 7)

Appendix I: Student Toolkit of Critical Lenses for Antiracist Reading for Younger Readers (Chapter 7)

Appendix J: Educator Toolkit of Critical Lenses for Antiracist Reading Instruction (Chapter 7)

Appendix K: Middle Grade and YA Recommendations

Appendix A
Antiracist Reading Framework (Chapter 1)

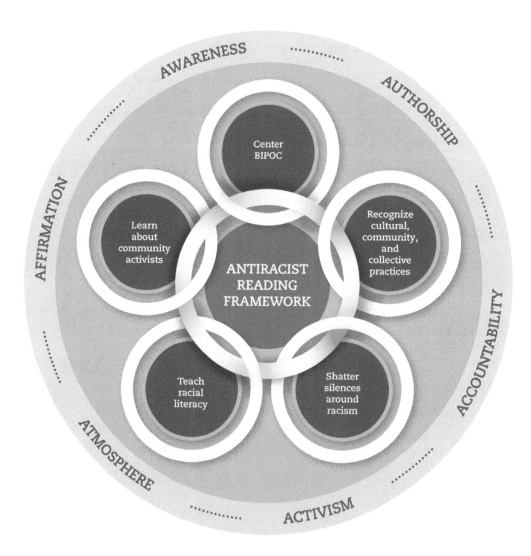

Appendix B

Recalling Reading Experiences in School (Chapter 2)

RECALLING READING EXPERIENCES IN SCHOOL		
BOOK TITLES	**IDENTITIES**	**PATTERNS**
Which books do you remember reading when you were in elementary or middle school?	What were some of your personal and social identities that felt important to you when you were a kid?	How many ways can you locate yourself on your Book Collage?
Which books were used in instruction?	Personal identities (talents, skills, abilities, hobbies, interests)	What patterns and truths are revealed as you look back at the books you read?
Which books were seen and celebrated in classrooms and libraries?	Social identities (race, ethnicity, gender, religion, language, economic status, dis/ability, sexuality)	How might this be similar/ different for students who are members of BIPOC/ multilingual/LGBTQ+/ dis/ability communities?

Appendix C
Historical and Sociocultural Understandings Chart (Chapter 3)

HISTORICAL AND SOCIOCULTURAL UNDERSTANDINGS—IMPLICATIONS AND APPLICATIONS			
THE FIVE Cs	What does this word mean to you?	What role has it played in your childhood?	What are the dominant archetypes in your reading instruction? How are they shaped by your understanding of and experiences with the Five Cs?
Culture			
Collective			
Collaboration			
Community			
Curriculum			

Appendix D
Every Book Is About Race! (Chapter 4)

EVERY BOOK IS ABOUT RACE!				
TITLE AND AUTHOR	What are the *hidden* rules students learn about race and racism?	What are the *clear* rules students learn about race and racism?	What is the *explicit* teaching about race and racism?	How is race and racism *silenced*?

Appendix E
K–12 Reflections (Chapter 5)

K–12 REFLECTIONS		
Think about your K–12 schooling. When, how, and what did you learn about the following people and events? What were you also learning about race and racism?		
PEOPLE AND EVENTS	WHEN, HOW, WHAT I LEARNED	WHAT WAS I LEARNING ABOUT RACE AND RACISM?
Christopher Columbus, 1492		
The arrival of the first Africans in Virginia, 1619		
Founding Fathers and the Constitutional Convention, 1787		
1819 Civilization Fund Act		
The Emancipation Proclamation, 1863		

PEOPLE AND EVENTS	WHEN, HOW, WHAT I LEARNED	WHAT WAS I LEARNING ABOUT RACE AND RACISM?
The first Memorial Day Commemoration organized by freed enslaved people on May 1, 1865		
Juneteenth, June 19, 1865		
Carlisle Indian Industrial School, 1879–1918		
1882 Exclusion Act		
Tulsa Race Massacre 1921		
Internment of Japanese Americans, 1942–1946		

(Continued)

(Continued)

PEOPLE AND EVENTS	WHEN, HOW, WHAT I LEARNED	WHAT WAS I LEARNING ABOUT RACE AND RACISM?
The murder of Emmett Till, 1955		
Civil Rights Movement, 1954–1968		
Dolores Huerta, 1962		
Malcolm X, 1963		
The Black Panther Party, 1966		
The Brown Berets, 1967		

PEOPLE AND EVENTS	WHEN, HOW, WHAT I LEARNED	WHAT WAS I LEARNING ABOUT RACE AND RACISM?
American Indian Movement and Wounded Knee, 1968–1973		
Marsha P. Johnson, 1969		
JoAnn Tall, 1993		

Appendix F

Racial Literacy Development and Reading Instruction (Chapter 5)

RACIAL LITERACY DEVELOPMENT AND READING INSTRUCTION		
COMPONENTS OF RACIAL LITERACY To be racially literate is to . . .	**BOOK (TITLE/AUTHOR)** Which books help me address one or more of the components of racial literacy?	**TEACHING** How does my instruction help students to become racially literate?
Recognize race as a contemporary problem		
Understand race as a construct		
Acknowledge intersectionality		
Identify Whiteness and White supremacy		
Develop language and lenses to discuss race and racism		
Acquire the ability to decode racism		

Appendix G
Considering Curriculum, Books, and Activism (Chapter 6)

CONSIDERING CURRICULUM, BOOKS, AND ACTIVISM	
Think about your own curriculum and instruction. What is the teaching that helps students develop ideas about activism—ways they, along with their communities, can make observations about issues and the collective work of change-making?	
Who are the activists your students learn about and under what circumstances?	
Which activists are silenced? Why? For what purpose?	
What understandings do your students have about activism? What has facilitated these understandings?	

Appendix H
Student Toolkit of Critical Lenses for Antiracist Reading for Older Readers (Chapter 7)

| STUDENT TOOLKIT OF CRITICAL LENSES FOR ANTIRACIST READING ||
CRITICAL LENS	GUIDING QUESTIONS
Affirmation	• Does this book/text affirm the racial and cultural identities of characters of color/people without generalizing, stereotyping, or misrepresenting? • Are characters of color/BIPOC portrayed in ways that reflect the full range of their lived experiences and humanity? • How does this book/text reflect and affirm my identities and lived experiences?
Awareness	• How does this book help me to think and talk about race and racism? • What opportunities does this book/text provide to analyze and interrogate systems of oppression? • In what ways does this book/text help me to develop ideas about disrupting inequities?
Authorship	• How many of the books/texts that I have access to are written by BIPOC authors? • In what ways do the identities of the author influence the book/text they've written? • If books are not written by BIPOC but are about BIPOC, what makes the author qualified to tell this story? Have they done so with authenticity and care?
Atmosphere	• Are the books/texts in my classroom relevant to my life today? • Do books/texts feature characters/people of color from various backgrounds, environments, settings? • How do the books/texts help me to understand the world around me?

STUDENT TOOLKIT OF CRITICAL LENSES FOR ANTIRACIST READING	
CRITICAL LENS	**GUIDING QUESTIONS**
Activism	• Which books/texts/authors/stories am I drawn to and why? • In what ways do the books/texts create opportunities for me to reflect, make connections, and think critically about my life and society? • What am I learning and possibly unlearning that helps me recognize what I will advocate for?
Accountability	• How am I being challenged and changed as a result of reading this book/text and discussing it with peers? • What about my own identities or the identities of others do I need to know more about? • What will I commit to doing that helps to advance the work of antiracism and equity?

Appendix I

Student Toolkit of Critical Lenses for Antiracist Reading for Younger Readers (Chapter 7)

STUDENT TOOLKIT OF CRITICAL LENSES FOR ANTIRACIST READING FOR YOUNGER READERS	
CRITICAL LENS	**GUIDING QUESTIONS**
Affirmation	• What makes the characters/people in this book feel happy, special, proud, and loved? • What are you learning about the things that the characters/people in this book like to do? What ideas do they have about themselves, their families, their communities, and the world? • In what ways does the story feel like it's about you and your life?
Awareness	• What problems does this book help you to think more about? • How does this book help you to understand who is harmed most by these problems? • What ideas does this book share about ways to make things better?
Authorship	• How many books in my classroom are written by authors who share one or more of my identities? • Why might the author have written this book? • What can I notice about whether books about Black and Brown characters/people are written with care and respect?
Atmosphere	• Which books feel like they are about me and my life? • Are there lots of different kinds of stories about Black and Brown characters/people in my classroom? • What am I learning about my life and the world from characters/people in the books I'm reading?

STUDENT TOOLKIT OF CRITICAL LENSES FOR ANTIRACIST READING FOR YOUNGER READERS	
CRITICAL LENS	**GUIDING QUESTIONS**
Activism	• Which books and authors are my favorite to read? • How do these books challenge me and inspire me? • What do these books make me care about and want to change in the world?
Accountability	• What does talking about this book with my friends and teachers help me to understand about myself and others? • What about my identity and others do I want to learn more? • How will I work to make my life and the life of others more peaceful, joyful, and free?

Appendix J

Educator Toolkit of Critical Lenses for Antiracist Reading Instruction (Chapter 7)

EDUCATOR TOOLKIT OF CRITICAL LENSES FOR ANTIRACIST READING INSTRUCTION		
CRITICAL LENS	**CONSIDERATIONS FOR BOOK SELECTION**	**IMPLEMENTATION**
Affirmation	• Are there a variety of books that affirm students' racial and cultural identities? • How are students' funds of knowledge (Moll et al., 1992) reflected? • Which books validate the cultural and linguistic competencies of students and their communities?	Ask questions that invite students to think about their multiple identities. Utilize the scholarship of Dr. Rudine Sims Bishop and Dr. Gloria Ladson-Billings. *In what ways might this book be a mirror, window, or both for you?*
Awareness	• Which books help students to recognize how the social, cultural, political, economic, and ecological systems they're embedded in can create and perpetuate inequity and injustice? • What opportunities do books provide for students to analyze and interrogate systems of oppression? • In what ways do books help students to develop ideas about disrupting inequities?	Ask questions that raise students' consciousness about the purpose and function of inequities. Utilize the scholarship of Dr. Barbara Love. *In what ways are you feeling empowered to recognize and challenge injustice and work toward a better future?*

EDUCATOR TOOLKIT OF CRITICAL LENSES FOR ANTIRACIST READING INSTRUCTION		
CRITICAL LENS	**CONSIDERATIONS FOR BOOK SELECTION**	**IMPLEMENTATION**
Authorship	• Does the library/curriculum reflect #ownvoice authors? • If books are not by #ownvoice authors, what makes the author qualified to tell this story? • In what ways does this book amplify the voices and experiences of underrepresented and historically excluded identities?	Ask questions that help students recognize the dedication of authors who write with cultural nuance that stems from being part of that culture. Utilize the scholarship of Dr. Sonja Cherry-Paul. *How do creators demonstrate the full range of humanity of characters/people/groups who have been marginalized? Are they doing this with authenticity and care?*
Atmosphere	• Are there numerous ways students of color can see themselves reflected in books made accessible to them? • Are there a variety of genres, time periods, settings, contexts, and issues? • Does the library include books that feature characters/people of color from various backgrounds, identities, and environments?	Ask questions that invite students to consider the ways books are reflective of who they are as well as the world around them. Utilize the scholarship of #DisruptTexts. *In what ways is this book relevant to you? How has it made a difference in your life?*
Activism	• Which books help students to develop racial literacy? • What opportunities do books provide for students to analyze and interrogate systems of oppression? • In what ways do books help students develop ideas about disrupting inequities?	Ask questions that invite students to consider how a book addresses antiracism. Utilize the scholarship of Dr. Yolanda Sealey-Ruiz. *What opportunities for conversations around justice and equity does this book offer?*

(Continued)

(Continued)

EDUCATOR TOOLKIT OF CRITICAL LENSES FOR ANTIRACIST READING INSTRUCTION		
CRITICAL LENS	**CONSIDERATIONS FOR BOOK SELECTION**	**IMPLEMENTATION**
Accountability	• Which books help students understand the meaning of solidarity and commitment? • In what ways do the books made accessible to students disrupt white saviorism and instead demonstrate the importance and value of working in community with BIPOC? • Which books are grounded in hope and love so that students understand the work of antiracism as sustained, ongoing actions?	Ask questions that invite students to consider ways they will advance the work of antiracism. Utilize the scholarship of Dr. Sonja Cherry-Paul. *What will stay with you, inspire you, and inform how you move forward with intentionality and humility to create a racially just world?*

Appendix K
Middle Grade and YA Recommendations

NOVELS

- *All You Have to Do,* by Autumn Allen
- *Warrior Girl Unearthed,* by Angeline Boulley
- *Undercover Latina,* by Aya de León
- *We Are Not Broken,* by George M. Johnson
- *You Are Here: Connecting Flights,* by Ellen Oh, editor
- *Imposter Syndrome and Other Confessions of Alejandra Kim,* by Patricia Park
- *Mascot,* by Charles Waters and Traci Sorell
- *Remember Us,* by Jacqueline Woodson
- *Nigeria Jones: A Novel,* by Ibi Zoboi

NONFICTION

- *Better Than We Found It,* by Frederick Joseph and Porsche Joseph

- *Revolution in Our Time: The Black Panther Party's Promise to the People,* by Kekla Magoon

- *The Sum of Us: How Racism Hurts Everyone*—YA Edition, by Heather McGhee

- *Stamped; Racism, Antiracism and You,* by Jason Reynolds and Ibram X. Kendi

- *Me and White Supremacy*—YA Edition, by Lalyla Saad

- *Just Mercy: True Story for the Fight for Justice,* by Bryan Stevenson

- *Caste—The Origins of Our Discontents*—YA Edition, by Isabel Wilkerson

Author's Note

The dandelion motif I have used across this book to represent antiracist teaching would not have been possible without research. In addition to observing dandelions throughout my life, I read several books that helped me learn about dandelions and their significance to the natural environment. To learn more about dandelions and how they benefit the soil, butterflies, bees, humans, and more, I recommend the following resources, which were a helpful guide as I contemplated dandelions as a powerful symbol for antiracism.

Northeast Foraging: 120 Wild and Flavorful Edibles from Beach Plums to Wineberries, by Leda Meredith

Medicinal Plants of North America: A Field Guide, by Jim Meuninck

Weeds of the Northeast, by Joseph C. Neal, Richard H. Uva, Joseph M. DiTomaso, and Antonio DiTommaso

Backyard Foraging: 65 Familiar Plants You Didn't Know You Could Eat, by Ellen Zachos

References

INTRODUCTION

Bishop, R. S. (Summer 1990). Mirrors, windows, and sliding glass doors. *Perspectives: Choosing and Using Books for the Classroom, 6*(3).

Buchanan-Rivera, E. (2022, July 25). Advancing equity through self-inquiry and thoughtful action. *ASCD.* https://www.ascd.org/blogs/advancing-equity-through-self-inquiry-and-thoughtful-action

Cherry-Paul, S. (2019). *Sparking courageous conversations: Exploring the racial-justice curriculum development and instructional processes of teachers for predominantly White middle-school students* [Doctoral thesis, Teachers College, Columbia University]. Academic Commons. https://academiccommons.columbia.edu/doi/10.7916/d8-syrf-7b03

Cherry-Paul, S. (2020). Becoming the architects of school. https://31daysibpoc.wordpress.com/front-page/

Cherry-Paul, S. (2023). From learning loss to a liberatory mindset. *Educational Leadership, 80*(5), 42–47. https://www.ascd.org/el/articles/from-learning-loss-to-a-liberatory-mindset

Cherry-Paul, S., & Johansen, D. (2019). *Breathing new life into book clubs: A practical guide for teachers.* Heinemann.

CRT Forward Tracking Project Team. (2023). *CRT forward.* https://crtforward.law.ucla.edu/

#DisruptTexts (n.d.). *What is #disrupt texts?* https://disrupttexts.org/lets-get-to-work/

Ebarvia, T. (2023). *Get free: Antibias literacy instruction for stronger readers, writers, and thinkers.* Corwin.

Everett, C. (2017, November 21). There is no diverse book. *Imaginelit.* https://www.imaginelit.com/news/2017/11/21/there-is-no-diverse-book

hooks, b. (2001). *All about love: New visions.* HarperCollins.

Kulger, T. (2012). Diversity in children's books 2012 [Online image]. *Reading Partners.* https://readingpartners.org/blog/discussing-diversity-in-childrens-literature/

Love, B. L. (2023). *Punished for dreaming.* St. Martin's.

Maher, J. (2020, January 29). New Lee and Low survey shows no progress on diversity in publishing. *Publishers Weekly.* https://www.publishersweekly.com/pw/by-topic/industry-news/publisher-news/article/82284-new-lee-and-low-survey-shows-no-progress-on-diversity-in-publishing.html

Milner, H. R., IV. (2020). Disrupting racism and whiteness in researching a science of reading. *International Literacy Association.* https://ila.onlinelibrary.wiley.com/doi/10.1002/rrq.347

Muhammad, G. (2023). *Unearthing joy: A guide to culturally and historically responsive teaching and learning.* Scholastic.

National Center for Education Statistics (NCES). (2020, September). *Race and ethnicity of public school teachers and their students.* U.S. Department of Education. https://nces.ed.gov/pubs2020/2020103/index.asp

Pendharker, E. (2023, February 23). AP African American studies: How other states are responding after Florida's ban.

Education Week. https://www.edweek.org/teaching-learning/ap-african-american-studies-how-other-states-are-responding-after-floridas-ban/2023/02

Reese, D. (2020, February 1). An illustrated record of my indigenous spotlight lecture at 2020 Ontario Library Association super conference. *American Indians in Children's Literature.* https://americanindiansinchildrensliterature.blogspot.com/search?q=curtains

SLJ Staff. (2019, June 19). An updated look at diversity in children's books. *School Library Journal.* https://www.slj.com/story/an-updated-look-at-diversity-in-childrens-books

We Need Diverse Books [@weneeddiversebooks]. (2020, June 26). *2019 by the numbers: Main characters in U.S. children's literature* [Online image]. Instagram. https://www.instagram.com/p/CB5mgWFlils/?hl=en

Chapter 1

Bishop, R. S. (Summer 1990). Mirrors, windows, and sliding glass doors. *Perspectives: Choosing and Using Books for the Classroom, 6*(3).

Cherry-Paul, S., Reynolds, J., & Kendi, I. X. (2021). *Stamped (for kids): Racism, antiracism, and you* (R. Baker, Illus.). Little, Brown.

Ladson-Billings, G. (1995). Toward a theory of culturally relevant pedagogy. *American Research Education Journal, 32*(3), 465–491.

Ladson-Billings, G. (2009). *The dreamkeepers: Successful teachers of African American children.* Jossey-Bass.

Love, B. (2010). Developing a liberatory consciousness. In M. Adams, W. J. Blumenfeld, R. Castaneda, H. Hackman, M. Peters, & X. Zuniga (Eds.), *Reading for diversity and social justice* (2nd ed., pp. 470–474). Routledge.

Love, B. (2019). *We want to do more than survive: Abolitionist teaching and the pursuit of educational freedom.* Beacon Press.

Moll, L. C., Amanti, C., Neff, D., & Gonzalez, N. (1992). Funds of knowledge for teaching: Using a qualitative approach to connect homes and classrooms. *Theory into Practice, 31*(2), 132–141.

Morrison, T. (1999). *The bluest eye.* Vintage. (Original work published 1970).

Paris, D., & Alim, S. (Eds.). (2017). *Culturally sustaining pedagogies: Teaching and learning for justice in a changing world.* Teachers College Press.

Parker, K. N. (2022). *Literacy is liberation: Working toward justice through culturally relevant teaching.* ASCD.

Price-Dennis, D., & Sealey-Ruiz, Y. (2021). *Advancing racial literacies in teacher education: Activism for equity in digital spaces.* Teachers College Press.

Quintero, I. (2019). *My papi has a motorcycle* (Z. Pena, Illus.). Kokila.

Sealey-Ruiz, Y. (2021). *Racial literacy* [Policy Brief]. National Council of Teachers of English. https://ncte.org/resources/policy-briefs/

Sullivan, J., Wilton, L., & Apfelbaum, E. P. (2020, August 6). Adults delay conversations about race because they underestimate children's processing of race. *Journal of Experimental Psychology: General, 150*(2), 395–400. http://dx.doi.org/10.1037/xge0000851

Chapter 2

Bishop, R. S. (Summer 1990). Mirrors, windows, and sliding glass doors. *Perspectives: Choosing and Using Books for the Classroom, 6*(3), 9–11.

Brechner, K. (2023, February 17). Hannah on "homeland." *Publishers Weekly.* https://blogs.publishersweekly.com/blogs/shelftalker/?p=34116

Crenshaw, K. (1989). Demarginalizing the intersection of race and sex: A black feminist critique of antidiscrimination doctrine, feminist theory and antiracist politics, *University of Chicago Legal Forum*, *1989*(1), 139–167. https://chicago unbound.uchicago.edu/uclf/vol1989/iss1/8

Fadel, L., & Balaban, S. (2019, August 25). "My papi has a motorcycle" pays loving tribute to a California childhood. *NPR*. https://www.npr.org/2019/08/25/753746555/my-papi-has-a-motorcycle-pays-loving-tribute-to-a-california-childhood

Hawthorne, B. [@britthawthorne]. (2020, June 2). *Pyramid of accountability* [Online image]. Instagram. https://www.instagram.com/p/CA8ihy_hH5J/?hl=en

Ladson-Billings, G. (2009). *The dreamkeepers: Successful teachers of African American children.* Jossey-Bass.

Lyons, K. S. (2020, February 22). *Day 22: Joshunda Sanders.* The Brown Bookshelf. https://thebrownbookshelf.com/28days/day-22-joshunda-sanders/

Palmer, C. (2023). *Biography.* Charly Palmer. https://www.charlypalmer.com/about

Pride and Less Prejudice. (2023). *Interview with DeShanna Neal, author of "My Rainbow."* https://www.prideandlessprejudice.org/meet-the-authors/neal-d

CHILDREN'S BOOKS

Barnes, D. (2020). *I am every good thing* (G. C. James, Illus.). Paulsen Books.

Behar, R. (2022). *Tía Fortuna's new home: A Jewish Cuban journey* (D. Holzwarth, Illus.). Knopf.

Bowles, D. (2021). *My two border towns* (E. Meza, Illus.). Kokila.

Chen, E. (2022). *I am golden* (S. Diao, Illus.). Feiwel & Friends.

Flett, J. (2014). *Wild berries.* Simply Read Books.

Gray, G. R., Jr. (2023). *I'm from* (O. Mora, Illus.). Balzer and Bray.

Hammond, T. (2023). *A day with no words* (K. Cosgrove, Illus.). Wheat Penny Press.

Moushabeck, H. (2023). *Homeland: My father dreams of Palestine* (R. Madooh, Illus.). Chronicle.

Neal, D., & Neal, T. (2020). *My rainbow* (A. Twink, Illus.). Kokila.

Quintero, I. (2019). *My papi has a motorcycle* (Z. Pena, Illus.). Kokila.

Sanders, J. (2019). *I can write the world* (C. Palmer, Illus.). Six Foot Press.

CHAPTER 3

Baker-Bell, A. (2020). *Linguistic justice: Black language, literacy, identity, and pedagogy.* NCTE-Routledge Research Series.

Campt, T. M. (2021). *A Black gaze: Artists changing how we see.* MIT Press.

Cherry-Paul, S., Reynolds, J., & Kendi, I. X. (2021). *Stamped (for kids): Racism, antiracism, and you* (R. Baker, Illus.). Little, Brown.

España, C., & Herrera, L. Y. (2020). *En comunidad: Lessons for centering the voices and experiences of bilingual Latinx students.* Heinemann.

hooks, b. (1994). *Teaching to transgress: Education as the practice of freedom.* Routledge.

Howell, D., Norris, A., & Williams, K. L. (2019). Towards Black gaze theory: How Black female teachers make Black students visible [Hillard/Sizemore Special Edition]. *Urban Education Policy and Research Annuals*, *6*(1).

Rose, C. (1998, January 19). *Toni Morrison beautifully answers an "illegitimate" question on race* [Video]. YouTube. https://www.youtube.com/watch?v=-Kgq3F8wbYA

Salesses, M. (2021). *Craft in the real world: Rethinking fiction writing and workshopping.* Catapult.

Thompson, R. F. (1984). *Flash of the spirit: African & Afro-American art & philosophy.* Vintage.

CHILDREN'S BOOKS

Ford, B. (2022). *Uncle John's city garden* (F. Morrison, Illus.). Holiday House.

Goade, M. (2022). *Berry song.* Little, Brown.

Kemp, L. Z. (2023). *A crown for Corina* (E. Chavarri, Illus.). Little, Brown.

Khalil, A. (2023). *The night before Eid: A Muslim family story* (R. Kheiriyeh, Illus.). Little, Brown.

Lindstrom, C. (2023). *My powerful hair* (S. Littlebird, Illus.). Abrams.

Peyton, B. (2023). *Dancing the tinikling* (D. Cerna, Illus.). Sleeping Bear Press.

Reynoso-Morris, A. (2023). *Platanos are love* (M. Rahman, Illus.). Atheneum Books.

Varadarajan, G. (2022). *My bindi* (A. Sreenivasan, Illus.). Orchard Books.

Wang, A. (2022). *Luli and the language of tea* (H. Yum, Illus.). Porter Books.

Zhang, K. (2019). *Amy Wu and the perfect boa* (C. Chua, Illus.). Simon & Schuster.

CHAPTER 4

Annamma, S., Jackson, D., & Morrison, D. (2017). Conceptualizing color-evasiveness: Using dis/ability critical race theory to expand a color-blind racial ideology in education and society. *Race Ethnicity and Education, 20*(2), 147–162.

Centers for Disease Control and Prevention. (2022, October 7). *Drowning facts.* U.S. Department of Health & Human Services. https://www.cdc.gov/drowning/facts/index.html

Centers for Disease Control and Prevention. (2022, October 7). *Drowning prevention.* U.S. Department of Health & Human Services. https://www.cdc.gov/drowning/prevention/index.html

Cherry-Paul, S., Reynolds, J., & Kendi, I. X. (2021). *Stamped (for kids): Racism, antiracism, and you* (R. Baker, Illus.). Little, Brown.

Cornwall, G. (2017) *Jabari jumps.* Candlewick.

Diaz, J. (2022, September 2). A swimming cap made for Black hair gets official approval after previous Olympic ban. *NPR.* https://www.npr.org/2022/09/02/1120761124/swimming-cap-black-hair-fina-approval

DiCamillo, K. (2000). *Because of Winn-Dixie.* Scholastic.

DiCamillo, K. (2020). *Because of Winn-Dixie.* Candlewick.

#DisruptText. (n.d.). *What is #disrupt texts?* https://disrupttexts.org/lets-get-to-work/

Ebarvia, T. (2023). *Get free: Antibias literacy instruction for stronger readers, writers, and thinkers.* Corwin.

FollettLearning. (2023, September 8). *Learn about Jabari Jumps with Gaia Cornwall* [Video]. YouTube. https://www.youtube.com/watch?v=IC3WGagY_UY

Freire, P. (2000). *Pedagogy of the oppressed.* Continuum.

Glenn, C. L., & Cunningham, L. J. (2009). Black magic: The magical Negro and White salvation in film. *Journal of Black Studies, 40*(2), 135–152. https://doi.org/10.1177/00219347073078

Grady, C. (2021, March 3). Dr. Seuss is a beloved icon who also drew some extremely racist stuff. *Vox.* https://www.vox.com/culture/22309286/dr-seuss-controversy-read-across-america-racism-if-i-ran-the-zoo-mulberry-street-mcgelliots-pool

Love, B. (2010). Developing a liberatory consciousness. In M. Adams, W. J. Blumenfeld, R. Castaneda, H. Hackman, M. Peters, &

X. Zuniga (Eds.), *Reading for diversity and social justice* (2nd ed., pp. 470–474). Routledge.

Martin, R. (Host). (2008, May 6). *Racial history of American swimming pools* [Audio podcast]. The Bryant Park Project. https://www.npr.org/2008/05/06/90213675/racial-history-of-american-swimming-pools

Morrison, T. (1992). *Playing in the dark: Whiteness and the literary imagination.* Harvard University Press.

Reese, D. (2021, March 20). Gone with the Wind is no longer in DiCamillo's Because of Winn Dixie. *American Indians in Children's Literature.* https://americanindiansinchildrensliterature.blogspot.com/2021/03/gone-with-wind-is-no-longer-in.html

Salesses, M. (2021). *Craft in the real world: Rethinking fiction writing and workshopping.* Catapult.

Thomas, E. E. (2019). *The dark fantastic: Race and the imagination from Harry Potter to the Hunger Games.* New York University Press.

USA Swimming. (2017, May 25). *USA swimming foundation announces 5-10 percent increase in swimming ability.* https://www.usaswimming.org/news/2017/05/25/usa-swimming-foundation-announces-5-10-percent-increase-in-swimming-ability

Wong, J. (1996). Quilt. In *A suitcase of seaweed and other poems.* McElderry Books.

CHILDREN'S BOOKS

Clarke, M. B. (2021). *When we say Black lives matter.* Candlewick.

Giddens, R. (2022). *Build a house* (M. Mikai, Illus.). Candlewick.

Hannah-Jones, N., & Watson, R. (2021). *The 1619 project: Born on the water* (N. Smith, Illus.). Kokila.

Sorell, T. (2021). *We are still here!: Native American truths everyone should know* (F. Lessac, Illus.). Charlesbridge.

Weatherford, C. B. (2021). *Unspeakable: The Tulsa race massacre* (F. Cooper, Illus.). Carolrhoda Books.

CHAPTER 5

Ainsley, J. (2023, February 24). U.S. has admitted 271,000 Ukrainian refugees since Russian invasion, far above Biden's goal of 100,000. *NBC News.* https://www.nbcnews.com/politics/immigration/us-admits-271000-ukrainian-refugees-russia-invasion-biden-rcna72177

Associated Press. (2021, August 18). Judge rules Philadelphia can't remove a Christopher Columbus statue. *NPR.* https://www.npr.org/2021/08/18/1029077566/christopher-columbus-statue-philadelphia-judge

Christopher Columbus statues taken down at 2 Chicago parks. (2020, July 24). *AP News.* https://apnews.com/article/ap-top-news-chicago-racial-injustice-il-state-wire-lori-lightfoot-62e35c71744cb154746cbefcda004e08

Elliott, D. (2022, August 11). Charlottesville was a wake-up call for many about the white supremacy movement. *NPR.* https://www.npr.org/2022/08/11/1116880047/charlottesville-was-a-wake-up-call-for-many-about-the-white-supremacy-movement

Freire, P. (2000). *Pedagogy of the oppressed.* Continuum.

Jackson, J. (2020, October 8). The Pen Ten: An interview with Yamile Saied Mendez. *Pen America.* https://pen.org/the-pen-ten-yamile-saied-mendez/

Joiner, L. (2017, June 27). Bree Newsome reflects on taking down South Carolina's Confederate flag 2 years ago. *Vox.* https://www.vox.com/identities/2017/6/27/15880052/bree-newsome-south-carolinas-confederate-flag

Mitchell, C. (2020, June 17). Data: The schools named after Confederate figures. *EducationWeek.* https://www.edweek.org/leadership/data-the-schools-named-after-confederate-figures/2020/06

Pfosi, N. (2020, June 11). Protesters tear down Christopher Columbus statue in Saint Paul, Minnesota. *Reuters.* https://www.reuters.com/article/us-minneapolis-police-saint-paul-statue/protesters-tear-down-christopher-columbus-statue-in-saint-paul-minnesota-idUSKBN23I04X

Pratt, G. R., & Yin, A. (2022, August 19). Chicago task force recommens removal of monuments, including Columbus statues, and the addition of others. Now what? *Chicago Tribune.* https://www.chicagotribune.com/politics/ct-chicago-monuments-columbus-statues-report-20220819-o5iqpfiomfexnn5apqlpuxkiey-story.html

Price-Dennis, D., & Sealey-Ruiz, Y. (2021). *Advancing racial literacies in teacher education: Activism for equity in digital spaces.* Teachers College Press.

Sealey-Ruiz, Y. (2021). *Racial literacy* [Policy Brief]. National Council of Teachers of English. https://ncte.org/resources/policy-briefs/

Smith, C. (2022). *How the word is passed: A reckoning with the history of slavery across America.* Little, Brown and Company.

Southern Poverty Law Center. *2020 Confederate symbol removals.* (n.d.). https://www.splcenter.org/data-projects/2020-confederate-symbol-removals

Treisman, R. (2020, July 5). Baltimore protesters topple Columbus statue. *NPR.* https://www.npr.org/sections/live-updates-protests-for-racial-justice/2020/07/05/887423624/baltimore-protesters-topple-columbus-statue

Twine, F. W. (2004). A white side of black Britain: The concept of racial literacy. *Ethnic and Racial Studies, 27*(6), 878–907. https://doi.org/10.1080/0141987042000268512

Whitepigeon, M. (2021, July 15). Native in the arts spotlight: Visual artist Andrea Carlson talks about her Chicago "you are on Potawatomi land" mural. *Native News Online.* https://nativenewsonline.net/arts-entertainment/native-in-the-arts-spotlight-visual-artist-andrea-carlson-talks-about-her-chicago-you-are-on-potawatomi-land-mural

CHILDREN'S BOOKS

Cherry-Paul, S., Reynolds, J., & Kendi, I. X. (2021). *Stamped (for kids): Racism, antiracism, and you* (R. Baker, Illus.). Little, Brown.

hooks, b. (2017). *Skin again* (C. Raschka, Illus.). Little, Brown.

Jewell, T. (2023). *The antiracist kid: A book about identity, justice, and activism* (N. Miles, Illus.). Versify.

Madison, M., & Ralli, J. (2021). *Our skin: A first conversation about race* (I. Roxas, Illus.). Rise.

Méndez, Y. S. (2019). *Where are you from?* (J. Kim, Illus.). HarperCollins.

CHAPTER 6

American Civil Liberties Union. (2005, November 23). Racial profiling: Definition. *ACLU.* https://www.aclu.org/documents/racial-profiling-definition

Bridges, R. (2009). *Ruby Bridges goes to school: My true story.* Scholastic.

Cherry-Paul, S. (2023). From learning loss to a liberatory mindset. *Educational Leadership, 80*(5), 42–47. https://www.ascd.org/el/articles/from-learning-loss-to-a-liberatory-mindset

Equal Justice Initiative. (2014). Racial profiling. https://eji.org/news/history-racial-injustice-racial-profiling

Gupta, E. (2021, September 16). Central York student speaks out on diversity book ban: "Enough is enough." *York Dispatch.* https://

www.yorkdispatch.com/story/opinion/
contributors/2021/09/16/central-york-
student-speaks-out-diversity-book-ban-
enough-enough/8362372002/

Ladson-Billings, G. (2017). The (r)evolution will
not be standardized: Teacher education, hip
hop pedagogy, and culturally relevant pedagogy 2.0. In D. Paris & H. S. Alim (Eds.),
*Culturally sustaining pedagogies: Teaching and
learning for justice in a changing world* (pp.
141–156). Teachers College Press.

Sealey-Ruiz, Y. (2021). *Racial literacy* [Policy
Brief]. National Council of Teachers
of English. https://ncte.org/resources/
policy-briefs/

Vulchi, P., & Guo, W. (2018, May). *Lessons of cultural intimacy* [Video]. TED Conferences.
https://www.ted.com/talks/priya_vulchi_and_
winona_guo_lessons_of_cultural_intimacy

CHILDREN'S BOOKS

Craig, M.-R. (2022). *We have a dream: Meet 30
young indigenous people and people of color protecting the environment* (S. Khadija, Illus.).
Abrams.

Lindstrom, C. (2023). *Autumn Peltier, water
warrior* (B. George, Illus.). Roaring Brook
Press.

Luzincourt, F. (2022). *Resistance: My story of activism.* Norton.

Tudor, A., Tudor, K., & Eaglespeaker, J. (2018).
*Young water protectors: A story about standing
rock.* CreateSpace Independent Publishing
Platform.

Wallace, G. (2023). *The light she feels inside* (O.
Duchess, Illus.). Sourcebooks Jabberwocky.

Woodard, B. (2022). *More than peach: Changing the
world…one crayon at a time!* (F. Liem, Illus.).
Scholastic.

CHAPTER 7

Brooks, G. (1992). *Maud Martha.* Third World
Press.

Cruz, M. C. (2021). *Risk. Fail. Rise. A teacher's
guide to learning from mistakes.* Heinemann.

Ebarvia, T. (2023). *Get free: Antibias literacy
instruction for stronger readers, writers, and
thinkers.* Corwin.

Ikeda, D. (2005). *A conversation with my wife.*
Daisaku Ikeda: Peace though dialogue.
https://www.daisakuikeda.org/main/profile/
recollections/conversation-with-my-wife.
html#sdendnote3sym

Moll, L. C., Amanti, C., Neff, D., & Gonzalez, N.
(1992). Funds of knowledge for teaching: Using
a qualitative approach to connect homes and
classrooms. *Theory into Practice, 31*(2), 132–141.

Morrison, T. (1999). *The bluest eye.* Vintage.
(Original work published 1970)

Index

Accountability lens, 37 (figure), 39
  BIPOC writers/topics and, 55, 58–59, 63, 67–68, 72, 76, 80, 84–85, 89, 93, 97
  community activists and, 231, 235, 239, 243, 247, 251
  cultural/community/collective practices and, 113, 117, 121–122, 126, 130–131, 135, 138–139, 143, 146–147, 150–151
  Educator Tool Kit of Critical Lenses for Antiracist Reading Instruction and, 263, 288
  racial literacy and, 203, 206, 209–210, 213–214, 218
  silences around racism and, 171, 174–175, 179–180, 184, 188
  Student Tool Kit of Critical Lenses for Antiracist Reading and, 258, 260, 283, 285
Activism, xvii
  accomplices and, 88
  active allies and, 88
  activists, teaching about, 28, 31–32
  antiracist mindset and, 2–3
  Black Lives Matter movement and, 4
  Black Panther Party and, 3–4
  Chicano Movement and, 4
  co-conspirators and, 88
  Greensboro Four and, 3
  intersectionality and, 88
  Little Rock Nine and, 3
  love, role of, 1, 2, 3, 4
  representation vs. liberation and, 2
  scholar activism, educational practices and, xxi, xxii
  systemic inequities and, 2–4, 5, 6, 30–31, 111
  Water Protectors of Standing Rock and, 4

  youth empowerment, transformative impact of, 3, 4
  See also Community activists; Human liberation movement; Sustained revolution
Activism lens, 37 (figure), 38–39
  BIPOC writers/topics and, 54–55, 58, 63, 67, 71, 75–76, 79, 84, 88–89, 92–93, 96–97
  community activists and, 230–231, 234–235, 238–239, 242–243, 246–247, 250–251
  cultural/community/collective practices and, 113, 116–117, 121, 125–126, 134, 138, 142, 146, 150
  Educator Tool Kit of Critical Lenses for Antiracist Reading Instruction and, 262–263, 287
  racial literacy and, 203, 206, 209, 213, 217
  silences around racism and, 170, 174, 179, 183, 187–188
  Student Tool Kit of Critical Lenses for Antiracist Reading and, 258, 260, 283, 285
Affirmation lens, 32, 35, 37, 37 (figure)
  BIPOC writers/topics and, 52–53, 56–57, 60–61, 64–65, 69–70, 73–74, 77, 81–82, 86, 94, 9091
  community activists and, 228–229, 232–233, 236–237, 240–241, 244–245, 248
  cultural/community/collective practices and, 110–111, 114–115, 118–119, 123–124, 127–128, 132–133, 136, 140, 144, 148
  Educator Tool Kit of Critical Lenses for Antiracist Reading Instruction and, 261, 286
  racial literacy and, 200–201, 204, 207, 211, 215

silences around racism and, 168, 172, 177, 181, 185–186

Student Tool Kit of Critical Lenses for Antiracist Reading and, 257, 259, 282, 284

Afrodiasporic voices, 246

Ali, Muhammad, 267

Alim, H. Samy, 6, 106

American Civil Liberties Union (ACLU), 237

American Indian Movement (AIM), 193, 279

American Indians in Children's Literatures (AICL), 10

American Library Association (ALA), 6

Amnesty International (AI), 61

Amy Wu and the Perfect Bao, 148–150

Anderson, Carol, 169

Angelou, Maya, xx

Annamma, Subini, 165

Anti-Muslim hate, 2, 82, 124

The Antiracist Kid: A Book About Identity, Justice, and Activism, 207–210

Antiracist Reading Framework, xvii, xx, 24–25, 25 (figure), 272

anti-CRT policies/legislation and, 6

antiracist teaching characteristics/critical lenses and, 39–41

authentic student-teacher engagement and, xxi

book clubs and, 20

canonical texts, allegiance to, 7–8, 9–10

class library contents, selection of, xxi, 8–13, 39–41

community of antiracist thinkers, fostering of, xxi, xxii, 107

curricula/units, planning of, 21

cycle of renewal, shedding process and, xxii

dandelion metaphor for, 23–24

#DisruptTexts movement and, 7, 157

diversity in children's literature and, 10–13

independent readers, support of, 20–21

liberation-grounded democracy, ascent to, 4, 41

lived experience, reflection of, xx, xxi, xxii, 9, 12, 26–27

mind work/heart work and, 25–26

mini lessons, development of, 19

mirrors and windows approach and, 9–13, 26–27

read-alouds, implementation of, 19

reading classrooms, practices of, 18–22

reading partnerships/groups and, 20

text sets, creation of, 21

transformative power of, xx, xxi, xxii

whole school/community reads, facilitation of, 21

See also Antiracist teaching; BIPOC writers/topics; Cultural/community/collective practices; Heroes/holidays curriculum; Justice centeredness; Racial literacy; Sustained revolution

Antiracist teaching:

accountability lens and, 37 (figure), 39

activism lens and, 37 (figure), 38–39

activists, teaching about, 28, 31–32

additive curricular approaches, disruption of, 5

affirmation lens and, 32, 35, 37, 37 (figure)

ancestral roots, connection to, xx

atmosphere lens and, 37 (figure), 38

authorship lens and, 37 (figure), 38

awareness lens and, 32, 34 (table), 35–36, 37–38, 37 (figure)

BIPOC in texts, centering of, 28–30, 29 (figure), 36, 38

Black women scholars, work of, 32, 33–34 (table)

book list recommendations for, 289–290

characteristics of, 27–32, 29 (figure)

community connections, nurturing of, 32

critical lenses for, 32–39, 33–34 (table), 37 (figure)

critical race theory, undermining of, 6

cultural/community/collective practices, recognition of, 28, 30

culturally relevant teaching and, xx, xxi, 6, 33 (table)

cycle of renewal, shedding process and, xxii

dandelion metaphor for, 23, 24

disciplinary measures, racial disproportionality in, 2–3

Educator Tool Kit of Critical Lenses for Antiracist Reading Instruction and, 260–263, 286–288

fairy dust approach to, 15

funds of knowledge focus and, 30
humanizing pedagogy and, xx, xxi, xxii
identity-inspiring instruction and, 11–12, 15
liberatory consciousness, development of,
    34 (table), 35, 36
lived experience, importance of, xx, xxi, xxii,
    26–27, 29–30
love/joy, role of, 1, 2, 3, 4, 15–16, 22, 35, 36, 254
mirrors and windows approach and, 9–10,
    26–27, 33 (table)
misunderstanding of, 8–13
ownvoices movement and, 29–30
race/antiracism conversations, resources for, 17
racial literacy, teaching of, 28, 31, 34 (table), 36
representation vs. liberation and, 2, 27
restrictive education policies and, 5, 6–7
silences around racism, shattering of, 28, 30–31
systemic inequities and, 2–4, 5, 6, 30–31, 111
teacher self-reflection and, 16–18
transformative potential of, xx, xxi, xxii, 2–3
See also Antiracist Reading Framework;
    BIPOC writers/topics; Community
    activists; Cultural/community/collective
    practices; Heroes/holidays curriculum;
    Human liberation movement; Racial
    literacy; Silences around racism; Sustained
    revolution
Arbery, Ahmaud, 5, 268
Assimilation, 128, 141, 142
Asylum Seekers, 61
Atmosphere lens, 37 (figure), 38
    BIPOC writers/topics and, 54, 58, 62, 66–67,
        71, 75, 79, 83–84, 88, 92, 96
    community activists and, 230, 234, 238, 242,
        246, 250
    cultural/community/collective practices
        and, 112, 116, 120, 125, 129–130, 134,
        137–138, 142, 146, 149–150
    Educator Tool Kit of Critical Lenses for
        Antiracist Reading Instruction and,
        262, 287
    racial literacy and, 202, 205–206, 208–209,
        213, 217
    silences around racism and, 170, 174, 178–179,
        183, 187

Student Tool Kit of Critical Lenses for
    Antiracist Reading and, 258, 259,
    283, 285
Authorship lens, 37 (figure), 38
    BIPOC writers/topics and, 53–54, 57, 62,
        65–66, 70–71, 74–75, 78, 83, 87, 91–92,
        95–96
    community activists and, 230, 233–234,
        237–238, 245–246, 249
    cultural/community/collective practices and,
        111–112, 115, 119–120, 124–125, 129,
        133, 137, 141, 145, 149
    Educator Tool Kit of Critical Lenses for
        Antiracist Reading Instruction and,
        262, 287
    racial literacy and, 202, 205, 208, 212, 216–217
    silences around racism and, 169, 173, 178, 182,
        186–187
    Student Tool Kit of Critical Lenses for
        Antiracist Reading and, 258, 259,
        282, 284
Autism spectrum disorder (ASD), 78, 88
Autumn Peltier, Water Warrior, 232–235
Awareness lens, 32, 34 (table), 35–36, 37–38,
    37 (figure)
    BIPOC writers/topics and, 53, 57, 61, 65, 70,
        74, 78, 82, 87, 91, 95
    community activists and, 229, 233, 237, 241,
        245, 249
    cultural/community/collective practices and,
        111, 115, 119, 124, 128–129, 133, 137,
        141, 144–145, 149
    Educator Tool Kit of Critical Lenses for
        Antiracist Reading Instruction and,
        261–262, 286
    racial literacy and, 201, 205, 207–208, 212, 216
    silences around racism and, 163, 169, 173,
        177–178, 182, 186
    Student Tool Kit of Critical Lenses for
        Antiracist Reading and, 257, 259,
        282, 284

Baker-Bell, April, 102
Baker, Rachelle, 200
Balaban, Samantha, 92

Baldwin, James, xx

Banks, James, 4

Barnes, Derrick, 52, 54, 55

Beals, Melba Patillo, 3

Because of Winn-Dixie, 158, 159–162

Behar, Ruth, 56

Bell, Kamal, 223

Berry Song, 114–117

BIPOC writers/topics, 28–30, 29 (figure), 38, 51

    accountability lens and, 55, 58–59, 63, 67–68, 72, 76, 80, 84–85, 89, 93, 97

    activism lens and, 54–55, 58, 63, 67, 71, 75–76, 79, 84, 88–89, 92–93, 96–97

    affirmation lens and, 52–53, 56–57, 60–61, 64–65, 69–70, 73–74, 77, 81–82, 86, 90–91, 94

    atmosphere lens and, 54, 58, 62, 66–67, 71, 75, 79, 83–84, 88, 92, 96

    authorship lens and, 53–54, 57, 62, 65–66, 70–71, 74–75, 78, 83, 87, 91–92, 95–96

    awareness lens and, 53, 57, 61, 65, 70, 74, 78, 82, 87, 91, 95

    book list for, 50

    dandelion metaphor and, 43, 49

    A Day With No Words, critical lens prompts/pathways for, 77–80

    environmental racism/injustice and, 229

    Homeland, critical lens prompts/pathways for, 81–85

    I Am Every Good Thing, critical lens prompts/pathways for, 52–55

    I Am Golden, critical lens prompts/pathways for, 64–68

    I Can Write the World, critical lens prompts/pathways for, 94–97

    I'm From, critical lens prompts/pathways for, 73–76

    lived experience, centering of, 45–47

    mirrors and windows approach and, 46

    My Papi Has a Motorcycle, critical lens prompts/pathways for, 90–93

    My Rainbow, critical lens prompts/pathways for, 86–89

    My Two Border Towns, critical lens prompts/pathways for, 60–63

    ownvoices concept, importance of, 69

    school-based reading experiences and, 44–49, 45 (figure), 273

    Tía Fortuna's New Home, critical lens prompts/pathways for, 56–59

    Wild Berries, critical lens prompts/pathways for, 69–72

    See also Cultural/community/collective practices; Racial literacy; Silences around racism; Sustained revolution

Bishop, Rudine Sims, 9, 10, 11, 26, 27, 33, 46, 261, 286

Black Gaze Theory, 105–106

Black History Month, 5

Black/Indigenous/people of color. *See* BIPOC writers/topics

Black Lives Matter movement, 4, 172–175, 201

Black Panther Party, 3–4, 193, 201, 221, 278

Black Power Movement, 267

Black Wall Street, 169

Blair, Ezell, Jr., 3

Bland, Sandra, 196

Boggs, Grace Lee, 267

Book bans, 6, 46, 163, 164, 196, 221, 255, 260–261

Born on the Water/The 1619 Project, 176–180

Bowles, David, 60, 62

Brechner, Kevin, 83

Bridges, Ruby, 3, 221

Brooks, Gwendolyn, 219, 254

Brown Berets, 4, 193, 278

Brown, Michael, 196

Brown, Minnijean, 3

Buchanan-Rivera, Erica, 16, 17

Build a House, 181–184

C-M-M (centered/marginalized/missing) analysis, 260

Campbell, Edith, 38

Campt, Tina M., 105, 106

Carlisle Indian Industrial School, 193, 196, 277

Carlson, Andrea, 190

Castille, Philando, 268

Cerna, Diobelle, 108, 132, 133

Change strategies. *See* Activism; Community activists; Sustained revolution

Chavarri, Elisa, 108, 118

Chen, Eva, 64, 66

Cherry-Paul, Sonja, 28, 101, 103, 104, 105, 161, 164, 198, 200, 202, 224, 262, 263, 287, 288

Chicago Monuments Project, 191

Chicano Movement, 4

Children's Crusade, 267

Chua, Charlene, 108, 147

Cisgender persons, 87, 208, 212

Civil Rights Movement, 21, 173, 193, 201, 221, 267, 278

Civilization Fund Act of 1819, 193, 276

Clarke, Maxine Beneba, 166, 172, 173

Collective/collaborative practices. *See* Cultural/community/collective practices

Colonization, 117, 133, 145, 169, 186, 190–192, 246

Columbus, Christopher, 191, 192, 193, 276

Colvin, Claudette, 3

Community activists, 219
   accountability lens and, 231, 235, 239, 243, 247, 251
   activism lens and, 230–231, 234–235, 238–239, 242–243, 246–247, 250–251
   affirmation lens and, 228–229, 232–233, 236–237, 240–241, 244–245, 248
   atmosphere lens and, 230, 234, 238, 242, 246, 250
   authorship lens and, 230, 233–234, 237–238, 241–242, 245–246, 249
   Autumn Peltier, Water Warrior, critical lens prompts/pathways for, 232–235
   awareness lens and, 229, 233, 237, 241, 245, 249
   book list for, 226
   community service, ethical commitment to, 223
   critical sociopolitical consciousness, nurturing of, 224–225
   curriculum/teaching approaches and, 221–223, 224, 225, 281
   dandelion metaphor and, 219, 225
   environmental racism/injustice and, 229
   The Light She Feels Inside, critical lens prompts/pathways for, 244–247
   lived experience of activism and, 220–221, 223

More Than Peach, critical lens prompts/pathways for, 248–251

Resistance: My Story of Activism, critical lens prompts/pathways for, 236–239

school-based exposure to, 221, 224, 225

teaching as activism and, 223, 224–225

We Have a Dream, critical lens prompts/ pathways for, 228–231

Young Water Protectors, critical lens prompts/ pathways for, 240–243

See also Activism; Cultural/community/ collective practices; Sustained revolution

Conversations, xvii, xxii
   antiracist teaching, reflective conversations and, xxi–xxii, 28–32
   race/antiracism conversations and, 16, 17, 108, 164–165
   relationships, becoming human and, xxiii
   safe discussions, conditions for, 16
   silences around racism and, 164–165, 166
   teacher self-reflection and, 17–18
   See also Cultural/community/collective practices; Human liberation movement; Racial literacy; Sustained revolution

Cooper, Floyd, 168, 169

Cooperative Children's Book Center, 11, 12, 13

Cornwall, Gaia, 158, 159, 162

Cosgrove, Kate, 77

COVID-19 pandemic, 3, 5, 66, 67, 196

Craig, Mya-Rose, 226, 228, 229, 230

Crenshaw, Kimberlé, 6, 88

Critical race theory (CRT), 6, 255

A Crown for Corina, 118–122

CRT Forward Tracking Project Team, 6

Cruz, M. Colleen, 255

Cultural assimilation, 141, 142, 186

Cultural/community/collective practices, xvii, xxi, 99
   accountability lens and, 113, 117, 121–122, 126, 130–131, 135, 138–139, 143, 146–147, 150–151
   activism lens and, 113, 116–117, 121, 125–126, 130, 134, 138, 142, 146, 150
   affirmation lens and, 110–111, 114–115, 118–119, 123–124, 127–128, 132–133, 136, 140, 144, 148

Amy Wu and the Perfct Bao, critical lens prompts/pathways for, 147–150

antiracist teaching and, 28, 30

atmosphere lens and, 112, 116, 120, 125, 129–130, 134, 137–138, 142, 146, 149–150

authorship lens and, 111–112, 115, 119–120, 124–125, 129, 133, 137, 141, 145, 149

awareness lens and, 111, 115, 119, 124, 128–129, 133, 137, 141, 144–145, 149

Berry Song, critical lens prompts/pathways for, 114–117

Black Gaze Theory, dominant ideologies and, 105–106

book list for, 108

collaborative action, understanding of, 102, 103 (table)

collective action, understanding of, 102, 103 (table)

community action, understanding of, 102, 104 (table)

A Crown for Corina, critical lens prompts/pathways for, 118–122

culture, understanding of, 102, 103 (table)

curriculum tool, understanding of, 102, 104 (table)

Dancing the Tinikling, critical lens prompts/pathways for, 132–135

dandelion metaphor and, 99, 107

Double Dutch jumprope activity and, 100–101

Five Cs, reflection on, 102, 103–104 (table)

historical/sociocultural understandings and, 102, 107, 274

linguistic/racial hierarchies, interconnectedness of, 102, 104–105

Luli and the Language of Tea, critical lens prompts/pathways for, 144–147

multiple ways of knowing, support of, 30

My Bindi, critical lens prompts/pathways for, 140–143

My Powerful Hair, critical lens prompts/pathways for, 127–131

The Night Before Eid: A Muslim Family Story, critical lens prompts/pathways for, 123–126

Plátanos Are Love, critical lens prompts/pathways for, 136–139

reading communities, nurturing of, 106–107, 108

truth-seeking/truth-telling and, 27

Uncle John's City Garden, critical lens prompts/pathways for, 110–113

whole school/community reads and, 21

See also BIPOC writers/topics; Community activists; Conversations; Racial literacy; Silences around racism; Sustained revolution

Cultural genocide, 128

Culturally relevant teaching (CRT), xx, xxi, 6, 33 (table)

Cunningham, Landra, 159

Dahlen, Sarah Park, 11, 12, 38

Dancing the Tinikling, 132–135

Dandelion metaphor, xv–xvii, xxii

Antiracist Reading Framework, vision for, 23–24

BIPOC in texts, centering of, 43, 49

community activists and, 219, 225

cultural/community/collective practices and, 99, 107

racial literacy development and, 189

silences around racism and, 153, 164, 165

sustained revolution and, 253, 254, 264

Davis, Angela Y., 221, 266, 268, 269

A Day With No Words, 77–80

Diao, Sophie, 64, 66

DiCamillo, Kate, 158, 159, 160, 161

#DisruptTexts movement, 7, 157, 262, 287

Diversity Baseline Survey (DBS), 14

Double Dutch jumprope activity, 46, 100–101

Douglass, Frederick, 266

Duchess, Olivia, 226, 244, 246

Duyvis, Corinne, 29–30

Eaglespeaker, Jason, 226

Ebarvia, Tricia, 7, 16, 17, 30, 105, 157, 161, 260

Eckford, Elizabeth, 3

Educator Tool Kit of Critical Lenses for Antiracist Reading Instruction, 260–261

accountability lens and, 263, 288

activism lens and, 262–263, 287

affirmation lens and, 260, 286
atmosphere lens and, 262, 287
authorship lens and, 262, 287
awareness lens and, 261–262, 286
C-M-M analysis and, 260
See also Student Tool Kit of Critical Lenses for
     Antiracist Reading; Sustained revolution
Ellis, Christina, 223
Emancipation Proclamation of 1863, 193, 276
English as a Second Language (ESL), 146
Environmental injustice/racism, 229, 241,
     242–243
Equal Justice Initiative, 245
Equity, xx
     achievement gap, education narratives/policies
          and, 3
     antiracist mindset and, 2–3
     critical race theory, undermining of, 6
     racial justice sentiments/policies, opposition
          to, 5–6
     silences around racism, shattering of, 28, 30
     systemic inequities and, 2–4, 5, 6
     youth empowerment, transformative impact
          of, 3, 4
     See also Heroes/holidays curriculum; Justice
          centeredness; Social justice
Espana, Carla, 104
Exclusion Act of 1882, 193, 196, 277

Fadel, Leila, 92
Five Cs, 102, 103–104 (table)
Flett, Julie, 69, 70, 71
Floyd, George, 5, 173, 191, 192, 196, 268
Forced assimilation, 128
Ford, Bernette G., 108, 110, 111
Frazin, Shana, 260
Freedom Rides, 267
Freedom Schools, 267
Freire, Paulo, 164, 197
Frias, Daphne, 243
Funds of knowledge focus, 30

Gay, Geneva, 6, 106
Genocide, 128, 188, 192
Gentrification, 27, 91, 245

George, Bridget, 226, 232, 234
Germán, Lorena, 7, 157
Giddens, Rhiannon, 166, 181, 182, 183
Glenn, Cerise, 159
Goade, Michaela, 108, 114, 115, 116
Gotanda, Neil, 6
Gray, Gary R., Jr., 73, 75
Green, Ernest, 3
Greensboro Four, 3
Griffin, Molly Beth, 11
Guide to Gender Identity Terms, 87
Guo, Winona, 223
Gupta, Edha, 223

Hammond, Tiffany, 77, 78
Hannah-Jones, Nikole, 166, 176, 178
Hawthorne, Britt, 17, 88
Heroes/holidays curriculum, 4
     African American studies programs,
          restrictions on, 6
     antiracist teaching, misunderstanding of, 8–13
     Black History Month and, 5
     canonical texts, allegiance to, 7–8
     contributions approach to curriculum and, 4–5
     disruption of, barriers to, 5–14
     #DisruptTexts movement and, 7
     meritocracy vs. antiracism and, 4, 5
     multicultural education movement and, 4–5
     oppression/racism, realities of, 4
     racial justice sentiments/policies, opposition
          to, 5–6
     racist history, acknowledgement of, 4–5
     restrictive education policies and, 5, 6–7
     systemic resistance to disruption of, 5–7
     teacher discomfort with disruption of, 7–8
     windows and mirrors approach and, 9–10
     See also Antiracist Reading Framework;
          Antiracist teaching
Herrera, Luz Yadira, 104
Historically Responsive Teaching Framework, 15
Holzwarth, Devon, 56
Homeland, 81–85
hooks, bell, 22, 107, 198, 204, 205, 206
Howell, D., 105, 106
Huerta, Dolores, 193, 278

Human liberation movement, 265
  collective struggle/mass movements and, 266–268
  hope as discipline/practice and, 268, 269
  hope/solidarity, reciprocal relationship between, 265, 266, 268
  individual responsibility, role of, 269
  obstacles to liberation and, 269
  solidarity, powerful impetus of, 268–269
  See also Liberatory consciousness
Huyck, David, 11, 12

I Am Every Good Thing, 52–55
I Am Golden, 64–68
I Can Write the World, 94–97
Ikeda, Daisaku, 264
I'm From, 73–76
Indigenization process, 115
Indigenous Peoples' Day, 187–188
Institute for Racial Equity in Literacy (IREL), 30, 205
Intersectionality, 88, 195, 223, 280
Islamophobia, 124

Jabari Jumps, 158, 159, 162–163
Jackson, Darrell, D., 165, 217
James, Gordon C., 52, 54, 55
Japanese American internment, 196–197
Jewell, Tiffany, 198, 207, 208
Johansen, Dana, 20
Johnson, Aeriale, 165
Johnson, Marsha P., 193, 196, 279
Juneteenth, 193, 277
Justice centeredness, xx
  antiracist mindset and, 2–3
  antiracist reading instruction and, xxi–xxii
  Black Panther Party and, 3–4
  environmental injustice/racism and, 229, 241, 242–243
  liberation-grounded democracy, ascent to, 4
  racial injustice, experience of, 35
  racial justice sentiments/policies, opposition to, 5–6
  systemic inequities and, 2–4, 5
  youth empowerment, transformative impact of, 3, 4
  See also Activism; Community activists; Equity; Human liberation movement; Marginalized voices

Kaba, Mariame, 265, 268
Karlmark, Gloria Ray, 3
Kemp, Laekan Zea, 108, 118, 119, 120
Kendi, Ibram X., 198, 200
Khadija, Sabrena, 226, 228, 230
Khalil, Aya, 108, 123, 125
Kheiriyeh, Rashin, 108, 123, 125
King, Bernice, 223
King, Martin Luther, Jr., 5, 221, 223, 267
Kochiyama, Yuri, 267
Kügler, Tina, 10

Ladson-Billings, Gloria, 6, 33, 35, 48, 106, 224, 261, 286
LaNier, Carlotta Walls, 3
Lee & Low Books Diversity Baseline Survey (DBS), 14
Lessac, Frané, 166, 185, 186
Letters for Black Lives, 268
Liberatory consciousness, 2, 27, 34 (table), 35, 36, 163–164
  See also Human liberation movement
Liem, Fanny, 226, 248, 249
The Light She Feels Inside, 244–247
Lindstrom, Carole, 108, 127, 129, 130, 226, 232, 234
The Little Rock Nine, 3
Littlebird, Steph, 108, 127, 129
Love, Barbara J., 34, 35, 36, 106, 163, 262
Love, Bettina, 2
Luli and the Language of Tea, 144–147
Luzincourt, Frantzy, 226, 236, 237, 238, 239
Lyons, Kelly Starling, 95

Ma, Yo-Yo, 183
Madison, Megan, 198, 211, 212
Madooh, Reem, 81
Magic Negro trope, 159

Malcolm, X, 193, 221, 267, 278

Marginalized voices, xvii, xx
    Afrodiasporic voices and, 246
    antiracist mindset and, 2–3
    antiracist teaching, reflective conversations and, xxi–xxii, 28–32
    BIPOC writers/topics and, 28–30, 29 (figure)
    critical race theory, undermining of, 6
    culturally relevant education and, xx, xxi, 6
    ownvoices concept and, 29–30, 69, 262, 287
    personal liberation/collective action and, xxi, 2–4
    racial justice sentiments/policies, opposition to, 5–6
    representation vs. liberation and, 2
    restrictive education policies and, 6–7
    youth empowerment, transformative impact of, 3, 4
    See also Antiracist Reading Framework; Antiracist teaching; BIPOC writers/topics; Community activists; Justice centeredness; Racial literacy; Silences around racism

Martin, Trayvon, 196
Martinez, Xiuhtezcatl, 197
McCain, Franklin, 3
McNeil, Joseph, 3
Méndez, Yamile Saied, 198, 216
Meza, Erika, 60, 62
Mi Papi Tiene una Moto, 90–93
Microaggressions, 65, 67, 216
Mikai, Monica, 166, 181, 182
Miles, Nicole, 198, 207, 208
Milner, H. Richard, IV, 20
Mirrors and windows approach, 9–10, 9–13, 26–27, 33 (table), 46, 157
Mis Dos Pueblos Fronterizos, 60–63
Mississippi Freedom Summer, 267
Montgomery Bus Boycott, 267
Mora, Oge, 73, 75
More Than Peach: Changing the World…One Crayon at a Time!, 248–251
Morrison, Deb, 165
Morrison, Frank, 108, 110, 111, 160, 163
Morrison, Toni, xx, 24, 105, 253, 254

Mothershed, Thema, 3
Moushabeck, Hannah, 81, 83
Muhammad, Gholdy, 3, 15, 106
Multilingualism, 26, 144–145
My Bindi, 140–143
My Papi Has a Motorcycle, 90–93
My Powerful Hair, 127–131
My Rainbow, 86–89
My Two Border Towns/Mis Dos Pueblos Fronterizos, 60–63

Nakba/catastrophe, 82
Neal, DeShanna, 86, 87
Neal, Trinity, 86, 87
Neurodiversity, 78
Newton, Huey P., 3
The Night Before Eid: A Muslim Family Story, 123–126
Norris, Aaminah, 105, 106

Oppression, 137, 156, 163, 166
Our Skin: A First Conversation About Race, 211–214
Ownvoices concept, 29–30, 69, 262, 287

Palmer, Charly, 94, 96
Paris, Django, 6, 106
Parker, Kimberly, 7, 30, 31, 32, 157
Parks, Rosa, 3, 5, 221
Patchett, Ann, 160
Peller, Gary, 6
Pelter, Autumn, 197, 243
Peña, Zeke, 90, 91, 92
Peyton, Bobbie, 108, 132, 133
Plátanos Are Love, 136–139
Pratt, Gregory R., 191
Price-Dennis, Detra, 31, 196
"The projects", 46, 111, 112, 220

Quintero, Isabel, 25, 90, 91, 93

Racial literacy, xx, xxi, 189
    accountability lens and, 203, 206, 209–210, 213–214, 218
    activism lens and, 203, 206, 209, 213, 217

affirmation lens and, 200–201, 204, 207, 211, 215

The Antiracist Kid, critical lens prompts/pathways for, 207–210

antiracist teaching practices and, 28, 31

atmosphere lens and, 202, 205–206, 208–209, 213, 217

authorship lens and, 202, 205, 208, 212, 216–217

awareness lens and, 201, 205, 207–208, 212, 216

book list for, 198

colonization, glorification of whiteness and, 190–192

components of, 195–196

contributions approach to curriculum and, 4–5

critical love and, 36

critical reading of texts and, 194

cultural competence and, 48

dandelion metaphor and, 189

development of, 28, 31, 34 (table), 36

historic people/events, race/racism and, 192–193, 196–197, 276–279

monuments to white colonizers and, 190–192

Our Skin: A First Conversation About Race, critical lens prompts/pathways for, 211–214

Racial Literacy Development model and, 194–195, 280

Skin Again, critical lens prompts/pathways for, 204–206

Stamped (For Kids): Racism, Antiracism, and You, critical lens prompts/pathways for, 200–203

systemic racism, recognition of, 190–193, 196–197

teacher/parent/caregivers, resources for, 17

Where Are You From?, critical lens prompts/pathways for, 215–218

See also BIPOC writers/topics; Heroes/holidays curriculum; Silences around racism

Racial profiling, 237

Racism. *See* Environmental injustice/racism; Racial profiling; Silences around racism

Rahman, Mariyah, 108, 136

Ralli, Jessica, 198, 211, 212

Raschka, Chris, 198, 204, 205

Reading instruction. *See* Antiracist Reading Framework

Reconciliation Park, 170

Reese, Debbie, 10, 38, 160, 164

Refugees, 61, 62, 197

Resistance: My Story of Activism, 236–239

Revolution. *See* Activism; Community activists; Sustained revolution

Reynolds, Jason, 1, 198, 200

Reynosso-Morris, Alyssa, 108, 136

Richmond, David, 3

Roberts, Terrence, 3

Rose, Charlie, 105

Roxas, Isabel, 198, 211, 212

Ruby Bridges Goes to School: My True Story, 221

Salesses, Matthew, 104, 105, 164

Sanchez, David, 4

Sanders, Joshunda, 94, 95

Seale, Bobby, 3

Sealey-Ruiz, Yolanda, 5, 31, 34, 35, 36, 194, 196, 223, 263, 287

Selma-to-Montgomery march, 267

Seven generations belief, 233

Silences around racism, 28, 30–31, 153

accountability lens and, 171, 174–175, 179–180, 184, 188

activism lens and, 170, 174, 179, 183, 187–188

affirmation lens and, 168, 172, 177, 181, 185–186

atmosphere lens and, 170, 174, 178–179, 183, 187

authorship lens and, 169, 173, 178, 182, 186–187

awareness lens and, 163, 169, 173, 177–178, 182, 186

Because of Winn-Dixie, critical lens prompts/pathways for, 158, 159–162

book list for, 166

book selection, examination of racism in, 158–164, 165, 275

Build a House, critical lens prompts/pathways for, 181–184

conversations on race and, 164–165, 166

critical evaluation practices and, 158, 163, 166

dandelion metaphor and, 153, 164, 165

environmental racism/injustice and, 229

Jabari Jumps, critical lens prompts/pathways for, 158, 159, 162–163

liberatory consciousness, application of, 163–164

literature, racialized disparities in, 157

Magical Negro trope and, 159

nostaligia bias and, 161

race-neutral/White-as-default stances and, 157, 158, 162, 164

racial consciousness, waking position and, 158, 163–164

racist behavior, leader response to, 154–156, 165

radical imagination, nurturing of, 157

reading instruction, potential power of, 156–157, 163–164, 165

The 1619 Project: Born on the Water, critical lens prompts/pathways for, 176–180

swimming activity, exclusion from, 162–163

systemic inequities and, 2–4, 5, 6, 30–31, 111, 162

Unspeakable: The Tulsa Race Massacre, critical lens prompts/pathways for, 168–171

When We Say Black Lives Matter, critical lens prompts/pathways for, 172–175

White Savior trope and, 159–160

See also BIPOC writers/topics; Racial literacy

Singleton, Glenn, 17

The 1619 Project: Born on the Water, 176–180

Skin Again, 204–206

Smith, Nikkolas, 176

Social justice, xvii

disciplinary measures, racial disproportionality in, 2–3

liberation-grounded democracy, ascent to, 4

systemic inequities and, 2–4, 5, 6, 30–31, 111

youth empowerment, transformative impact of, 3, 4

See also Activism; Community activists; Justice centeredness; Marginalized voices; Silences around racism

Socialization process, 36, 50, 108, 166, 198, 226, 249

Solidarity, xvii, 265, 266, 268

Sorell, Traci, 166, 185, 186, 187

Southern Poverty Law Center (SPLC), 192

Sreenivasan, Archana, 108, 140, 141

Stamped (For Kids): Racism, Antiracism, and You, 200–203

Stereotypes, 74, 75–76, 157, 161, 190

Sterling, Alton, 268

Stonewall riots, 196

Student Tool Kit of Critical Lenses for Antiracist Reading, 256

accountability lens and, 258, 260, 283, 285

activism lens and, 258, 260, 283, 285

affirmation lens and, 257, 259, 282, 284

atmosphere lens and, 258, 259, 283, 285

authorship lens and, 258, 259, 282, 284

awareness lens and, 257, 259, 282, 284

older readers and, 257–258, 282–283

younger readers and, 259–260, 284–285

See also Educator Tool Kit of Critical Lenses for Antiracist Reading Instruction; Sustained revolution

Sustained revolution, 253–255

activist mindset and, 255

change activism, ongoing need for, 255

dandelion metaphor and, 253, 254, 264

Educator Tool Kit of Critical Lenses for Antiracist Reading Instruction and, 260–263, 286–288

hope/solidarity, reciprocal relationship between, 265

love, impact of, 254

Student Tool Kit of Critical Lenses for Antiracist Reading/Older Readers and, 257–258, 282–283

Student Tool Kit of Critical Lenses for Antiracist Reading/Younger Readers and, 259–260

tool kits for, 255–256

See also Activism; Community activists; Human liberation movement

Systemic racism, 2–4, 5, 6, 30–31, 111, 190–193, 196

Tall, JoAnn, 193, 197, 279

Taylor, Breonna, 5, 196

Taylor, Mildred D., 46

Teaching practices. *See* Antiracist Reading Framework; Antiracist teaching; BIPOC writers/topics; Racial literacy

Tell Me Who You Are, 223

Thomas, Ebony Elizabeth, 38, 157, 164

Thomas, Jefferson, 3

Thomas, Kendall, 6

Thunberg, Greta, 197, 229

Tía Fortuna's New Home, 56–59

Tiger Rising, 161

Till, Emmett, 169, 193, 278

Torres, Julia, 7, 157

Transgender persons, 86–89, 196

Tubman, Harriet, 3

Tudor, Aslan, 197, 226, 240, 242, 243

Tudor, Kelly, 226, 240, 242

Tulsa Race Massacre, 168–171, 193, 277

Turner, Henry M., 267

Tutu, Desmond, xxiii

Twine, France Winddance, 195

Twink, Art, 86, 87

Uncle John's City Garden, 110–113

Unspeakable: The Tulsa Race Massacre, 168–171

Varadarajan, Gita, 108, 140, 141

Vulchi, Priya, 223

Wallace, Gwendolyn, 226, 244, 246

Wang, Andrea, 108, 144, 145

Water protectors, 4, 233, 240–243

Water Protectors of Standing Rock, 4, 240–243

Watson, Renée, 166, 176, 178

We Are Still Here!, 185–188

We Have a Dream: Meet 30 Young Indigenous People and People of Color Protecting the Plant, 228–231

Weatherford, Carole Boston, 166, 168, 169

Wells, Ida B., 267

When We Say Black Lives Matter, 172–175

Where Are You From?, 215–218

White savior trope, 159–160, 164, 263, 288

White supremacy ideology, 28, 29, 37, 50, 108, 111, 117, 129, 142, 145, 169, 182, 191, 192, 198, 267

Wild Berries, 69–72

Williams, Krystal L., 105, 106

Wong, Janet, 154

Woodard, Bellen, 226, 248, 249, 250

Woolworth's lunch counter protest, 3

Yglesias, Natasha, 17

Yin, Alice, 191

Young Chicanos for Community Action, 4

Young Water Protectors...A Story About Standing Rock, 240–243

Yum, Hyewon, 108, 144, 145

Zhang, Kat, 108, 147, 149

A Sage Company

Helping educators make the greatest impact

CORWIN HAS ONE MISSION: to enhance education through intentional professional learning.

We build long-term relationships with our authors, educators, clients, and associations who partner with us to develop and continuously improve the best evidence-based practices that establish and support lifelong learning.